Love, Violence, and the Cross

Love, Violence, and the Cross

How the Nonviolent God Saves Us
through the Cross of Christ

GREGORY ANDERSON LOVE

CASCADE *Books* · Eugene, Oregon

LOVE, VIOLENCE, AND THE CROSS
How the Nonviolent God Saves Us through the Cross of Christ

Cascade Publications
An Imprint of Wipf and Stock Publishers
199 W. 8th Ave., Suite 3
Eugene, OR 97401

"On Turning Ten" from *The Art of Drowning*, by Billy Collins © 1995. Reprinted by
permission of the University of Pittsburgh Press.

Excerpts from "Revelation" from EVERYTHING THAT RISES MUST
CONVERGE by Flannery O'Connor. Copyright © 1965 by the Estate of Mary
Flannery O'Connor. Copyright renewed 1993 by Regina O'Connor. Reprinted by
permission of Farrar, Straus and Giroux, LLC.

www. wipfandstock.com

ISBN 13: 978-1-60899-042-9

Cataloging-in-Publication data:

Love, Gregory Anderson.

Love, violence, and the cross : how the nonviolent God saves us through the cross of
Christ / Gregory Anderson Love.

ISBN 13: 978-1-60899-042-9

x + 306 p. ; 23 cm. Includes bibliographical references and indexes.

1. Atonement — History of doctrines. 2. Jesus Christ — Crucifixion — History of
doctrines. 3. Motion pictures — Religious aspects — Christianity. I. Title.

BT263 L70 2010

Manufactured in the U.S.A.

Contents

Introduction

THE CENTER NO LONGER HOLDS

A T THE CENTER OF the story of Jesus of Nazareth is a series of claims that are strange, offensive, and scandalous: That he befriends all groups yet associates himself with none. That he proclaims a kingdom or new world that is all around us and even within us, yet which is "not of this world."[1] That "the last" will walk into this new world at the front of the line, "the first" tailing behind. That he speaks in intimate tones to a God he calls *Abba* yet speaks harshly at times to his mother and siblings. Even John the Baptist wondered whether Jesus really was "the one who is to come."[2]

There is more: beyond the strangeness of his way of being in the world, there is the greater strangeness of the resurrection appearances.

These gospel narratives of the man Jesus slowly led to the offensive claim of the incarnation, and its implied portrayal of a God who suffers. The Creator of heaven and earth becomes one of the creatures, a man from the backwater town of Nazareth in an occupied territory of an empire. This offensive idea led to another: that the one God is a triune community of three persons who exist in love. It smacks of bad math.

Most offensive and scandalous of all is the claim that each of the gospel writers, and Paul himself, felt compelled to place at the center of this man's story: that God's saving act in and through Jesus of Nazareth finds its center in the moments of Jesus's story which seem most devoid of either God or saving power—his torture and death on the cross. There is a dark comedy to this claim, readily apparent when Jesus, in Mel Gibson's cinematic retelling, is stumbling toward Golgotha after being tortured to within a breath of his life, sees his mother and whispers to

1. John 18:36. All Scripture references and quotations are from Metzger and Murphy, eds., *New Oxford Annotated Bible: New Revised Standard Version.*

2. Luke 7:18–23.

her, "See, Mother, I make all things new."[3] But mostly what is scandalous is the claim that the God who is in Christ reconciling the world to Godself does so "through the cross," putting all hostility to death "through it."[4] "We proclaim Christ crucified," Paul insisted, "a stumbling block to Jews and foolishness to Gentiles, but to those who are the called, both Jews and Greeks, Christ the power of God and the wisdom of God. For God's foolishness is wiser than human wisdom, and God's weakness is stronger than human strength."[5] He had to make a case because the assertion stuck in everyone's craw. Not only that, the assertion became the center of the Christian witness to the salvation come in the person and work of Jesus.

Today the Christian church is losing this center, and with it, the good news that the end of divine-human estrangement and its reverberations in intrahuman and human-creaturely rifts has been accomplished in the work of Jesus. That loss of its central gospel message makes the Christian community's proclamation timid and unclear, its members alienated, and its theological narrative shattered into incoherent pieces. The loss of the central Christian assertion that God in Christ reconciles the world to Godself brings about the loss of the gospel itself, because it divides the message of salvation from the message of atonement.

Atonement, an element of salvation, is a relational concept. In Christian theology, atonement assumes human beings are estranged from God and one another and are powerless to restore harmony. Christianity identifies the divine act by which harmony is restored as atonement; it occurs in the incarnation, life, death, and resurrection of Jesus.

Salvation is a restoration concept. It describes the act by which God restores all things to wholeness, to God's intended "right order" of justice and mercy. This comprehensive restoration is imagined by the prophets and apostles as *shalom*, and as the "kingdom of God" and the "new heaven and new earth" of Jewish apocalyptic expectation. Human beings, incapable of bringing this salvation, must call upon God to save. When God comes, God restores the divine-human relationship torn by human sin and guilt (atonement). But God also overcomes human and animal suffering by lifting the dead to life, breaking chains of external

---

3. See Rev 21:5; see also 2 Cor 5:17.

4. Eph 2:16. Those who were far off have been brought near "by the blood of Christ" (Eph 2:13).

5. 1 Cor 1:23–25.

and internal oppression, bringing hope to the despairing, and healing broken bodies, souls, and spirits. When God appears, God not only judges, but saves.

Some critics of the idea that God reconciles us through the event of Jesus's death reject not only certain models of atonement but the need for atonement altogether. They keep salvation but not atonement, and the locus of salvation is moved off the cross back onto the power of Jesus's life and ministry, or forward to his resurrection and to our roles as partners with God in healing the world.

However, when the concept of divine-human atonement is put aside, the concept of incarnation also becomes unnecessary for these theologians. With incarnation set aside, the concept of God as a triune community of divine persons in a sociality of love is also lost. Finally, the paradoxical nature of human beings as free yet bound in their sin, and the Protestant rejoinder that if we and the world are to be saved, God must do the saving, are rendered unnecessary.

The loss of a cohesive understanding of atonement has the effect of unraveling the Christian faith and jeopardizing not only the doctrines of the incarnation and the Trinity but also a complex and serious interpretation of the human condition under sin and the concept of grace.

Concerning the meaning of the death of Christ, the church has become mute, divided, and adrift. This book explains the saving significance of the death of Christ in ways that speak to us today.

LOVE, VIOLENCE, AND THE CROSS

The loss of the central Christian hope of reconciliation in Christ and its restoration have their source in differing answers to one crucial question: *What is the relationship between divine love and violence in regard to the saving significance (or lack of it) of the cross of Christ?*

This book creates eight models of atonement that reveal the power of this one question and of its basic but radically different and opposing answers. No one model can capture the complex ways in which human beings and the created order are broken and in need of wholeness. Nor can one model convey the depth and breadth of the saving power of God's act in the life, death, and resurrection of Jesus. For example, imagining Jesus as a victor speaks to our experience of feeling helplessly bound by destructive forces, while imagining Jesus as offering a sacrifice speaks to our experience of having polluted ourselves through sin and betrayal.

Beneath the differences of the models run common patterns of response to the basic question, which enable certain models to be grouped together into families. Models within a family all give the same answer to the basic question. These family groupings make clear that *there are three basic responses to the crucial question of the relations of love, violence, and the cross; and these responses are radically different and mutually opposing.*

The first response, from the advocates of the penal substitutionary theory of atonement or the idea that Jesus in his death assumed for us the punishment we deserved, understands divine love and violence conjoined mysteriously at the cross, and the cross as the apex of God's saving work. God brings about redemption through violent means, and the torture and death of Jesus is seen straightforwardly as the will of God. Part One investigates this view and why it has so long captured the imaginations of Christians.

The second response, from certain feminist and womanist theologians[6] as well as from Marcus Borg, believes the message of divine redemption through violence functions not only to portray God as abusive but also to legitimate human uses of violence. These theologians, in complete opposition to penal substitution, argue that God saves through the power of love, not through Jesus's torture. The locus of salvation is moved off the cross to what occurs beforehand, in Jesus's life and ministry, and to what occurs after, in the resurrection, the descent of the Spirit, and the actions of the new community founded by Jesus. Part Two investigates both these theologians' deep problems with the penal-substitutionary model and their alternative models.

The third response is my own. In it, I argue that *God is nonviolent,* while retaining the core idea presented in the New Testament witnesses: that *reconciliation occurs in the work of Christ, and the cross plays a role in that divine work.* In Part Three, I present five constructive models that embody this third response.

---

6. Though not all feminist and womanist theologians fit under this second response, as well shall see in Part Three. (For instance, cf. 158 n. 39, 208 n. 30.)

PART ONE

Penal Substitution

The Atonement Theory Most Prevalent in North American Popular Christian Piety

Jesus the Reconciler of Divine Justice and Mercy

Penal Substitution

T HE THEORY OF ATONEMENT with which most Christians in North America are familiar is one that answers two cravings of the human heart: A longing for justice upon perpetrators of violence, and ironically, a plea for mercy—that our sins of violence and omission can somehow be forgiven.

An offshoot of Anselm's eleventh-century theory of *satisfaction*,[1] the theory of *penal substitution* was developed by medieval theologian Thomas Aquinas and solidified with the rise of the nation state and its rule of law in the sixteenth century. Reformation theologians Martin Luther and John Calvin were influenced by these prevailing concepts of law. To help us understand this model, we shall follow two guides who provide well-thought-out justifications for it: Charles Hodge (1797–1878), a professor of systematic theology at Princeton Theological Seminary and defining shaper of American Presbyterianism; and John R. W. Stott (b. 1921), a prolific and influential Anglican and Evangelical scholar and evangelist.

We begin, however, with stories of the human condition, for it is to this which atonement responds: two from recent movies, and one from a historic instance. Each story sheds light on how we humans offend, punish, and are wronged, and how we try to resolve those inter-human ruptures. They are stories and responses to which we will return again and again throughout this book.

---

1. This we shall look at in chapter 9.

UNFORGIVEN

Deep at night in Big Whiskey, Wyoming, in 1880, it is raining hard.[2] The man with the knife tells his partner to "hold her." He cuts her face, again and again and again. "Do you think it's funny?"

Finally, Skinny, the owner of the saloon, gets him off her with a gun to his head. He wants to shoot them both.

Rousted out of bed, the sheriff, Little Bill, finally arrives. "She gonna die?"

Alice, the leader of the women, says, "She's gonna live . . . She didn't steal nothing. She didn't even touch his pecker . . . All she done when she seen he had a teensy little pecker is give a giggle. That's all . . . You should hang them, Little Bill."

Alice, Little Bill, and Skinny go downstairs, where the men are tied to a post. Little Bill tells the deputy, "Go over to the office and get the bullwhip."

Alice interjects, "A whipping? That's all they get after what they done?"

"A whipping ain't no little thing, Alice."

"But what they done, they should get more than . . ."

"Alice, shut up!" Skinny turns. "Little Bill, a whipping ain't gonna settle this."

"No?"

"This here's a lawful contract between me and Delilah Fitzgerald, the cut whore."

Thinking of Skinny's damaged financial investment, Little Bill turns to the two men. "You boys off the Bar-T. You got your own string of ponies?" They do. "Guess you just as soon not have a trial, no fuss, huh? All right. You did the cutting. Come the thaw, you bring in five ponies and you give them over to Skinny. And you bring in two . . ."

His deputy brings him the bullwhip. "Maybe we don't need this whip now."

Alice again interjects. "You ain't even gonna whip them?"

---

2. The opening scene to the movie *Unforgiven*, directed by Clint Eastwood.

"Well, I fined them instead, Alice."

"For what they done, Skinny gets some ponies, and that's it? That ain't fair, Little Bill. That ain't fair!"

The next morning, the women are in Alice's room. "I got eighty-five dollars," says one. They are pulling together their savings to see if they can hire someone to execute the two men who cut up Delilah.

"I don't know . . . If Delilah doesn't care one way or another, what are we getting so riled up about?" says another.

Alice responds, gritting her teeth. "Just because we let them smelly fools ride us like horses don't mean we gotta let 'em brand us like horses! Maybe we ain't nothing but whores, but by God, we ain't horses!"

After a pause, another says, "I got $112."

When the word of a thousand-dollar reward reaches William Munny at his hardscrabble farm, he thinks of his children, living in poverty, and sets off toward Big Whiskey. He collects his old friend Ned Logan on the way. That night, they talk around the campfire. (Later in the movie, it becomes clear that Will, a thief and expert killer, has killed women and children, a U.S. Marshall, "and just about everything that walks or crawls at one time or another.")

Will refers to his encounter with Sally, Ned's wife. "She knew me back then. She knew what a no-good-son-of-a-bitch I was. She just ain't allowing I've changed. She don't realize I ain't like that no more. I ain't the same, Ned. Claudia (his deceased wife), she straightened me up. Cleared me of drinking whiskey and all. Just cause we're going on this killing don't mean I'm gonna go back to being the way I was. I just need the money. Get a new start for them youngsters . . ."

"Ned, you remember that drover I shot through the mouth and his teeth came out the back of his head? I think about him now and again. He didn't do anything to deserve to get shot. At least nothing I could remember when I sobered up."

The next evening in Big Whiskey, William gets kicked and beaten to near-death by Little Bill. The women find an abandoned shack outside of town for the men. In the midst of a three-day delirium, Will awakens briefly from a nightmare and talks to Ned. "Claudia . . . Is that you, Ned?

I seen 'em, Ned. I seen the Angel of Death. I've seen the river, Ned. He's got snake eyes."

"Who's got snake eyes?"

"It's the Angel of Death. Oh, Ned, I'm scared of dying."

Late in the movie, after shooting both men, Will is speaking with the young man who was the third partner. "It's a hell of a thing, killing a man. You take away all he's got, and all he's ever gonna have."

"Well, I guess they had it coming," says the young man.

"We all have it coming, kid."

25TH HOUR

His father is driving him to the state prison in upstate New York to begin his seven-year term.[3] Montgomery Brogan, face beat-up to disfigure himself so he is less likely to be abused in prison, looks out the passenger window. He knows he deserves it. He was greedy, he waited too long to stop drug-dealing. Not for the money; he didn't grow up poor. For what he called "the sway."

"It's gonna be okay, Monty," his father says softly.

Daydreaming, he sees the faces of all those he cursed, smiling back, friendly toward him. He tries to reach out to them through the window.

"Give me the word, and I'll take a left turn. Take the GW Bridge and go west. Get you stitched up somewhere and keep going. Find a nice little town."

"They'll take your bar."

His father dismisses this.

"They'll find me, sooner or later."

"You go, and never come home. They won't find you. We'll keep driving. Head out to the middle of nowhere . . . The desert's for starting over."

Monty imagines them in the desert in the West. His father leaves. He gets a job in a bar. He pays cash. He makes himself a home out there.

---

3. From the movie *25th Hour*, directed by Spike Lee.

He works hard. He gets papers, a driver's license. He takes the name "James."

"You forget your old life," his father says, still talking. "You make a new life for yourself, and you live it. You live your life the way it should have been."

Monty daydreams again. After a few years, he imagines Naturelle, his beloved, coming to join him there. He is loved; he loves her. New Year's Eve, a baby in her tummy, "a New Year," they say as they look at one another.

He gives his family what they need. He has children, grandchildren, there in that town in the West. When they get old, they sit the family down and tell them the truth.

Monty wakes from the daydream as his dad has finally become quiet. They continue on the Palisades Parkway, heading north to Albany.

NAJMA

Najma speaks in a cautious monotone, eyes dull, like a captive. Don Belt writes of the story this sixteen-year-old Pakistani girl told him.[4]

"Two weeks ago, at one in the morning, five men, maybe six, burst through the door of the family's mud-brick home, which sits on a tiny plot of land in the village of Nizampur in southern Punjab. They identified themselves as police and said they were searching for weapons. One held a pistol to her mother's chest while another pinned her nine-year-old brother, Rizwan, to the floor. And then two men held Najma down on the bed while a third raped her."

Despite the scarf, the mother recognized the raspy voice of their neighbor as the leader—a police officer who wants the plot of wheat held by Najma's family. If they do not leave, he says, they will be back to rape the other daughter.

Rashid Rehman, a veteran human rights lawyer, said that if a family does not comply with such threats, they are often killed. "Who's going to stop them?"

Though the family obtained a medical report the next morning confirming the rape, the local police—of the same clan as the police officer—refused to file charges.

4. Belt, "Struggle for the Soul of Pakistan," 50–54.

Rehman is off to hear the outcome of an appeal he has filed. Najma speaks to him quietly. "I don't know what my life will be in the future, but I'm ready to face my attackers in public and demand justice for what they did." Of the rapist she says, "He must be hanged. He must."

When Rehman talks to the acting superintendent at the police station, he claims the forensic evidence for the case has been "unfortunately, misplaced."

When Rehman then speaks to the supervisor, the man claims that the truth is that Najma is lying to protect her (almost-disabled seventy-year-old) father from charges of assaulting a police officer. Further, she is a known "fornicator," and "60 or 90 people in the village mosque" declared the accused police officer incapable of committing such a crime. The case, he says, is closed.

Rehman knows that if the family does not leave immediately, they are in danger.

THE HUMAN LONGINGS FOR JUSTICE AND MERCY

The theory of penal substitution often conjures up images of guilty humans prostrate before a God who is a stern judge, a hard master, one who knows the exact specifications of the law and holds the guilty parties firmly in hand. This model, however, begins in a surprising way: With two questions that reflect two deeply-felt human longings.

We begin with the very human question of theodicy: *Is God just?* Does God judge like Little Bill judges, who makes a deal with Skinny to let it go for seven ponies, ignoring Alice's demands; or like the Pakistani police superintendent and supervisor, related to the perpetrators of the crime, saying the evidence is lost and the victim a liar? *Is God like that?*

As Yahweh was described by the Israelite prophets, and as Calvin perceived, God is one who *judges rightly*, sees truly, and cannot be bought off. God refuses to "look the other way" for the "right people." In Calvin's 1536 edition of the *Institutes of the Christian Religion*, he does call God a "stern judge, a strict avenger of sin" who will come to punish those who flout the duties of the law; this description fits the popular notion of God in the penal theory of atonement.[5] Yet Calvin combines this image of the just judge with the military image of "the strong hand of the Lord, coming forth armed to deliver the poor from their afflictions, and punish

---

5. Calvin, *Institutes of the Christian Religion*, 1536 edition, xxix.

their despisers."[6] Like the God who frees the oppressed in the Exodus, and like the prophesied Messiah, God is the defender of the poor and the oppressed, including from unjust human judges. When Calvin references Scriptures that describe God as coming to "repay according to each one's deeds,"[7] the context is often one in which humans lack integrity, speak falsehoods in order to ruin another, and judge differently depending upon one's high or low status.[8]

In like fashion, Hodge confronts opponents[9] who say God accepts Christ's saving work "as if" it satisfied divine justice, rather than doing so based upon its inherent worth, for then "a thing avails for whatever God chooses to take it."[10] His description of his opponents' view of God reminds one of the corrupt nature of human judges (including Pontius Pilate): "It amounts to saying there is no truth in anything. God may . . . take anything for anything; a whole for a part, or a part for the whole; truth for error, error for truth; right for wrong, or wrong for right . . . This is impossible."[11] Precisely here Calvin and Hodge appeal to God's immutability. God is "savior" in that God can be trusted, unlike human judges.

Paradoxically, though understandably, a second question forms a root of the theory of penal substitution. The context here, however, is not the corruptibility and capriciousness found in one's neighbors and social systems, but that found in oneself. The scene is that of William Munny, waking up from his nightmare, afraid of the Angel of Death who is coming to get him, for he knows he "has it coming." It is that of Monty Brogan, daydreaming out the window of the car that is heading toward prison, where he knows he will be brutalized and leave, seven years later, with nothing of his former life unscathed.

Aware of one's sin and guilt, people ask: If there is a God, *is this God merciful?*

For Christians, the fulfillment of these two seemingly contradictory longings is more than a bare hope.

---

6. Ibid., 14.

7. Rom 2:6. See also Ps 7:9–11; 62:12; Matt 16:27.

8. Calvin, *Institutes of the Christian Religion*, 1536 edition, 15. Cf. Pss 7 and 62.

9. Scotists, Hugo Grotius, Remonstrants.

10. Hodge, *Systematic Theology*, 2:487.

11. Ibid.

THE DEATH OF JESUS AS THE CENTER OF HISTORY

Our first surprise is that the penal substitution model of atonement begins not with the stern face of the legalists, but with the theodicy question and the longing for mercy when faced with the weight of one's own human sin. Hodge and Stott surprise us a second time, for they find resolutions to such questions and longings in the cross of Christ. A place of execution such as the cross hardly seems an obvious place to discover a solution to the human desire for either ultimate justice or mercy. As theologian Jürgen Moltmann stresses, the cross only deepens the theodicy problem; for Christ's brutal torture and execution add deicide to the unreconciled pains of the past and sufferings of the dead which can never be made good.[12] Nor does one expect to find an answer to one's longing for mercy in this man who himself experiences abandonment by God in his hour of deepest need.[13] Crucifixion was regarded with horror in the ancient world—as it is today. It was meant to be cruel, deliberately delaying death for days to increase the torture. It was reserved for slaves, foreigners, and other 'non-persons,' being unworthy of a Roman citizen and a free man. To Paul's Gentile hearers, Paul's 'message of the cross' was "madness" (1 Cor 1:18, 23). Jews also looked on crucifixion with horror, for in light of their scriptures, "anyone hung on a tree is under God's curse" (Deut 21:23). For Jews and Gentiles, the idea of worshipping a crucified man was therefore particularly contemptible.

The early Christian martyrs were patient and joy-filled at their coming torture "for the Lord's sake." Jesus, in contrast, reacted with sorrow and horror at his coming abuse. At Gethsemane and on the cross he expressed dismay not only at his physical pain, but the mental anguish of betrayal and desertion by his friends, of mockery and torture by his enemies, of abandonment by his God.

Yet advocates of the penal substitution theory of atonement believe that beneath Jesus's reluctance was a deeper stream of purposefulness. It was Christ's intent to endure these sufferings and die on the cross. The centrality of the cross in Jesus's mission originated in Jesus's own mind, they say. In his own self-understanding, Jesus combined the *Son of*

---

12. Moltmann, *Way of Jesus Christ*, 189–92. See also his discussion of Israel's conception of messianism as entailing the redemption from all evil, in a public way, from which the crucifixion of Jesus only brings a deeper distance, in chapter 1.

13. Ibid., 165–67.

Man imagery from Daniel with the *Suffering Servant* figure from Isaiah[14] to develop the surprising notion that when the Son of Man or Messiah came, the reason he came would be to die; this death was the fulfillment of the Israelite prophecies. Jesus's teachings, moral example, and works of compassion and power were not central to his mission. The death was the apex of the Messiah's work, not its untimely end. Indeed, according to Stott, his life's mission was accomplished in the last six hours.[15]

The same startling perception of the central role of the cross was adopted by the apostles after the resurrection. Though Jesus died under the divine curse (Deut 21:22–23), they began to understand that it was our curse which he was bearing. Paul ends his first letter to the Corinthians by passing on a succinct summary of the early Christian witness: "For I handed on to you as of first importance what I in turn had received: that Christ died for our sins in accordance with the scriptures, and that he was buried, and that he was raised on the third day in accordance with the scriptures, and that he appeared to Cephas, then to the twelve" (1 Cor 15:3–5).

In his letter to the Romans, Paul connects the blood of Jesus with being put right before and reconciled with God: "But God proves his love for us in that while we still were sinners Christ died for us. Much more surely then, now that we have been justified by his blood, will we be saved through him from the wrath of God. For if while we were enemies, we were reconciled to God through the death of his Son, much more surely, having been reconciled, will we be saved by his life" (Rom 5:8–10).

The authors of Hebrews, 1 Peter, 1 John, and Revelation perceived similarly to Paul the central role the cross played in bringing humans into a renewed relation with God.[16]

The apostles persisted in this message despite opposition. They did so not only because of Jesus's own statements concerning his death's meaning, but because they perceived the death to be God's plan.

---

14. For examples of the figures, see respectively Dan 7:13–14 and Isaiah 53.

15. Stott, *The Cross of Christ*, 66–67. See also 25–32; 60–61; 146–47.

16. See Hebrews 8–10; 1 Pet 1:18–19; 1 John 1:7; 2:1–2; 3:16—4:9, 14; 4:10; Rev 1:5–6; 7:9–14, 16–17; 13:8; 14:1ff.; 21:27.

THE DIVINE DILEMMA: HOW CAN GOD FORGIVE SINNERS WITHOUT COMPROMISING HOLINESS?

Why is it that a violent execution becomes the center of God's plan to redeem and reconcile a fallen, suffering world? Due to the gravity of human sin, "there was no way by which the righteous God could righteously forgive our unrighteousness, except that he should bear it himself in Christ ..."[17]

> God's love must be wonderful beyond comprehension. God could quite justly have abandoned us to our fate. He could have left us alone to reap the fruit of our wrongdoing and to perish in our sins. It is what we deserved. But he did not. Because he loved us, he came after us in Christ. He pursued us even to the desolate anguish of the cross, where he bore our sin, guilt, judgment and death. It takes a hard and stony heart to remain unmoved by love like that. It is more than love. Its proper name is 'grace', which is love to the undeserving.[18]

If God is to forgive the offenses of human beings, this theory says, God must do so in a way that is "consistent" with God's justice, rather than overlooking that justice. In Christ's atoning work, God is simultaneously just and merciful.

Why is it that the merciful God cannot simply forgive human beings, without the cross? The penal substitution theory bases its response on three premises. First, the justice of God, a justice by which God structured the world's order, entails what sociologists call *retributive justice*, or *distributive justice*.[19] Briefly, distributive or retributive justice means that "people should get what they deserve." Thus, righteousness deserves to be rewarded, and sin deserves to be punished, for God is "a righteous judge."[20] Hodge writes, "as the Scriptures teach, every sin deserves God's wrath and curse, both in this life and in that which is to come ..."[21] "In

---

17. Stott, *The Cross of Christ*, 83. Hodge repeats this central thesis of the penal-substitution theory of atonement numerous times. Christ suffered and died "in order that God might be just in justifying the ungodly" (474). See also 471, 478, 488, 493, 499, 508, 520, 579.

18. Ibid., 83.

19. Hodge at times also terms it *vindicatory justice*, for "it vindicates and maintains the right"; *Systematic Theology*, 2:489.

20. Ibid.

21. Ibid., 485.

the Old Testament and in the New, God is declared to be just, in the sense that his nature demands the punishment of sin; that therefore there can be no remission without such punishment, vicarious or personal."[22]

The requirement that all offenses against the divine law receive their due penalty would not be grievous if human offenses were minor, or if our ill behavior were somehow beyond our ability to control (and thus not ascribable to us). The second premise, however, dashes this hope. *We are grave sinners and are responsible for our acts.* All our offenses against the divine law are rooted in a more-fundamental Godless self-centeredness, an active rebellion against and hostility toward God. And while acknowledging that we are conditioned by our genes and socialization and other forces beyond our control, our moral responsibility is only diminished, not destroyed. We have a choice between good and evil.[23]

"We are all without excuse, since we have all known our duty, and none of us has done it."[24] Responsible for our sins, we are thus liable for the just penalty of our wrongdoing. And what is that penalty? For Hodge and Stott, Scripture clearly shows that "the wages of sin is death."

The situation would not be dire if despite our sin and the necessity of punishment, we would not lose our God. The third premise, however, is that *God, in God's holiness, cannot abide sin.* God "cannot have fellowship with the unholy."[25] God is repelled by all unrighteousness and ungodliness of human beings, and thus sinners do not have the liberty of access to God.[26]

These three basic premises of the penal substitution theory are reflected in the inter-human ruptures that began this chapter. Alice is incensed that Little Bill does not think the cowboys' knife assault on Delilah deserves genuine punishment, just as Najma and her lawyer Rehman are beside themselves that the police are turning a blind eye to the rape and extortion by one of their own, a policeman who is part of their clan. Alice fumes further when Little Bill implies the cowboys'

---

22. Ibid., 478. See also 488, 490. Stott concurs concerning this first premise: "according to Scripture, evil deserves to be punished" (*The Cross of Christ*, 310; see chap. 12). When Stott says that love without justice is appeasement, not peace making (296), he has retributive/distributive justice in mind.

23. See Stott, *The Cross of Christ*, 88–102.

24. Ibid., 97.

25. Hodge, *Systematic Theology*, 2:492.

26. Ibid., 464.

crime was not serious—they did not kill her!—and that they were not really responsible for their acts, since "they were just hard working boys that was foolish." To Alice, the boys are grave wrongdoers who knew what they were doing. And in all three stories, there is the sense that human righteousness and integrity cannot abide the winks and nods by which perpetrators and bystanders turn that blind eye. "Just because we let them smelly fools ride us like horses don't mean we gotta let 'em brand us like horses!" Alice tells the other women. Even some of the perpetrators who previously turned a blind eye recognize the moral force of the three premises. Will Munny knows he's done grave acts toward innocent people and deserves a righteous recompense of terror. Monty knows his daydream is just that; he has tainted everything he's touched.

And so, grounded by these three very human moral premises, the collision of divine perfection and human rebellion brings a dilemma to the divine-human relationship. God, being *merciful*, wants to forgive sinners and bring them into renewed relationship with Godself. However, God, being *holy*, cannot abide sin; and being *just*, demands that the penalty for human sin—death—be satisfied.[27] Forgiveness is a divinely-commanded duty to human beings, but a problem for God. How can God forgive sinners without compromising God's holiness?

If the holy and merciful God is to forgive guilty sinners and have new fellowship with them, the divine justice must first be *satisfied* or fulfilled. In commercial dealings, "satisfaction" of claims occurs when a debtor pays the monetary demand of her creditor in full; she is then entirely free of any further demands. In criminal cases, however, the claim is upon the offender herself, not her money. The penalty need not be identical to the offense, but must be "proportional" to it in terms of injury inflicted. When that penalty is paid, the claim of justice upon the offender is "satisfied" and ceases.[28]

Alice reflects this principle of proportionality:

> Little Bill tells the deputy, "Go over to the office and get the bullwhip."
>
> Alice interjects, "A whipping? That's all they get after what they done?"
>
> "A whipping ain't no little thing, Alice."
>
> "But what they done, they should get more than . . ."

---

27. See Stott, *The Cross of Christ*, 88.

28. See Hodge, *Systematic Theology*, 2:470–71; also 492, 571.

The concept of "the satisfaction of divine justice" was connected in the Hebrew Scriptures with that of "the day of the Lord's wrath." God's forbearance of human sinfulness during the Old Testament period only deepened the theodicy problem for God: Why did God allow God's law to be flouted? Why did God allow the wicked to prosper, the righteous to be "ground into the dust" by those who mock them? On the coming "day of wrath," it was believed, God would finally uphold God's name as "just" by bringing judgment upon Israel and the nations. God would enact the penalties humans had incurred with their sins, and thereby "satisfy" the claims of justice. Like a consuming fire, the divine anger would burn until evil was consumed. Like Will Munny's snake-eyed, silent visitor, the Angel of Death comes with divine recompense.

According to Stott, Christians also held this belief in the satisfying action of God to come, but saw the "day of the Lord's wrath" as now split into two days. On the cross, God decisively judged sin; and at the end of history, God would conclude the punishment of evil.

Does this not explain Jesus's dread at Gethsemane, when he anticipates the agony of the Lord's wrath poured out upon him, with its alienation from God the Father and the punishment of humanity's sin upon him?[29]

In popular versions of the penal substitution theory of atonement, with guilty humans prostrate before the divine judge, and both surrounded and held by the exact specifications of the law, God's dilemma is imagined as God needing to satisfy something *external* to God's own being—some independent form of "justice" or "law" or "moral order," some code of honor, or even some being like the devil who has "just claims" upon humans. Hodge and Stott, however, clarify that if something *extraneous* to God constricted God's options in relation to God's creation, then God would not be sovereign.

Instead, what must be satisfied in face of horrendous human sin and evil is not something exterior to God's being, but *God's very being* itself. God, being holy love, is repelled by evil and cannot abide it. The "divine law" and "divine justice" are simply expressions of God's own moral being, and it is this innate moral sensibility in God which must be satisfied before God can pardon and have fellowship with sinful humans.[30] If

29. On the wrath of God, see Stott, *The Cross of Christ*, 88, 102–10, 133–34, 206–11; on Jesus's dread at the coming divine wrath, see 74–82, 88, 125.

30. See Stott, *The Cross of Christ*, chap. 5: "Satisfaction For Sin," and 88–89. Hodge likewise speaks of justice as "a quality of moral excellence" in God that ensures that "the

God's justice were not satisfied, God would not have integrity, and the concern of those who cry out for justice would end in dereliction: even God cannot be trusted to be just.

SACRIFICES AND SUBSTITUTIONS

God must uphold God's innate sense of justice if God is to forgive sinners and have new fellowship with them. But since God's justice entails retributive justice—"sins deserve to be punished"—and the just penalty for sin is death, fulfillment of God's justice would kill all human beings.

For Hodge and Stott, this logic is witnessed in a principle found in the Hebrew and Christian scriptures, in all religions, and in the human conscience: *there can be no forgiveness without the shedding of blood.* While sin pollutes, the shedding of blood washes sinners clean, because the shedding of blood—death—pays off the just penalty for sin.[31] In the Hebrew law codes, for example, a murder pollutes the land and the community with the blood of the innocent. Because God is holy and cannot abide evil, God can remain present only if the land and community are cleansed, the blood "expiated," by the shedding of the perpetrator's blood as the just penalty for her or his murderous act.

Since all sin deserves the penalty of death, however, and all humans are sinners, divine justice would bring death to all. However, Hodge and Stott notice that religions, the Jewish religion included, offer another possibility—that *a substitute* may receive the penalty instead of the perpetrator.

On one level, in the Hebrew Scriptures, *the priest* acts as a substitute, for he acts as a mediator between guilty sinners and holy Yahweh. Guilty sinners could not approach God and live. The priest alone could enter the veil sheltering the "holy of holies" in which God made Godself present, and only with blood which the priest offered for himself and for the sins of the people. The priest offered gifts, sacrifices for sin, and made intercession with God on behalf of the people.

On the stricter level, it is *the animals* killed in the sacrificial ritual who act as substitute for guilty sinners before Yahweh. While Hodge and

---

judge of all the earth will do right; punishing or pardoning, just as moral excellence demands" (540). See also Hodge, *Systematic Theology*, 2:468, 489ff., 567.

31. "Indeed, under the law almost everything is purified with blood, and without the shedding of blood there is no forgiveness of sins" (Heb 9:22). Hodge, *Systematic Theology*, stresses this point frequently (cf. 2:478, 492, 496, 501).

Stott acknowledge that there are other forms of sacrifices offered to God in the Hebrew Scriptures—such as offerings of grain and first fruits to signify thanksgiving and peace with God—it is the animals offered in "sin offerings" that redeem from guilt. On the great Day of Atonement (*Yom Kippur*) held once a year, for example, two animals are chosen with physical perfection, to symbolize freedom from sin. With the first, the sin-offering, the priest lays hands upon the animal, saying "I have sinned," and delineates those sins. "Now I repent. Let this victim be my expiation."[32] The animal's throat is slit, the blood drained into a vessel, and then sprinkled on the Ark of the Covenant (ten commandments) in the holy of holies, proving the death of the victim. In similar fashion, the laying on of hands transfers the obligation to pay the penalty for sins from guilty humans to the second animal, the scapegoat, which is then driven off into the wilderness, outside the community's presence.[33]

In sin, guilt, and atonement sacrifices such as these, God takes the death of an innocent victim—an animal—in lieu of the death of the transgressor. The *criminality* of the transgressor cannot be transferred to the animal. However, *the obligation to satisfy the claims of divine justice*— to pay the penalty demanded by that justice—may be transferred from one to another.

It is this offering of the animal's life to God which changes God, not the repentance and reformation of the presenter. (Repentance and refor- mation of behavior are essential, but must come before the sin offering is made.) In Isaiah 53, it is the Suffering Servant's *death*—not his attitude or moral transformation—which frees the community from guilt and its corresponding penalty.[34] Guilt is cleansed by the shedding of blood: by the giving of soul for soul, life for life, which the Jews believed was located in an animal's blood. Once the penalty for sin is paid, God—or God's quality of moral excellence which includes retributive justice—is *propitiated*. Because of the sacrificial cleansing, a change occurs in God, not in us. The cleansing of human guilt does not awaken love in God. God loves us while we are sinners, and before the satisfaction to justice is rendered. But because the just penalty for sin has been paid, it becomes possible for God to reconcile justice with love.

---

32. Outram, one of Hodge's sources, quotes this prayer from Jewish authorities as one form of confession connected with the imposition of hands on the victim.

33. Hodge *Systematic Theology*, 2:503–4.

34. Ibid., 466, 498, 501.

CHRIST OUR SACRIFICE

The sacrificial rites are not humanly initiated attempts to placate an angry God. It is God who graciously initiates the sacrificial system in order that the penalty demanded by God's moral sensibility be paid, the individual's or community's guilt cleansed, divine forgiveness given in such a way that it does not contradict justice, and fellowship with God renewed. Both Hodge and Stott, however, follow Hebrews in describing the sacrificial rites of the Old Testament as mere "shadows" until the appearance of Christ, who is the true priest and the perfect vicarious sacrifice. Jesus saves us sinful humans by performing, in a perfect way, all three functions of a priest.[35] He acts as mediator between sinners and God, and intercedes with God on our behalf.

Most important, however, Jesus acts not only as the priest of the sacrificial rite, but as the sacrifice itself. For Hodge, two traits are significant in the efficacy of a sacrifice for guilt. First, the substitute animal or person *must suffer somewhat either in kind or in degree the suffering the sinner would have been required to endure as penalty for sin.* The divine law must be fulfilled. It demands perfect obedience; and, in the case of transgression, the penalty of death. Christ substituted himself in our place in order to fulfill the law's demands, living a life of perfect obedience, and volunteering his death on our behalf.[36]

Since the penalty for sin is death, Jesus's death is "adequate" to satisfy divine justice. Yet even Hodge acknowledges that Jesus did not suffer either in kind or degree what sinners would have suffered as penalty for their sins (eternal torment in hell).[37] But in the second trait for an efficacious sacrifice for guilt, Jesus excels. The value of one's sufferings increases or decreases depending on *the inherent dignity and value of the life of the one suffering.* "The death of an eminently good man would outweigh the annihilation of a universe of insects."[38] If the victim offered

---

35. Ibid., 464–65.

36. A criminal's penalty for a crime, while it need not be of the nature of the injury inflicted, should be a just equivalent. The penalty must bear an adequate proportion to the crime committed: "To fine a man a few pence for wanton homicide would be a mockery; but death or imprisonment for life would be a real satisfaction of justice." See Hodge, *Systematic Theology*, 2:471. On Christ substituting himself to fulfill the law, cf. 494–95.

37. See ibid., 471, 483.

38. Ibid., 471.

for sacrifice had no inherent dignity or worth, the suffering would not be of value sufficient to pay the penalty for the sin. In offering the blood of irrational animals, the Old Testament sacrifices were inadequate in cleansing from sin, purifying ceremonially and externally but not truly.[39] In contrast, the blood of an eternal spirit, or of a divine nature, offered without spot to God, effects "the real expiation of sin."[40] "So the humiliation, sufferings, and death of the eternal Son of God immeasurably transcended in worth and power the penalty which a world of sinners would have endured."[41] Hodge refers to Hebrews 9:11–14 to describe Christ as both final priest and sacrifice:[42]

> But when Christ came as a high priest of the good things that have come, then through the greater and perfect tent (not made with hands, that is, not of this creation), he entered once for all into the Holy Place, not with the blood of goats and calves, but with his own blood, thus obtaining eternal redemption. For if the blood of goats and bulls, with the sprinkling of the ashes of a heifer, sanctifies those who have been defiled so that their flesh is purified, how much more will the blood of Christ, who through the eternal Spirit offered himself without blemish to God, purify our conscience from dead works to worship the living God!

The combination of the infinite dignity of his nature with the depth of his fatal sufferings perfectly satisfies the penal demands of justice upon guilty sinners. Once met, justice's claims upon sinners cease; no further punishment can justly be demanded.[43] By Jesus's vicarious death, humans have been freed from the law, sin, and death. This new freedom would be experienced by perpetrators like Will Munny, Montgomery Brogan, and the Pakistani police rapist as the effect of a surprising and liberating act of mercy. They all get what they do not deserve: a second chance.

It was for the power of this vicarious death and this second chance that Jesus, the second person of the Trinity, came to earth. "He, therefore, assumed our nature in order that he might die, and by death

---

39. See Heb 10:4: "For it is impossible for the blood of bulls and goats to take away sins."

40. Hodge, *Systematic Theology*, 2:509.

41. Ibid., 471. See also ibid., 497.

42. Ibid., 483–84.

43. See ibid., 482.

effect our reconciliation with God."[44] He came to offer his blood as a propitiation to God, "to satisfy justice, that God might be just in the forgiveness of sin."[45]

GOD PAYS THE PRICE

In the sections surrounding his discussion of the atoning work of Christ, Hodge affirms the orthodox "two-natures" understanding of Christ's person. Jesus is fully divine as well as fully human. However, in Hodge's description of Christ's vicarious sacrifice, Christ is usually portrayed as a mediating figure between the holy God and guilty sinners, thus highlighting the distinction between God the Father and Jesus. In taking on the penalty humans deserve, Jesus experiences the wrath of God the Father.

John Stott argues that this portrayal of Christ as mediator misses the very heart of the theory of penal substitution and clouds the depth of the costliness to God involved in the atoning work. For Stott, there are only two sets of actors involved in the atoning drama—God and sinful humans, not three—God, sinful humans, and a mediator. It is God who pays the penalty for sin *in and through* the person and work of Christ. It is *God* who propitiates God's own wrath. Jesus is not a man who intervenes to pacify God. Nor does God the Father intervene to punish an innocent victim, Jesus of Nazareth. The story of atonement is the story of *God's* love and mercy, for the entire atoning work is initiated and accomplished solely by God.[46] The satisfaction of God's own moral sensibility occurs through God's substitution of God's own self for guilty sinners. God pays the penalty for our crimes.

This is where the penal substitution theory of atonement perceives the grace of God. God could have abandoned us to our fate, leaving us lawbreakers to endure the just penalty for our sins—death. But freely, God chose to take our place and endure our penalty of death, in order to free us from that death, by Godself satisfying the claims of divine justice. We did not cause or deserve this. It comes solely from the love of God.[47] Hence, in John 3:16 we read, "For God so loved the world that he gave his

---

44. Ibid., 513.
45. Ibid., 508–9.
46. Stott, *The Cross of Christ*, 212–17.
47. See Ibid., 83; and Hodge, *Systematic Theology*, 2:478, 481.

only Son . . ."; and in Romans 5:6–8 that: "while we were still weak, at the right time Christ died for the ungodly. Indeed, rarely will anyone die for a righteous person—though perhaps for a good person someone might actually dare to die. But God proves his love for us in that while we still were sinners Christ died for us."

Those who believe we must correct our ways and reclaim our righteous character through our own efforts before God can act to forgive us and reconcile us to Godself, miss this central core of grace, and turn the gospel on its head.

THE RESULT OF GOD'S ATONING WORK IN CHRIST

. . . and the curtain of the temple was torn in two.[48]

God's atoning work in Christ saves sinners from their sins. This salvation is manifest in multiple ways. First, God's atoning work brings *the justification of the sinner* before a holy God. Because of Christ's work, God justifies or "acquits" guilty sinners. This is shocking, for this atonement model is founded on a strident assertion that God is just: Unlike corrupt human judges, God does not wink and pronounce criminals "innocent." God justly acquits the innocent and condemns the guilty to the penalty of the law.[49]

Justified before God, we also find ourselves *redeemed from captivity* to sin and the consequent curse and penalty of the law, death. The cost of being bought out of slavery is Christ's blood.[50] Jesus died under the curse of the law, the withdrawal of God, so that we would not have to.[51] In Jesus Christ, God has acted as deliverer, just as God did in saving the Israelites from slavery in Egypt.[52]

Acquitted and freed from the curse of the law, the ultimate goal of the work of God in Christ is the *reconciliation* of God's beloved but sinful humans with Godself. Stott clarifies that the alienation of God and humanity was mutual, not one-sided. In our sin, we are hostile to God.

48. Luke 23:45b; see also Exod 26:31–35; Heb 9:8; 10:19–20.

49. God never acquits the guilty. See for example Exod 23:6–8; Prov 17:15.

50. This picks up the ransom themes of the New Testament; see for example Mark 10:45; 1 Pet 1:18–19.

51. See, for example, Gal 3:13.

52. For redemption as a consequence of the cross, see Stott, *Cross of Christ*, 175–82; and Hodge, *Systamtic Theology*, 2:516–18.

God's wrath is God's responding hostility to everything evil, God's active opposition to it (see Rom 5:9–11). But in and through Christ, God takes the initiative and acts to bring an end to God's enmity toward sinners, with "peace" the result—peace between God and sinful humans, and also peace between hostile human groups. "Therefore, since we are justified by faith, we have peace with God through our Lord Jesus Christ, through whom we have obtained access to this grace in which we stand ..." (Rom 5:1–2a; see also Eph 2:11–22).

For Stott, this initiative of God to act in Christ to end God's enmity toward sinners is "the key to the whole of the New Testament."[53] Sinners, polluted with their crimes, were not free to approach God; but because of Christ, the wall that separates humans from a holy God has been torn down, split in two, and we are free to approach God with boldness, and have renewed fellowship with God (see Eph 2:17–18; 3:12).

THE FAITH THAT CLAIMS THE NEW FELLOWSHIP

These fruits of Christ's atoning work—justification before God, redemption from the penalty of the law, a new fellowship with God—are already real in Christ's work; we do not need to make them real. However, we must receive these fruits as a gift, through believing they have been given to us by God, and taking them for our own through the act of *faith*. Such a reception in faith demands that we abandon all ground in our selves for forgiveness and acceptance by God, and acknowledge Christ alone as ground; it requires humility. "For by grace you have been saved through faith, and this is not your own doing; it is the gift of God—not the result of works, so that no one may boast" (Eph 2:8–9).[54]

53. Stott, *Cross of Christ*, 200 (quoting James Denney, concerning God's making Christ the victim who bears the penalty for our sins, thus freeing us from the claims of justice). For Stott's discussion of reconciliation as the ultimate goal of the cross, see 192–201; for Hodge's, see *Systematic Theology*, 2:515.

54. Concerning the necessity of faith for gaining the reconciling fruits of Christ's atoning work on the cross, see Stott, *Cross of Christ*, 70–71, 84; and Hodge, *Systematic Theology*, 2:494, 497, 508, 522. Hodge (ibid., 2:497) references Heb 10:26–31. For recent presentations of the penal-substitution theory by American evangelicals, see, for example, New Testament scholar Thomas Schreiner's arguments in Beilby and Eddy, *Nature of the Atonement: Four Views*. While Bruce Demarest mentions other models of atonement in *Cross and Salvation*, he argues that the penal-substitution theory is the master model; see chap. 4/III/C, "The Big Idea of Atonement: Penal Substitution." John Piper has written some books in response to the negative reaction to Mel Gibson's *Passion of the Christ* by some Christians. Among his fifty reasons why Jesus came to die,

The three stories with which we began are not overtly religious. Yet they hint at this human role in the reconciliation which overcomes rupture. The Pakistani rapist is not ready for mercy or reconciliation, for he lacks the requisite humility and hope found in the human act of faith. In resisting personal responsibility for his crimes, he clings to self-justifying postures and exhibits no longing for mercy. In contrast, Will Munny's nightmares, and his statement to his young partner that concerning the taking of our life and its hopes, "we all have it coming, kid," reveal the humility and longing for grace that fund faith. And Monty Brogan imagines the faces of those he contemptuously wronged smiling back at him in peace, with a second chance to live his life "the way it should have been," and simultaneously knows he doesn't deserve it. For both men, such freedom for a new life must come from beyond themselves, from God.

---

the first two are "to absorb the wrath of God," and "to please his heavenly Father." See *Fifty Reasons Why Jesus Came to Die*; and *Seeing and Savoring Jesus Christ*, chap. 9. For a succinct presentation by the famous British evangelical, see Packer, *Concise Theology*. A recent book by British evangelical and pastor Steve Chalke, in which he criticizes the penal-substitutionary theory of Charles Hodge and current evangelicals (comparing the view to divine child abuse) and subscribes instead to the *Christus Victor* theory, has contributed to the ending of a fourteen-year conference partnership and has instigated a heated debate among British evangelicals concerning "the very definition of what is an evangelical" (Trammel, "Cross Purposes," 16). See Chalke, *Lost Message of Jesus*.

PART TWO

Beyond Penal Substitution

Problems and Alternatives to the Atonement of Popular Christian Piety

The Abusive God

THE THEORY OF PENAL substitution is not clear about God's intent toward us, or the meaning of our own self-sacrificing. It is this ambiguity of the "gospel message" on which patristics scholar Roberta Bondi reflects and which funded her unconscious understanding of God's—and her father's—compromised attitude toward her.

THE QUALIFICATION OF DIVINE LOVE

Revival at Pond Fork Baptist Church

By her own description, Roberta Bondi was a timid little girl who was afraid of everything; she longed for bravery. Growing up in New York City, she spent summers at her grandparents' farm in Union County, Kentucky. The second week of each visit, she would attend Vacation Bible School and the revival at Pond Fork Baptist Church. She enjoyed memorizing Bible verses and hearing Old Testament stories of God rescuing children from bad situations, and she enjoyed Kool-Aid and cookies, and crafts in the afternoons.

Yet this enjoyment was tempered by the nightly revivals. Brother Smith's message was always the same, she recounts. "'Sinners!' he would shout. 'You are all sinners! Are you ready for hell? Do you think you can keep your sins hidden from your heavenly Father? Don't you think your own Father knows what you do in secret? Do you think he can't see into your hearts? That there will be no day of reckoning? Well, I'm here to tell you judgment is coming and it's coming soon! Aren't you afraid?'"

Sitting in her starched sundress between her two big aunts, Bondi listened, trembling, for a good long while until Brother Smith would shift gears and start preaching John 3:16:

"'Yes,' he would say, 'you are a sinner,' his voice dropped to a whisper. 'But your heavenly Father loves you. He *loves* you enough to send his Son to *die* for you and your sins. Only believe, only believe God loves you, or he'll send you to hell for ever!'"

What Bondi heard was this four-point message:

1. Each of us is so rotten to the core that we deserve to die and roast in hell forever.

2. God is enraged at us enough to kill us.

3. In spite of everything, God loves us enough to rescue us by sending his son as a sacrifice to die a terrible death in our place.

4. Jesus believed this sacrificial death was the only reason he had been born in the first place.

Bondi could not believe God's love for her, despite the message of love. "How could God love me in spite of my sins if they were bad enough to make God's own Son die?"[1]

The Character and Intention of God

While Brother Smith's intent was to impress upon his hearers the depth of God's love, his four-point message painted a portrait of God in which God's character traits and intentions toward human beings are conflicted and ambiguous. For Bondi, God was described by Brother Smith as a strong father whose "strength" was found in self-sufficiency, in being "above" the children within a hierarchy, and in being "perfect."[2] Perfect in his own performance, this father also had perfectionistic expectations. Though brilliant and loving and full of life, this father focused on faults, on how the children failed to measure up to his expectations, and the difficulty in making up for those sins and absolving such guilt.[3] Tolerating no imperfections, this father found his children to be imperfect at obeying his commands, and therefore rejected them as contemptible.[4]

In the presence of a strict, perfect, and perfectionist God, we can never measure up. Somebody has to die. God is in the business of bring-

---

1. Bondi, *Memories of God*, 21–24, 116.

2. See ibid., 83–84, 183–84.

3. See ibid., 28, 157.

4. See ibid., 24, 87–90, 123.

ing death to people. While the extended explanation for this divinely-caused death was that it was needed to pay off some unspeakable debt the father's children had run up, it was unclear to Bondi to whom the debt was to be paid—to God's justice? To the devil?

As a child, Roberta could only conclude that just below the surface of love, the father simmered with anger, fired up by the child's sin of disobedience.

That God is in the death business is evident in this divine father's solution to his own rage and his contemptible children's sinful disobedience: the killing of Jesus.

God Loves Us, But . . .

Brother Smith's message speaks of the divine father's qualified love: God does not accept us "just as we are," but in spite of who we are.[5] As Brother Smith says, what we do "in secret," and the inner movements of our hearts, bring the father's judgment and his sending us to suffer in hell. As Charles Hodge said, God hates what we make of ourselves, but loves what God has made of us.

The divine father's love for us is further qualified with the father's seemingly greater concern for abstract principle over particular individuals with all of their "messiness." The father does not attempt to see and love the struggles and messiness of the child's particular personhood. Rather, the divine father knows and loves only what they might become, or were supposed to become. This father knows ideals, and as the perfect one who is a perfectionist, this father's first concerns are whether or not the ideals fulfill their calling. The children fall short of the ideal, and this makes them contemptible.[6]

The divine love is qualified again because, as Roberta Bondi sensed at the Pond Fork revival meetings, it is surrounded by the divine father's rage and his threat of condemnation, violence, and even death. The God "who loves us" is also "in the death business." The latent violence behind the divine love is seen in the context prior to God's saving act in Christ: all persons are judged as lawbreakers who deserve to die and roast in hell. The holy divine father cannot endure their presence. It is seen in the two conditions demanded for divine forgiveness and reconciliation:

5. See ibid., 48.
6. See ibid., 77–78.

someone has to be punished with death to pay for the sins of the people, and individuals must have faith in the one who paid that price. Bondi's subconscious understanding of the meaning of Jesus's death was that the divine father was going to kill her, but decided to kill Jesus instead, because he "loved her."

The fatherly love revealed on the cross is qualified in a fourth way. "The wages of sin is death," as Deuteronomy says. The justice of the divine father will be satisfied only when lawbreakers receive their just punishment, which is execution. But Jesus's death was not a mere execution. Crucifixion was meant not merely to kill, but above all to humiliate. The "love" of this divine father for us has within its purview the father's torture of the man Jesus, in order to convey to all that he is a "nonperson."

A GOD WHO SUPPORTS VIOLENCE: HOW PENAL SUBSTITUTION'S IMAGE OF GOD FUNCTIONS IN PERSONAL AND SOCIAL LIFE

There are images of God, of ourselves, and of the world that can be destructive instead of life-giving. They bind us and take away life within us. And this is true of the image of God, ourselves, and the world found in the penal substitution theory of atonement. At its root, the theory's ambivalent message about a loving, death-dealing, conflicted God makes it impossible to trust God, and this has catastrophic psychological, interpersonal, and intercommunal effects.

The Shaming God

If a person commits rape, murder, and plunder, they may hear the message concerning God's character and intention correctly in the penal substitution theory of atonement. They are lawbreakers against God's very ways who deserve the just punishment of death. Yet in spite of their rebelliousness and brutality, God loves them, and God has trod a path to save them that involves great cost to God's own self.

By the same token, if someone has had a nurturing, positive relationship with her primary caregiver(s), and/or had wonder-filled, supportive experiences in the larger world, then they may hear the note of deep divine love within the ambiguous message of God's character and intent found in the penal substitution theory.[7] The shaming, condemning, threatening notes are overcome by the dominant sound of love.

However, there are many people who do not fit in either of the two categories. With their main experiences in life being ones of failing in others' eyes and being shamed by others, they find in penal substitution a shaming God. Roberta Bondi illustrates this third situation.

Roberta could never measure up to her father's expectations of her. She was always a disappointment. When she was eleven and a half, her parents suddenly divorced. After that, she saw her father only once a year, and the visits were very painful, for she was never really sure of his love.[8]

Roberta Bondi's relationship with her father affected her hearing of the divine love in Brother Smith's gospel message. Sitting between her aunts, she heard that her "badness"—her lying, her disobedience, her unhappiness, her femaleness—was the actual cause of the divine father's sending of the son to be killed. She was unsure exactly what her sin was. But she was sure she was the reason for the murder.[9]

In response to God's violent choice of remedy for her "badness," Bondi felt a plethora of emotions. She longed for her divine father, yet perceived she could never meet his expectations. She grieved Jesus's death, while feeling guilt and shame as its source. She shifted between perfectionist behavior and depression. Since Roberta could never please God, she felt unhappy, yet unable to escape.[10] Accordingly, she felt rage: at God, others, the world, herself. Later in life, she recognized that she hated this God: a God of wrath, so focused on human imperfection; an all-powerful, angry parent God whose love somehow demanded the

---

7. Pastoral theologian Carroll Saussy builds on Ana-Maria Rizzuto's work on the formation of God images in *Birth of the Living God* to identify three sources that fund a person's image of God: A child's interaction with her or his primary caregiver(s), which results in both positive and negative memories and representations of oneself and one's caregiver(s); talk about God in church or school, at which the child is taught the "official" view of God; and the child's positive and negative experiences with the larger world found in nature, art, literature, music, neighborhood, daycare, school, and extended family. Saussy, *God Images and Self-Esteem*, 46–53.

8. Bondi, *Memories of God*, 25.

9. See ibid., 114–15, 125, 132.

10. See ibid., 25. On Bondi's connection between her similar inabilities to please her human and divine fathers, see also 118, 153.

blood-payment of God's own child for the sins and imperfections of the world, regardless of the son's lack of wrongdoing.[11]

Upon hearing this message of a divine parental love so qualified, the consequence was an increase in Roberta's sense of shame, resulting in self-hatred. Instead of being a source of new life, the images of God and herself which Roberta gained from the penal substitution theory of atonement took away her life and left her impotent. More important, she could not turn to God in her pain, for though she was told God loved her, the qualifications on this divine love created doubt about God's trustworthiness. No one, particularly the shamed and impotent, will reach out in trust, or share something genuine of themselves if they feel they may once again be judged, condemned, and violated.

Persons like Roberta Bondi whose core experiences of themselves in relation to their primary caregivers and/or the larger world are ones of shame and condemnation respond to the version of the gospel presented by the theory of penal substitution by becoming complicit in their own self-destruction. They help God by hating and punishing themselves.

The Abusive God

SACRIFICE AS REDEMPTIVE

For many persons whose primary self-destructive pattern is shame rather than lawlessness, the images of God, self, and world presented by the penal substitution theory of atonement function to make those persons more deeply alienated from their true self,[12] and complicit in their own self-hatred, punishment, and destruction. The images also function to reinforce abusive patterns in relationships, for two primary reasons.

First, the theory says that the suffering of the innocent is redemptive. As a child, Roberta Bondi watched her mother's family relationships. She noticed that "sacrifice," as it was displayed in her household and talked about at church, meant both "giving up" and "suffering for."

11. See ibid., 140–41.

12. In Object Relations Theory of psychological development, the "true self" is the original self as "whole" and integrated. It exists prior to a person's encounter with a lack of unconditional love from caregivers and the world. This lack leads the person to substitute admiration for love in relationships, with a resulting swing between grandiosity and depression concerning the ability to become admirable. The part of the self that seeks admiration is deep, but deeper still resides the original or "true" self that longs for love.

Sacrifice meant giving up what you most wanted—and a pure person would not want anything at all for her- or himself. God had demanded Abraham to sacrifice Isaac because Abraham had wanted Isaac so much. Sacrifice also meant suffering for the good of others: "'sacrifice' also had a specialized, particular meaning that applied to women in family life. Real women were supposed to suffer on behalf of their husbands and children, and this suffering was called 'sacrifice.' If the mother was exhausted with a new baby and the baby cried in the night, it was mama who got up because daddy needed his sleep. If there were two pieces of chicken and three family members, mother smilingly went hungry. If there were three silver forks and one battered, black fork, that was the one mother took."[13]

Not wanting anything for the self, and being willing to suffer pain for the sake of others' betterment, the two traits of sacrifice point to its base meaning: being selfless. God and Jesus, perfect in holiness, "sacrifice" for us. God the heavenly father gives up his own Son, sending him for the express purpose of being killed. Jesus gives up his life for us. Sin, in contrast, is thinking only of oneself.

Why were these pains endured, indeed, lifted up as sacred? Because the lesson culled from the penal substitution theory is that the suffering of the innocent is salvific. Just as Jesus's tortured execution saves humanity from the divine rage and threat of hell, so salvation becomes linked with sacrificial pain. Primarily, it is the violent perpetrator who will be saved by the victim's endurance of pain, just like violent humans are saved by the blood of Jesus. Secondarily, the victim is also redeemed, for by such endurance of pain, she or he shows that necessary holy trait of selflessness, of not wanting anything for oneself and being willing to suffer pain for others' redemption. Jesus's mark of goodness is that he chose his death freely, "for others," in obedience to God the heavenly father.

The redemptive power is strengthened when the suffering is endured in silence. For to speak, to resist, is to call attention to oneself and one's own needs.

The second reason the penal substitution theory of atonement functions to support abusive relationships is that God supports the sacrifice of the innocent, for God intends to redeem precisely through the

---

13. Bondi, *Memories of God*, 121. See also ibid., 129–30.

sacrifice of the innocent. Jesus's silent walking to his torturous execution is the will of the heavenly father.[14]

When the two-fold message is conveyed to a person caught in an abusive relationship, it leads the victim to accept abuse not only because they deserve to suffer, but also for supposed holy reasons, chief among them because they believe that their innocent suffering can save someone—the perpetrator of the violence but also themselves. Further, they endure the suffering—in silence—because they believe this is what God wants them to do.

Ironically, however, the victim's willingness to accept violation can deepen the cycle of abuse.

TRAUMA WITHIN MIXED-MESSAGE RELATIONSHIPS

When an abusive relationship is familial or intimate, the mixture of love and pain deepens self-fragmenting and self-destructive patterns in the victim. This amplification is borne out in clinical research of trauma victims.[15] The two core experiences of sexual, domestic, or war time abuse are helplessness and isolation.

The initial experience for the victim is of disempowerment. In relation to the abuser, the victim experiences a loss of control, and fears annihilation.[16] When the natural "fight or flight" impulse is ineffective in extricating the victim from the danger, the victim experiences a fragmentation of the self, and also loses the ability to integrate the memory of the violent events into her life (dissociation).[17] She becomes numb.

The abuse also severs the victim's connections with the outside world, leaving him isolated. Due to the betrayal innate to violence, the victim's basic trust in others is replaced by mistrust, and attachments to loved ones are called into question.[18] Belief in the goodness of the

14. In a telling statement by Hodge, he writes that Jesus's sufferings and death on the cross "were divine inflictions. It pleased the Lord to bruise him. He was smitten of God and afflicted" (Hodge, *Systematic Theology*, 2:517).

15. Psychiatrist Judith Lewis Herman spent two decades in research and clinical work with victims of sexual and domestic violence. In *Trauma and Recovery*, she describes common traits of victims of trauma.

16. See ibid., chap. 2: "Terror." See also Marie Fortune, *Sexual Violence*, chap. 1.

17. The abusive moments are imprinted on her psyche, yet fail to become integrated into her narrative. On repression and the creation of a false self, see also Poling, *The Abuse of Power*, 36, 44.

18. Erikson's developmental theory states that the most basic developmental move for the child is to develop a fundamental trust in reality, rather than mistrust. This basic

world, of God, and of self diminishes. The severing of these attachments deepens the loss of self for the victim.[19]

In the context of helplessness and isolation from the world, victims who survive develop survival strategies, including altered states of consciousness. These altered states allow the growth of somatic and psychological symptoms. Symptoms may include intractable depression, smoldering anger, murderous and/or suicidal impulses, somatic illnesses, a confusion of pain and emotional entrapment with love, or of pain with pleasure, and a turning of violence toward the self.[20]

When the victim receives both painful punishment and loving support from the abuser—as occurs to the son by the father in the penal substitutionary theory of atonement—the damaging effects are heightened. The abused spouse or child, for example, links abuse with love.[21] Further, the selves of victim and perpetrator are fused, for violence obliterates boundaries.[22] Because love is mixed with violence, and boundaries are weakened, the victim may have impulses to care for the needs of the perpetrator or the relational bond at the expense of her or his self-protection. Is not this mixture of love with violence at the heart of the penal substitutionary theory of atonement?

The Theological Function of Penal Substitutionary Atonement for Victims of Abuse

The penal substitutionary theory not only sanctifies abusive patterns; it also hinders movement toward healing for the victim.

As the core experiences of trauma are helplessness and isolation, so recovery comes about from the empowerment of the survivor and

---

trust develops in relation to the child's primary caregiver(s). If trauma shatters that fundamental trust, it affects the victim's psyche at its most basic level.

19. Through a combination of force, intimidation, and enticement, the perpetrator also seeks control over the victim's mind, affect, and self-assessment. Total control is achieved when the victim believes the perpetrator's assessments are correct (a result gained easily with children, who are predisposed to assume that adults are correct). The victim loses belief in her or his innate goodness, and thinks she or he deserves the suffering; otherwise, why would God allow it? (Herman, *Trauma and Recovery*, 83).

20. Perhaps through rituals of self-mutilation, addiction; eating disorder, suicide. See Fortune, *Sexual Violence*, 167–68.

21. The emotional bonds of abusive love are perceived as more compelling than intimacy of distinct selves.

22. See Herman, *Trauma and Recovery*, chap. 4; and Brock and Parker, *Proverbs of Ashes*, 155–57.

the creation of new connections to the world. A community of caring persons—whether other survivors, a therapist, or a network of friends and family—plays a significant role by aiding the survivor's empowerment and reconnection, and by countering the previous dynamics of dominance through new forms of relationality rooted in equality and mutual regard.[23] The community also aids in the victim's reassembly of the self by listening to the story without judgment, validating that the victim did nothing to deserve this violation, and reaffirming that she or he contains innate goodness and worth. This process brings mourning for the part of the self lost by the trauma. The survivor then forges a new self, one which integrates the past traumatic events while looking toward the future with desires and hope enkindled. The self holds a narrative that tells the whole truth.

The penal substitutionary theory of atonement functions to undercut just these moves toward healing. It hinders the creation of a narrative about a violation which should not have occurred by telling a different story, one in which the violation plays a redemptive role. Their suffering may save someone, and God supports it precisely for that redemptive power. It is hard for the victim to describe the violence as outrageous and try to extract her- or himself from it when it is deemed holy and God-willed. Further, the theory identifies Christian virtue with love, and identifies love with selflessness.

The very acts by the survivor needed for her or his healing—the creation of a narrative in which the violation is named as abomination utterly destructive of good; the intentional creation of a supportive network; the mourning of the self broken by the trauma; the forging of a new self; the affirming of desire and grasping of hope—all demand the victim's rightful claim to self-protection and life. All these acts are undercut by penal substitution's sanctification of selflessness as virtue. What is needed for the victim's healing is something quite contrary to the penal substitutionary theory: a definition of love as *the loving of life instead of death*, a definition which would include loving the life of the self as well as that of the perpetrator. What is needed is a definition of Christian virtue in the plural: Obedience and resistance are both holy, and the adult Christian is called to gain the wisdom to know when to

23. See Herman, *Trauma and Recovery*, 133–36.

continue in a relationship and when to distance oneself for the sake of self and the other.[24]

The penal substitutionary theory also blocks healing for victims in another way. The victim's forging of a new self may involve forgiveness, which can neither be hurried nor orchestrated by outsiders. If it occurs, it must come after the survivor's appropriate "righteous anger" is directed at the source of abuse—the perpetrator—and after the survivor places the responsibility for the abuse there, rather than upon the self.[25] Forgiveness is conditioned upon the offender's confession and repentance, including some concrete expression of the fact that the victim has been wronged;[26] that it should never have happened; and that the offender is responsible. Further, the perpetrator must change his behavior, and promise not to repeat the offense. The survivor cannot be forced to forgive the perpetrator. And if it happens, it may take one year, or thirty.[27]

This integrative and empowering role of forgiveness for the victim is subverted by penal substitutionary theory's trumpeting of unconditional forgiveness as divine command. Victims are thus forced by the church to forgive the perpetrator for the abuse prematurely, preventing the emergence of the repressed but necessary anger the victim has about the abuse, and the reassembly of the facts of what occurred into a coherent narrative. Healing is blocked.[28]

Penal substitutionary theory prevents victims from escaping abusers for a final reason: the reality of tragedy is lost in penal substitution's narrative. The insistence that the suffering resulting from abuse is redemptive disallows the victim to call it a crime, and to see her suffering as meaningless. Without the categories of criminal evil and of tragedy,

---

24. On the need for an alternative understanding of "imitating Christ," which includes both the virtue of obedience and the virtue of resistance to abuse and injustice, see Poling, "The Cross and Male Violence," 54; and Soelle, *Beyond Mere Obedience*.

25. To forgive is to give up one's right to hurt the perpetrator back. Further, it is also letting go of and thereby disarming the power the offense has over the victim's life. It involves acknowledging the humanness of the offender, without condoning what was done.

26. Such as restitution—for example, paying for medical expenses or supporting a rape-crisis center.

27. On the role, and protocol, for forgiveness as part of recovery from sexual or domestic abuse, see Fortune, *Sexual Violence*, 204–15.

28. On the victim's being pressured and hurried to forgive the perpetrator, see Fortune, *Sexual Violence*, 204–15.

confusion of violence with love and of meaninglessness with sacred meaning abounds. Such confusions contribute to the victim's psychological fragmentation, and steal her or his power to resist.[29]

These reasons help explain why penal substitutionary theory keeps victims in abusive situations, rather than freeing them. It promotes sadomasochism as virtue, thus supporting the victim's self-blame, repression of the crimes, silence concerning them, and splitting of the self, all of which ultimately leads to the self's destruction. The victim is not encouraged to "get out," to describe the story of abuse and name the abuser as culpable, or to fight for one's own right to self-determination and wholeness. Finally, penal substitutionary theory blocks redemptive change in dominance-victim dynamics, changes necessary if the victim and perpetrator are to find a new basis for self-identity in relations of equality and mutual regard.

FROM DIVINE SADISM TO DIVINE MASOCHISM

Advocates of the penal substitutionary theory of atonement often respond in three ways to the charge that the theory imagines God as a cosmic sadist, and encourages victims of abuse to remain in abusive situations.

First, they insist that their theories never say that God the father kills Jesus.[30] The New Testament makes it clear that human beings, supported by institutions with vested interests in silencing him, kill Jesus, and that it is a murderous crime against Jesus and against God. To make this assertion cohere with their claim that Jesus's death is the will of God, they make use of the concept of *double agency* for understanding the relation of divine and human agency. God works in and through evil human hearts and deeds to bring about the divinely-willed effect—the salvation of the world. Thus God and humans both act to bring about Jesus's death, but the humans involved in Jesus's execution have evil desires and intentions, while God's desires and goals are benevolent.

The concept of double agency may be helpful in understanding the complex relations between God's goodness and sovereign action and events of evil, including God's relationship to Jesus's murder. But it is

---

29. On the loss of the category of tragedy, due to the search for sacred meaning in the abusive event, and a source in someone other than the abuser, see Fortune, "Transformation of Suffering"; and in *Sexual Violence*, 193–208.

30. See n. 14 above, however.

not helpful in countering the claim that penal substitutionary theory supports victims' continued surrender to abusive patterns. As we saw with Hodge and Stott, the concept was not used in a significant way. When it is used by theologians or preachers, it is a subtle theological argument difficult to grasp, allowing the simpler explanation to come to the fore: God the father wanted Jesus dead to solve the problem of God's wrath toward us and allow a new relationship. Further, whether the idea of double agency is used or not, the two core reasons penal substitution theory functions to support abusive relationships remain: The suffering of the innocent is redemptive, and God supports the sacrifice of the innocent.

Second, God is not a child abuser, because Jesus is not a child when he goes to his death; he is an adult around thirty. Further, Jesus is not a victim, because he chooses to go freely to Jerusalem and the death he anticipates. Nor is Jesus the victim of the father's abusive will, for the three persons of the Trinity share in one will and purpose: the world's redemption by means of a self-sacrifice on the cross.

This appeal to the unanimity of mind amidst the Trinity, however, leaves the basic patriarchal structure intact. The father sends the son. The son, despite hesitation and pleading, plays the role of obedience to and subordination of self to the will of the father, because someone will be saved by this violence. This pattern glorifies suffering, sacralizes violence, and makes the "virtue of revolt" against abusers impossible.

Third, while some theories cast three players in the divine drama of salvation—God the father, sinful humanity, and Jesus the intermediary—other versions such as Stott's clarify that it is not God's will that another pay the price of suffering to release humankind from the bondage of sin and death. Rather, in Christ, God pays the price.

This version may be a bit more palatable, but does not change how the theory functions for victims of abuse. The "God of the cross" moves from cosmic sadist to cosmic masochist. The principles that good still comes from surrender to torture and suffering, and that such surrender is God's will, remain as model for abused victims.

A stronger counter to the criticisms of penal substitution theory is this: If God felt superior to guilty humans, if God ridiculed and held them in contempt—as every abuser does his or her victim—then God would never have *died for* them. This kenotic movement counters forcefully the charge that God is a cosmic abuser.[31] Abusers objectify and seek total control over their victims, behavior opposite that of a kenotic God who stoops in order to see us eye-to-eye and endure our fate to lift us up.

The Violent God

The theology inherent in the penal substitutionary theory of atonement functions in ways that contribute to violence. On the psychological level, for those whose primary spiritual problem is not self-assertive lawlessness but rather self-negating shame, the theology functions to deepen their sense of shame and make them accomplices in their own destruction. On the interpersonal and systemic levels, the theology functions to keep victims of abuse fragmented, silent, and willing to endure abuse in order to punish the self or save someone else. On the national and international levels, the theology functions to sanctify human violence against others.

Violence towards humans entails the violation of inalienable subjects, and the maintenance of relations of dominance and submission. This objectification, involving harm and damage to bodily and/or psychic integrity, can be done to the self, or to the Other.[32] Christianity has a history of complicity in, and perpetration of, such violence, calling into question its loyalty to its central figure.[33]

The penal substitutionary theory of atonement provides a metaphysical sanction of violence because of the ambivalent God-image it presents, and its understanding of how human life is secured.

31. On the impact of the kenotic movement upon the view of God for first-century Christians, see Placher, *Narratives of a Vulnerable God*, chap. 1, "The Vulnerable God"; and Thomas Cahill, *Desire of the Everlasting Hills*, esp. chaps. 1 and 5.

32. For Weaver's definitions of violence and nonviolence, see *Nonviolent Atonement*, 8–9; and "Violence in Christian Theology," 226.

33. As Weaver writes: "Is Christianity characterized by the medieval crusades, warrior popes, the multiple blessings of wars by Christians over the centuries, wars religious and otherwise fought in the name of the Christian God, support for capital punishment, justifications of slavery, worldwide colonialism in the name of spreading Christianity, corporal punishment under the guise of 'spare the rod and spoil the child,' the systemic violence of women subjected to men, and more? Or does it reflect its eponymous founder, who is worshiped as 'Wonderful Counselor, Mighty God, Everlasting Father, Prince of Peace' (Isa. 9:6); whose Sermon on the Mount taught nonviolence and love of enemies; [and] who faced his accusers nonviolently and then died a nonviolent death . . . ?" (in "Violence in Christian Theology," 225).

A God of Help and Terror: Penal Substitution's Ambivalent God-Image

The penal substitutionary theory of atonement did not create an ambivalent image of God. However, its logic contains elements which undergird that ambivalent picture of God's character and intent toward humankind: It presents a form of religion rooted in fear and self-abasement, rather than trust and self-acceptance; it employs as premise the logic of mimetic exchange; it deletes the role of "the Devil" from atonement models; and it conceives an a-historical account of atonement.

A Religion Rooted in Fear

German Catholic theologian Eugen Drewermann traces the descent into fratricide to an ambivalent God-image that introduces fear and a sacrificial mentality into individual and group psychology. Yahwist accounts in Genesis portray this tragic fall of the God-image and resulting introduction of violence.[34] In Genesis 2, humans are living in harmony with God, the earth, and themselves. They love without dominating one another. How is this possible? God confirms the true longings and wishes of human beings, and allows them to love their own life. Because of this divine advocacy, humans rely upon God in trust; the relation is completely lacking in fear.[35]

The transition from harmony with God to an ambivalent relation with a God perceived as heteronomous emerges with a shift from confident trust to fear, a shift brought on by the role of the serpent in Genesis 3:1–7: "Now the serpent was more crafty than any other wild animal that the Lord God had made. He said to the woman, 'Did God say, "You shall not eat from any tree in the garden"?'" (3:1).[36]

Through the question, the serpent paints for the woman, for the first time, a tyrannical portrait of God by wrongly suggesting that God forbade humans to eat from *any* of the trees in the garden, and by claiming that God gave the command not as guiding information (2:16b–17) but to jealously prevent humans from becoming like God (3:4–5).

---

34. This explication of Drewermann's logic is based on the first secondary source in English on Drewermann's work: Beier, *Violent God-Image*.

35. On the original harmony, see ibid., 33, 38; on God 's confirming true human longings, 127; on humans' relying completely on God, 109, 119–20.

36. For Beier's description of Drewermann's interpretation of Gen 3:1–7, see *Violent God-Image*, 38–39, 42.

The woman wants to hold onto God, as seen in her attempt to defend God by correcting the serpent (3:2). The change in the woman's perception of God, however, becomes clear in her confusion as she attempts to defend God. In her retelling of God's instructions, she adds an element not originally present—the taboo of touching the tree (3:3). She remembers God's instructions within a feeling of fear, changing a guiding instruction to a commandment, and remembering it as more severe than it is.

She fears being shunned and rejected by God, fears losing God, the source of her and all life. For God is now perceived as a moralist. Similar to the God of the first part of the Flood Story, God insists on a "clean" world without human defilement, and will punish them, depending on what the humans do. The woman's motive for following God's instruction shifts from trust in God as life-giving source, to fear that God would punish her with death. She seeks to "obey" God by doing her moral duty. Later, the fear will include hell as well.

As Drewermann reads it, the Yahwist's account of the fall is one of deeper tragedy beneath genuine moral culpability. The consequences of the fall are that though God walks in the Garden as ever, now the humans are able to see God only in ambivalence. They hide from God. The humans introduce into the God-image a deep contradiction. From God now comes both protection and annihilation; salvation and doom; security and deadly threat. Though God seems jealous and unjust, humans also retain the sense that God wants to save them from the spiral of fear and violence that engulfs them.[37] But they perceive that how God will appear to them depends on what humans do. God's love is now conditioned.

While life with God was good before, now humans know what life feels like without God: Being human feels like a lack. Nakedness turns to shame. From within this field of fear and sense of lack, the humans attempt to recover God's lost love by becoming admirable. Yet this tragic response employs a sacrificial mentality that brings either internal or external violence, or both. Since God is now perceived as a moral watchdog unwilling to accept that perfections and imperfections can live together, the human will not accept such compromises either and so attempts to become flawless. This effort splits the self into parts that are permitted to be seen and acknowledged and expressed, and parts that must

37. See the Yahwist accounts in Genesis 3–11.

be repressed. This combination of performance and masochistic self-abasement in the fight for lost love is an internally violent moral effort.

Contempt for the self creates an environment in which contempt for the Other appears. Feeling far from God, and believing God needs his free self-giving in order to accept him, Cain slowly feels that the "other," his brother, is a competitor for the blessing of a lost God (Gen 4:1–16).[38] Either the other is idolized, or subjugated, by murder if necessary.[39]

The sacrificial mentality also encourages violence in a second way, by enticing the human being to liquidate her independent personality in order to be accepted by the dominant social group. Such sacrifice of the individual and of everything human—kindness, reason, morality, humanity, an inner sense of self, freedom of conscience—for the sake of group acceptance is easily harnessed by heteronomous leaders through the use of fear.[40] The willingness to step forward to protect the threatened Other is weakened.

The penal substitutionary theory of atonement inflames all these existential and spiritual dynamics that lead to human violence. The intense contradictions humans introduced into the God-image tumble forth in its interpretations of the cross of Christ. It promotes the sacrificial mentality that is the source of Christianity's destructive power. God, as enemy, out of love, wants humans to die. A God who needs the death of a human being in order to reconcile the world to Godself is untrustworthy, barbaric, sadistic.[41]

38. Drewermann believes Cain did not originally seek to resolve the tension with his brother through murder; initially, he wanted to talk with him. Leaning on Buber's translation of Gen 4:8, Drewermann translates: "Cain talked with Abel, his brother. But then as they were in the field Cain rose up against Abel, his brother, and killed him" (Beier, *Violent God-Image*, 46 n. 6).

39. On the rise of competition and deep-seated attitudes of jealousy, envy, and rage, which then bring on idolization or violence toward one's Other, see ibid., 45–46, 106–7, 128, 213. For an analysis of these dynamics of envy, see Ann and Barry Ulanov, *Cinderella and Her Sisters*.

40. On the manner of a person's self-projection entailing the liquidation of an independent personality, see Beier, *Violent God-Image*, 3, 12, 29, 31–32, 107–8. On the person with diminished personality then projecting the self as only "good"—a good citizen, or father—and also lacking resistance to peer pressure toward violence, see 6, 23, 29, 31. On authoritarian institutions stabilizing power by means of fear and accessing the sacrificial mentality, see 3, 8–9, 20–21, 128.

41. See Drewermann in ibid., 218.

Is it any wonder that with such a contradictory image of God, within a field of fear and sacrificial mentalities, we should imitate the saving, violent God?

The Logic of Mimetic Exchange

We can now clearly see that the penal-subsitution theory of atonement emerges from and supports a form of religion rooted in fear and self-abasement, undergirding an ambivalent God-image that entices human violence. The theory also employs the logic of mimetic exchange, to similar effect. That logic is both judicially and anthropologically rooted.

In Roman law, if a person harms another, he must compensate the other for damages. If he is wise, he acts before the aggrieved party strikes back for the perceived violation; a "gift" may defer the violent response of the other. Alternately, beneficial action earns merit which deserves to be repaid by the other.

This logic of mimetic exchange conceives human life grounded on violence and the logic of an eye for an eye, rather than the logic of forgiveness, the former intertwined with the majority tradition of criminal justice in the Christian West.[42] The majority thread embraces retributive justice, which is grounded on the idea that offenders must endure retributory sufferings commensurable with the evils they have inflicted if the "balance" of justice is to be restored.

The idea that sacrificial suffering saves people from righteous wrath is present at the tribal level as well. Anthropologist René Girard argues that when rivalry over a limited desired object leads to escalating violence between multiple groups, the crisis of violence is surprisingly solved when a figure (or minority group) is singled out by any arbitrary mark of difference or weakness, and warring parties find commonality in attacking this one. The brutalization of the surrogate deflects attention from the previous object of desire and brings peace. The startling peace is felt as holy, and the sacrificial death of the surrogate deemed "sacred," the will of God who brought about peace through those violent means.

The notion of a juridically absolute and punitive God who upholds the logic of mimetic exchange is used to explain the violence suffered by Jesus. God uses violence to solve violence, and does so through victim-

---

42. The minority thread advocates *restorative justice*, in which the community focuses on the needs and rights of victims, on education and reintegrative shaming for perpetrators, and on restitution and reconciliation.

ization of a chosen surrogate. Such an ambivalent God-image, in which cruel reciprocities are combined with motherly mercy, is used by humans to justify their own victimization of the marginalized, a victimization with an imagined and miraculous "saving power."[43]

DELETING THE ROLE OF THE DEVIL

If a religious field of fear and an embraced presupposition of mimetic exchange move groups toward divinely-sanctioned violence, the deletion of "the Devil's" role from the penal substitutionary theory of atonement heightens their effect.

During the first millennium of Christianity, the Devil had a role in atonement. The era's dominant theory of atonement, *Christ the Victor*, imagines three parties in the redemptive narrative—God, captive humans, and Satan—with God and Satan battling over the human beings. For example, the subset of this model, the *ransom* theory, imagines God bargaining with the Devil for the release of humans who, through their sin, had made themselves subject to the Devil. By becoming incarnate in human form, appearing weak, the second person of the Trinity lures the Devil into grabbing hold of Christ as well and condemning him to death. The Devil had no right to kill the sinless human being, Jesus of Nazareth. Overstepping his bounds, the Devil justly lost control of humanity to Christ, who restored human beings to the original status in creation.

In *Christ the Victor*, it is the Devil who needs the death of Jesus. The death is neither God's desire, nor Christ's. Further, the Devil is the agent of Jesus's death. God and Christ remain mostly nonviolent, focused solely on liberating captive humans.

In *Cur Deus Homo?* Anselm (1033–1109) deleted the Devil from that triangular relation, leaving only the sinners and God. Instead of the death of Jesus being a sacrifice from God and Christ to the Devil in order to free human beings, the death now moves from sinful humanity (embodied in Jesus as mediator) to God the Father, to satisfy God's offended honor. God orchestrates the violence to satisfy God's just nature.

In Luther's notions of the cross and the "alien work of God," the conflict that once occurred between God and the Devil now is brought within God. God experiences a conflict between wrath and love, two

---

43. For Girard's theory about conflictual relations among our hominid ancestors, see Girard, *Violence and the Sacred*.

warring factions within God's own self. God's heart is ambivalent, but with the death of Jesus, wrath is overcome by love.

In *Christ the Victor*, God is the advocate and helper of humans in time of fear. With the satisfaction and penal substitution theories of atonement, the dark hypostasis, once residing in the figure of the Devil, is now fixed into the heart of God. Alongside God's saving impulses, God emerges as vengeful toward human beings, judgmental, abusive, the ultimate punisher. This violence in God then sanctions human violence as punishment and saving satisfaction.[44]

By altering the triangular relation in the passion narrative into a morality tale between God and guilty sinners, penal substitution's deletion of the Devil brings about the loss of *the concept of tragedy* as well, a concept helpful in countering the sacrificial mentality which, according to Drewermann and victim advocates, contributes to violence.

An Ahistorical Model of Atonement

By moving from an historical to an a-historical view of how Jesus saves us, penal substitutionary theory folds violence into saving motifs in the God-image, against the intentions of Jesus. It understands the divine-human relationship through an abstract legal formula, allowing it to locate the salvific work of God solely in the cross. By focusing on supposed "universal" principles—sin as disobedience; the need for retributive punishment before divine forgiveness is possible; the saving role of an innocent substitute—rather than the concrete elements of the gospels' narratives involving Jesus's birth, message and ministry, execution by an empire, and appearances after the resurrection, the political elements of Jesus's statements and actions, death and resurrection can be ignored, as can the theorists' own political interests. Jesus's consistent nonviolence becomes irrelevant to the atonement model, and fails to inform its God-image.[45]

Such an ahistorical penal substitution permits a person to claim Jesus' saving work while ignoring his ethical practice. A person or group may embrace Jesus's redemptive death while wielding the sword Jesus

---

44. On the deletion of the Devil from atonement theories introducing metaphysical dualism into God's self, resulting in an ambivalent God-image that sanctions human violence, see Bartlett, *Cross Purposes*, 58–62, 72–94, 130–34. See also Weaver, "Violence in Christian Theology," 227–29; and *The Nonviolent Atonement*, 72–73, 197–204.

45. See Cone, *God of the Oppressed*, 52.

had forbidden. The atonement models allow for the accommodation, and often outright support, of a group's institutions of social order based in violence—institutions such as slavery, racism, militarism, and capital punishment in the penal system. Society's violence is left unchallenged.[46]

THE MYTH OF REDEMPTIVE VIOLENCE

By rooting religion in fear and self-abasement, employing the logic of mimetic exchange, deleting the Devil from the atonement narrative, and creating an ahistorical model, the penal substitutionary theory of atonement supports the transposition of violence into the divine nature, leaving an ambivalent God-image. God is both redeemer and source of fear. This ambivalent God-image functions to support accommodation or outright support for inter-human violence, as well as violence against self and nature.

However, through three of its ideas, the penal substitutionary theory of atonement further functions to support violence. The myth of redemptive violence, the assertion of divine support for such violence, and the sanctification of the selfless endurance of violence as "love" which "mimics Jesus" all converge in the notion of the innocent substitute. This idea of a surrogate who undergoes suffering and thereby redeems others often claims the figure of the "suffering servant" from Isaiah 52–53 for inspiration.

Beyond its effect upon parties in abusive relationships, the hallowed figure of the innocent substitute functions to support violence between groups and nations. For perpetrators of violence, it suggests that violence against other groups is salvific in some mysterious fashion, and that God has chosen the innocent group for the role of substitute.[47]

46. Cone acknowledges that in their personal ethics, white theologians such as Jonathan Edwards, Harold DeWolf, and Paul Tillich may have been against black oppression, and for the civil-rights movement. But their theological theories, being "universal," were able to talk about the God-human relationship, sin, and reconciliation, without reference to political structures. See Cone, "White American Theology," in ibid., 45–53. His entire third chapter, "The Social Context of Theology," is relevant here; and see 212.

Womanist theologian Kelly Brown Douglas connects the accommodation to institutions of violence in society by the powerful classes to the "Platonization" of Christianity, in other words, interpretations of the cross developed apart from an investigation into the historical circumstances of the murder of Jesus. See Douglas, *What's Faith Got To Do With It?* 53–56.

47. Orlando Patterson argues that black lynching was seen as redemptive by many fundamentalist whites in the American South after the Civil War, in a way analogous

For the victimized group, it may move them to endure such suffering in order to play the role of innocent substitute, and gain the benefits of divine approval and a blessed reward in the hereafter.

The violence between human beings, and of individuals upon themselves, finds support in the message that such violence has saving power, and in the image of a God who also saves through violent means.

METHODOLOGICAL FAILURE

By far the most damaging effects of the penal-substitutionary theory upon the gospel are its introduction of violence, and thus ambivalence, into the divine love, and the way the resulting ambivalent God-image and myth of redemptive violence function to support human violence. The theory, however, also fails methodologically, ethically, and evangelistically.

Theology draws its content from four sources: scripture, the Christian theological and practical traditions, reason, and contemporary human experience (which includes the sciences). The penal substitutionary model fails to cohere with all four sources.

At first glance, the claim that penal substitution lacks coherence with Scripture and tradition is startling. After all, every theorist of the model draws heavily from texts and verses in both testaments, and penal substitution has been a predominant model in Catholicism since Aquinas, and Protestantism since Luther and Calvin (who both continued the Thomistic line of thought). Clearly, the Bible and tradition present texts concerning the seriousness of human sin, the divine judgment of and wrath against that sin, and the role of sacrifices to cleanse the guilty (whether of animals or of the Son).

But the gaping hole in the penal substitutionary theory's coherence with the New Testament and Christian traditions is itself what is startling: The theory has no saving role for the resurrection of Jesus from the dead. How is such a theory viable when it leaves out the central and methodologically-originating event of the Christian faith—the shocking and hope-inducing resurrection of the Crucified One? By reducing Jesus's resurrection to irrelevancy, the theory allows for a static and/or cyclical understanding of the sinner's relation with God that replaces the

---

to the redeeming power in Christ's crucifixion. The ambivalent view of God, combined with the notion of the suffering, redemptive substitute, supports the lynching mentality. See Patterson, *Rituals of Blood*, chap. 2, esp. 215–22. See also Douglas, *What's Faith Got to Do with It?* 61–70.

apocalyptic clash of powers which forms the New Testament context for Jesus's death and resurrection. Instead of seeing God the Mother/Father, Jesus, and the Holy Spirit countering the principalities and powers that use violence to subjugate persons, groups, and nature—with Jesus's death and resurrection being decisive moments in that battle—the penal substitutionary theory removes the cross from this intra-historical clash. It becomes, instead, an ahistorical cultic moment of sacrifice by which God's conflict between justice and mercy is resolved.

The removal of the resurrection from God's saving act allows for the previously-discussed problems to emerge: The lifting up of the suffering of the innocent, and of death, as sacred though difficult moments on a personal journey from death to everlasting life, thus underwriting sacred violence; the separating of salvation from history and its socio-political movements, and thus from ethics; and the loss of the unambiguous import of the resurrection—that God is against death and its powers, and for us. Without the resurrection, the penal substitutionary theory diabolically distorts the gospel narratives.[48]

Because penal substitutionary theory fails to cohere with reason and experience, its incredibility weakens it further. The theory unreasonably asks believers to trust in a psychologically-conflicted God. A follower is asked to believe that, without the sacrificial punishment and death of Jesus, God the father is enraged enough at her sins to kill her. Her sin is so wicked that she deserves to die and to roast in hell forever. Yet this father loves her so much, he sent his beloved One to be tortured and executed in her place. However, this offer of love includes the caveat that if she doesn't believe in the story's truth, she will roast in hell forever!

The believability is also undercut by its assertion that the Son came only to die, and he himself thought of his mission solely in terms of his sacrificial offering during the last six hours of his life. Rather, Jesus approaches his proclamation, healings, and social interactions with a focus which suggests he believes God's eschatological presence is breaking into the world precisely through the actions of his life and ministry; this seems true even if he later developed the recognition that he was going to be killed.

---

48. On the eclipse of the resurrection's challenge to suffering and death in the sacrifice and penal-substitutionary theories, see Weaver, *The Nonviolent Atonement*, 49–58; and Finlan, *Problems with Atonement*, 73–74.

Credibility is further undercut because the conceptual premises of the penal substitutionary theory are no longer accepted by those in modern/postmodern cultures. Most today find the concept of an innocent substitute incomprehensible as well as unjust. How can one person's sin or goodness be transferred to another? Or how could the death of Jesus change God's view of the rest of humankind? The punishment of a substitute does not make us any less guilty. Without this notion of the innocent substitute, the entire penal substitutionary theory of atonement collapses.

Another premise of satisfaction and penal substitutionary theories of atonement is that the predominant, if not only, disabling human problem is guilt. Many individuals and groups, however, are bound more by self-destructive shame, or by suffering, than by guilt.

ETHICAL FAILURE

The penal substitutionary theory of atonement has no ethical requirement because it is ahistorical and ignores the resurrection. A person may never live differently—yet be reconciled to God and admitted to an afterlife.

As penal substitutionary theory describes salvation as an event of intra-divine drama that happens above human history, it similarly negates the need for social transformation. The prophets understood divine salvation as the restoration of *shalom*, in which wholeness spread to nature, human bodies and personalities, and social structures. Jesus forgave sins, called followers to repent, and invited them into a new relationship with God. But like the prophets, he combined this person-focused effort with strong challenges to "the powers and principalities" that used violence to maintain unjust social orders. By dropping this element of social challenge, the penal substitutionary theory allows people to become "right with God" while perpetrating—or enjoying—the benefits of unjust social relations.

EVANGELISTIC FAILURE

The great strength of the penal substitutionary theory of atonement is in its core message: Reconciliation with God comes as gift, and that divine-human reconciliation is an accomplished fact in Jesus Christ. This is a message filled with hope.

That strength is evangelistically compromised, however. First, by describing the problem through an ahistorical, abstract legal formula, narrowing God's response to Jesus's six hours of suffering at Golgotha, and avoiding the triune God's eschatological confrontation with the powers, the broad saving work of the triune God falls from view altogether. Without cosmic conceptions of Christ and the Spirit, the notion that the triune God is creating a process of world transformation that is at the heart of Christianity, but also the other world religions, is lost. Evangelism becomes haughty and imperialistic. Christians approach non-Christians to speak and never to listen. They tell the news of a saving sacrifice and call for faith, yet fail to consider that Christ and the Spirit may have preceded their arrival. They perceive no need to listen to Christ's voice or the Spirit's truth in and through the voice of the non-Christian "Other."

What is most tragic is the compromise of the gospel itself. The prodigal father of the lost son is replaced by the exacting judge who upholds the cosmic order of justice, whose forgiveness is contingent upon the penalty of suffering unleashed upon someone, and obedient faith in the saving effect of that death.

That the penal substitution theory should reflect the transactional logic of mimetic exchange rather than the shocking logic of grace should not surprise us, given the psychological proclivity human beings have for the principle of *quid pro quo*. People should get what they deserve, we have come to accept. Nothing is free.

Yet deep at night, we long for mercy.

3

God, the Lavish Lover of All Life

WHEN I WAS SIXTEEN, I worked at a summer camp as a counselor-in-training. Many peers and youth leaders at a local Presbyterian church had played a role in shifting my attitude toward religious faith. Among the most significant of those persons was Ben. Ten years my senior, he was one of the directors of the high school youth ministry.

Though I had loved the excitement and new friendships at the summer camp, it had also been a bit lonely for me. Ben decided to encourage me by giving a visit. After driving six hours, he called to say he had arrived. At *Camp Firwood*, we had to walk a half mile along the forest road to the locked gate to meet visitors. When I crested a hill in the road, I saw him at the gate. He broke into a huge smile, and lifted his right hand in a wave. I smiled and waved back. Neither of us said anything. As I walked the still considerable distance toward him, he didn't relax his smile or lower his arm. Instead, his left hand went up as well. Both arms wide in the air, a smile and gleaming eyes between them, as in a bodily benediction. As I walked, his enthusiasm only increased. He began waving the arms, then jumping in the air.

My summer feelings of loneliness eased. Most of all, I thought, "This must be what God is like." Ever since, when I have wondered what God is like, and how God feels about me, I remember that face at the gate; the arms, waving; the promise, never in doubt from his end, that I am wanted, that my existence matters.

It never occurred to me that God might or would reject me. Mine has never been a faith rooted in fear.

THE CRITICS' UNDERSTANDINGS OF SALVATION

Similarly, the sharp critics of penal substitutionary theory of atonement do not root faith in fear. Drewermann identifies the critics' fundamental shift in thinking about salvation. As we have seen, for Drewermann, the root of Christianity's often-destructive violence in society, interpersonal relations and the human psyche is its early, tragic return to an ambivalent, violent God-image. This distorted portrait of God's character and intent created a religion founded in fear, which itself led to a sacrificial mentality in order to ease those fears, a way of death which supported violence against self and others.

Drewermann corrects the faulty Christian praxis of violence by shifting from an ambivalent, violent God-image to a nonambivalent, nonviolent image of God. All other changes in soteriology come in relation to this fundamental shift. In this approach, Drewermann is not alone among critics.

SIX TRAITS OF THE ALTERNATIVE SOTERIOLOGIES

There are common patterns that emerge in a study of the alternative soteriologies offered by many critics. Here, Marit Trelstad in her *Cross Examinations* can help us. She describes a feminist alternative understanding of how God saves us which illuminates six traits common to many alternative soteriologies.

Ground Clearing

The first common trait is methodological. The sharp critics of penal substitution mentioned in chapter 2 form a new basis for conceiving how God saves us by negating or reversing all of the premises held by advocates of penal substitution, for in the modern/postmodern world, the premises are no longer viable. They reject:

- the premise that the predominant problem of the human condition is guilt, rather than shame, suffering, tragedy, or meaninglessness

- the equation of divine justice with retributive justice and its logic of mimetic exchange

- the notion that an innocent substitute may justly pay the price of punishment for someone else's guilt

- the presupposition that God, in God's holiness, cannot abide sin, and so cannot have fellowship with the unholy

- the conclusion that God cannot forgive until the guilty party's punishment is paid in full, vicariously or otherwise.

They also reject the premises that lead to the ambivalent God-image that qualifies the divine love. In particular, they reject:

- the premise that God loves us in spite of who we are, rather than as the very people we are

- the premise that God has greater concern for abstract principle over particular individuals (as in Abraham's near-sacrifice of Isaac, and the Great Flood)

- the conception of the divine love surrounded by the divine father's rage and his threat of condemnation, violence, and death; that humans are so bad that God wants to kill them, and thus they are the reason for Jesus's vicarious, sacrificial death.

In terms of portraying the character and intention of God, these qualifiers of the divine love are simply negated.

Planting Anew

With the premises behind the penal substitutionary theory rejected, the way is cleared for the critics' second trait: the shift from an ambivalent, violent God-image to a nonambivalent, nonviolent image of God. Countering the serpent's questions which distorted the God-image, making Eve wonder if God was trustworthy, Drewermann and the others assert that God gives us unconditional acknowledgment, acceptance, love. Our life is precious to God. God whispers that our name is always on God's lips. While faith is about transformation of the individual, society, and cosmos, God loves us as the very persons we are, not in spite of who we are. God will not sacrifice any of us for the furtherance of abstract principles. The divine love is not mixed with rage or threats of condemnation, violence, and death. It is pure, and nonviolent. This is what Trelstad means when she says our relation to God and reconciliation with God are "ontological." We live within the divine embrace because that embrace depends solely on the unconditional and irrevocable commitment God makes to be our God and to love us. The gift of relationship is offered freely, without limit, and without regard for the moral or spiritual nature of the recipient. While it is true we sin gravely, there is no alienation on God's part toward us. Further, our reconciliation with God occurs simply on the basis of God's gracious choice to love and redeem us and all creation.[1] God is a lover who lavishly pours God's love and gifts upon us, as Trelstad portrays when she introduces her soteriology with a speech from General Lorens Lowenhielm at the end of an extravagant dinner in Isak Dinesen's *Babette's Feast*:

> [W]e imagine divine grace to be finite. For this reason we tremble
> . . . We tremble before making our choice in life, and after having
> made it again tremble in fear of having chosen wrong. But the
> moment comes when our eyes are opened, and we see and realize
> that grace is infinite. Grace, my friends, demands nothing from
> us but that we shall await it with confidence and acknowledge it
> in gratitude. Grace . . . makes no conditions and singles out none
> of us in particular; grace takes us all to its bosom and proclaims
> general amnesty.[2]

Surrounded by this unconditional, lavish love, we need not fear God. Thus, the fear and consequent sacrificial mentality that are the inner funds of human violence are intercepted and disarmed by the now unambiguous, nonviolent image of God.

In a surprising way, these alternative soteriologies share common ground with the penal substitutionary theory of atonement. Both proclaim the fundamental message that we are justified to exist in the world. This justification provides a new basis for self-identity, for living, and for reconciliation. However, the theories base the claim upon radically different foundations. For the penal substitutionary theory, we are justified to exist in the world because the punishment for our sins has been fully paid by the Son's death. God's alienation from us due to sin, and the internal tension between justice and mercy within God, have been resolved. With the conditional covenant of the moral law fulfilled, God can now be all-merciful.

On the other hand, for Drewermann, Trelstad, and the other sharp critics, it has always been true that we are "justified to exist," and that God conveys unconditional mercy toward us, for both truths are based solely upon the unlimited nature of the divine love, and the irrevocable commitment of God toward God's beloved creatures. God's actions in

1. See Trelstad, "Lavish Love," 110–11.

2. Dinesen, *Anecdotes of Destiny and Ehrengard*, 52, as quoted in Trelstad, "Lavish Love: A Covenantal Ontology," 109 (inclusive language changes are Trelstad's).

history take the form of clarifying these constant truths, rather than reestablishing them after they have faltered. "We are justified to exist in the world" is the first and ultimate word in the alternative soteriologies. This is in direct opposition to Hodge and Stott who insist the unalterable word is this: "The law must be kept."

Feeding the Plant

Negating the premises behind the penal substitutionary theory clears the ground for the portrayal of God in nonambivalent, nonviolent God image. With the final four common traits, the sharp critics bolster their nonviolent image of God.

First, the prime source of agency for salvation shifts from Jesus to a combination of God and the believer, for these alternative soteriologies are based upon a reciprocal model of God's relation to the world. The salvific process is synergistic, one in which God and human agents cooperate in mutuality and reciprocity toward the shared goal of healing the world.

This shift in understanding the agency of salvation supports a corresponding shift toward a nonambivalent, nonviolent God-image. This shift supports intra-creaturely relations of equality and reciprocity in which power is shared. This makes it much easier to imagine God acting redemptively through other religions, thus erasing the arrogant and imperialistic Christian exclusivism found in penal substitution. The synergistic model also heightens the role of the believer in her or his salvation and that of the world as one that is cooperative and in which behavioral, ethical and spiritual change is required in the believer.

The shift in agency makes the second constructive move possible. The critics' alternative soteriologies shift the locus of salvation off the cross to what happens before and after Jesus's crucifixion.[3] Salvific are Jesus's vision of the reign of God and its portrayal of God's inviolable, covenantal love; Jesus's healings, exorcisms, and actions to subvert social injustice; non-hierarchical social relations of equality, mutual respect, love and reciprocity; and the human reception of this vision of God's reign and actualization of relations of mutuality and reciprocity. These cooperative actions by Jesus and human agents are ultimately salvific

---

3. See Trelstad, "Lavish Love," 110.

because they clarify the eternal covenant between God and creation and highlight that God is the God who raises the dead.

In their third constructive move, the critics support a nonambivalent, nonviolent God-image by dissolving the distinctions between atonement, salvation, and creation. Creation and salvation are seen as one continuous, organic process by which God and creatures cooperate to bring the world to its fulfillment. The divine-creaturely processes of creation and redemption become synonymous.

The dissolution of the distinctions between creation, redemption, and at-one-ment has the further advantage, once again, of removing an exclusivistic view of Jesus's saving role amidst religious pluralism. When redemption and atonement are separated from creation, faith becomes particularized in Jesus Christ as savior. In contrast, by bringing together creation with redemption and at-one-ment in one overall divine movement toward creation, God's unity with all creatures is strengthened, and faith is able to focus its attention upon the one Creator behind all religious traditions. It is to divine creative grace that we turn our attention, not toward a specified (and exclusive) divine redeeming grace acting in a unique way in Jesus of Nazareth.

Finally, the sharp critics make a definitive, negative claim. In their alternate soteriologies, they ascribe a meaning to the cross which could not be more opposed to that found in the penal substitutionary theory of atonement. They insist that the crucifixion of Jesus is not salvific in any way whatsoever. As Delores Williams writes, "There is nothing of God in the blood of the cross."[4] It is a tragedy, a martyr's noble death, a crime, and nothing more.

This rejection of the cross as a locus of redemption brings great advantages to the alternate soteriologies. It supports the nonambivalent, nonviolent portrait of God by asserting that God did not want, will, or bring about the murder of Jesus, but rather, reacts in horror at his torture and execution by humans.

Most significantly, by rejecting the saving role of the cross, these authors reject the idea that human life is secured by means of violence; that God supports the suffering of the innocent as somehow "saving"; and that Christian virtue is identified with love, and love with selflessness, an ethic which converges upon the suffering surrogate concept which lies behind the continuance of all forms of human violence.

4. Williams, "Black Women's Surrogacy," 32.

The deletion of the redeeming role of Jesus's crucifixion also aids, once again, in overturning an exclusivistic view of salvation that a focus on the cross inevitably brings. For those who have trouble understanding how the death of one man two thousand years ago in Palestine can save humanity from its sins, the cross's removal from soteriology may aid the believability of the argument. Finally, the problem of conditional grace, located in the penal theory's interpretation of the cross, is overcome by the cross's removal. God's grace toward us is not contingent upon someone's death to pay the price for sins, and upon human belief in the saving efficacy of that death. Grace is unconditional and unearned, and thus, a gift.

THE CONCRETE MODELS

Multiple concrete theories of salvation may fit under the overarching soteriological framework presented in this chapter. In the following two chapters, we shall look at two common models, within which most of the sharp critics who gave voice to the criticisms found in chapter 2 find themselves. The first conceives God's saving actions as effected through the generative power of compassion; the second, through the enlightening power of truth-telling.

4

Jesus, the Strong Mother and Friend

Generative

FOR THE MAJORITY OF the sharp critics, God saves a broken humanity through means vastly different from the sacrificial act imagined in the penal substitutionary theory of atonement. And Jesus, imagined as one who nourishes the life of God's beloveds, bears no resemblance to the silent lamb baring his neck for the slaughter. The story of Andy Dufresne illustrates this new vision of God's saving act for one bound by forces without and forces within.

ANDY DUFRESNE

Andy first walked into Shawshank State Prison in 1947, convicted of murdering his wife and her lover—wrongly, he claimed, and as was corroborated eighteen years later. He was sentenced to two life sentences back-to-back.[1] The warden, Mr. Norton, told Andy to put his trust in the Lord, while simultaneously telling Andy, "Your ass belongs to me." Andy's old life as the vice president of a large bank in Portland, Maine, blew away in a moment of time.

Andy was assigned to the laundry. Bogs, one of the Bull Queers, and two others beat him, kicked him, and raped him. This became Andy's routine. Sometimes he could fight them off, sometimes not. Two years later, when they beat Andy to within a breath of his life, the captain tore

---

1. From the movie, *Shawshank Redemption*, based on the short novel *Rita Hayworth and Shawshank Redemption*, by Stephen King. Ellis Redding, "Red," a seasoned convict who is the middleman for desired outside goods in the prison like cigarettes and playing cards, is played by Morgan Freeman. Andy Dufresne is played by Tim Robbins.

into Bogs, and afterward sent his crippled body to a minimum-security prison.

In the spring of 1949, several men were on an outside work detail, tarring a roof. Andy, with his background in finance, overhearing the captain complaining about the government taking most of an inheritance windfall that had come his way, offered to fill out the tax forms to protect his assets. "I'd only ask three apiece for each of my coworkers. A man working outdoors feels more like a man if he can have a bottle of suds. That's only my opinion, Sir." Andy's co-prisoner and best friend Red recalled,

> And that's how it came to pass that on the second-to-last day of the job, the convict crew that tarred the factory roof in the spring of '49 wound up sitting in a row at ten in the morning drinking ice-cold bear, courtesy of the hardest screw that ever walked a turn at Shawshank State Prison . . . We sat and drank with the sun on our shoulders and felt like free men . . . As for Andy, he spent that break hunkered in the shade, a strange little smile on his face, watching us drink his beer. "You want a cold one, Andy?" "No thanks. I gave up drinking." Perhaps he wanted to curry favor with the guards, or make friends with us cons. I think he did it just to feel normal again, if only for a short while.

When one of the men, Brooks, was paroled after spending fifty years of his life in prison, he reacted by attempting to slit the throat of one of his fellow prisoners so they'd keep him locked up. Red tried to explain to them that Brooks wasn't crazy, or a murderer; he was just "institutionalized." "These walls are funny. First you hate 'em. Then you get used to 'em. Enough time passes, you begin to depend on 'em. That's 'institutionalized.' They send you here for life. That's exactly what they take."

Andy had been working in the library with Brooks. For years, he had written a letter twice a week to the State Senate, asking for money for new books. One day, after six years, Andy got a check for two hundred dollars, and a collection of used books, *National Geographics*, and music. When the guard in the office hit the john, Andy thumbed through the music. He put on a record: Italian opera, with two women singing. As he sat in the Warden's chair listening to sounds he had not heard in years, he had an impulse. Locking the bathroom door, he flipped the switch and placed the microphone next to the phonograph, sending the sounds to the yard and prison workhouses. Everyone stopped and looked up at the speakers. The convicts did not know what the two Italian women were saying, but said Red, "I tell you, those voices soared, higher and farther than anybody in a gray place dares to dream. It was like some beautiful bird flapped into our drab little cage and made those walls dissolve away. And for the briefest of moments, every last man at Shawshank felt free."

> It pissed the warden off something awful. Andy got two weeks in isolation.
>
> "Was it worth it?"
>
> "Easiest two weeks ever . . . In here. (Andy points to his head.) In here. (Andy points to his heart.) That's the beauty of music. They can't get that from you . . . Here is where it makes the most sense. You need it so you don't forget . . . that there are places in the world that aren't made out of stone. That there's something inside that they can't get to, that they can't touch. That's yours."
>
> "What are you talking about?" Red said with a cock of his head.
>
> "Hope."
>
> "Hope? Let me tell you something, my friend. Hope is a dangerous thing. Hope can drive a man insane. It's got no use on the inside. You'd better get used to that idea."
>
> "Like Brooks did?"

Several years later, Andy and Red were talking in the yard. Andy was telling Red of his dreams for his life in the future. Red told Andy to stop that thinking; it would ruin him. Frustrated, Andy looked Red in the eye. "I guess it comes down to a simple choice. Get busy living, or get busy dying."

After his escape in 1966, the Warden found the note Andy inscribed in the Bible he left: "Warden, you are right. Salvation lies within."

UPRISING

This chapter presents an alternative understanding of how God saves us, drawn from many of penal substitutionary theory's sharpest critics—certain feminist and womanist theologians, as well as theologians with existentialist and psychological approaches. Their central motif is *uprising*—meaning rising up from death into life, and rising up in resistance to those persons and systemic forces and internal voices which malevolently seek to keep one imprisoned, and thus slipping toward death. As

Andy Dufresne found out, rising up to embrace life in a fallen world inevitably entails resistance to those forces which do not want your resurrection. In Andy's case, and for the theologians supporting this model, that resistance is essential to one's salvation. Fundamentally, these soteriologies bespeak a theology of life.[2]

Throughout this and the rest of the chapters of this book, we will follow a common pattern of questions, questions that we also ask about Andy at Shawshank and others in this fallen and redeemed world:

- What is the theological method of these theologians?

- From what does humanity need saving?

- What is the meaning of the term 'salvation,' and what core metaphor is used to portray it?

- In that event or process of salvation, what is God's role in bringing it about?

- What is Jesus's role?

- What is the Holy Spirit's role (if any)?

- Finally, what is our role in bringing about salvation?

By using identical questions for each of the soteriologies, it will be easier to discover their similarities and differences.

THEOLOGICAL METHOD

Theologians who support this model of soteriology use a functional theological norm: Does the view of how salvation occurs *function to serve and save life*?[3] Does it empower people, first to rise up and affirm their own agency and moral responsibility and power, as Andy Dufresne did,

2. Feminist theologians from whom I draw extensively for this model are Rita Nakashima Brock, Rebecca Parker, Mary Grey, Roberta Bondi, and Elisabeth Moltmann-Wendel. Other feminist soteriologies will include: Joanne Carlson Brown, Elisabeth Schüssler Fiorenza, Carter Heyward, Marjorie Suchocki, Ivone Gebara; homileticians Christine Smith and L. Susan Bond; and authors Marit Trelstad, Mary Streufert, Rosemary Carbine, and Deanne Thompson from Trelstad's *Cross Examinations*. Womanist theologians include Delores Williams and Kelly Brown Douglas.

3. Parker (43), and Brock (158), in Brock and Parker, *Proverbs of Ashes*. In "For God So Loved the World?" Parker and Joanne Carlson Brown assert that that human claim to passionate and free life "is paramount" (27). Elizabeth Johnson judges a Christology by its life-giving impulse, inclusive of all women and the entire cosmos ("Redeeming the Name of Christ," 120).

and then to resist the abuse and terror that will be unleashed upon them by the forces of death? With its central norm rooted in God generating new capacities and energies for living in those persons and communities in which life-forces are dissipating, I term this model *the generative model of salvation.*

Patriarchy provides another way to see this model's norm. For Catholic theologian Eugen Drewermann and these feminist and womanist theologians, forces of death are rooted in the dominative structures found in patriarchal social systems, as well as the image of God as omnipotent Father who uses coercive force to create unity. Thus, atonement models that support patriarchal images of God are rejected. Such a theological norm explicitly excludes the soteriological image of a divine father requiring the death of his son.

Christian theologians draw upon four classic sources for developing doctrine: Scripture; theological tradition; reason; and human experience. Alongside the theological norm and these sources, every theologian also uses three criteria to judge the adequacy of a theological statement:

1. Does the theological position cohere externally with Christianity's Scriptures and traditions?

2. Is the position internally coherent; in other words, do the various parts of the argument cohere, or do they clash?

3. Is the position externally coherent with lived human experience?

Hodge and Stott give most emphasis to the first criterion, some to the second, and least to the third.[4] In contrast, the authors of this life-giving model reverse the weighting. Thus,

1. Theologies must cohere with *lived human experience.* This includes listening to the voices of the wounded, oppressed and marginalized, and taking into account what social analyses tell us about the world and its structures of power.[5]

4. Hodge acknowledged that while the notion of substitution—the vicarious suffering of the innocent to pay for others' crimes before God—might strike modern people as abhorrent, it was to be affirmed because of its biblical support.

5. "The weight of our argument was in our lives. Our theological questions emerged in our daily struggles to teach, minister, and work for social change, and from personal grappling with how violence had affected us," write Parker and Brock (*Proverbs of Ashes,* 6).

2. Portrayals of Christ and of salvation must *make sense*, internally and to the modern/postmodern mind.

3. Though Scripture is perceived as a document flawed by the patriarchal premises and God-images of its authors, it holds glimpses of God's saving, life-giving power. Their theological norm guides the weighting of scriptures—*does the text serve life, or forces of death?* They prioritize Jesus's ministry and affirmation of life, and frequently draw upon the Hebrew wisdom literature (which describe a figure, Sophia, to which Jesus likens), synoptic descriptions of his life, and Johannine traditions. Other Hebrew genres, the gospel passion narratives, Paul and other New Testament letters (Hebrews, for example), and Revelation appear infrequently as resources, if at all. As chapter 2 made clear, they sharply criticize the tradition. They use Wisdom traditions, borrow elements of the doctrine of the Holy Spirit to talk about God's saving actions, and frequently draw on process theology to provide a philosophical framework for the model.

4. One final criterion is employed frequently. An adequate Christian soteriology must affirm that other religions contain truths about God's nature and provide peoples with valid routes toward salvation. Christian exclusivism is rejected.

THE PROBLEM WITHIN THE HUMAN CONDITION

In the penal substitutionary theory of atonement, the problem from which humans need salvation is the guilt that comes from sin. In the generative model the problem is that people are dying. It is the dissipation of life, human and creaturely: the loss of vivacity, the lack of flourishing, a bleeding to death. Like Red and the other prisoners in *The Shawshank Redemption*, their life is being caged in and drained away. Sometimes the lack of human flourishing is described as a person's woundedness, damage, or brokenheartedness; sometimes as disintegration or fragmentation of one's personhood.[6]

The dissipation of life is rooted in a creaturely breakdown of relationality, and a loss of connection with God who is the source of life-giving power.

---

6. Similar to the description of the effect of violence and abuse on victims in chapter 2.

The inflicted suffering which fragments persons and communities is rooted in *the distortion of relationality*, which blocks the flow of life-giving, mutual power between persons and communities. The breakdown is due to a betrayal of trust: A refusal of the God-given command to love our neighbor as we love ourselves.[7] The resulting estrangement or "tribalism" is seen in the boundaries and boxes that separate us.[8] The distorted world reflects a "kyriarchal reality," a reality suffused with multiplicative and intertwined privileged male systems of domination.[9] In these social systems, relations are structured in a subject-to-object fashion, such that the subject has control and "does something to" the other person or group of persons. The relation is not one in which the persons or groups live in mutual subjectivity, association and empowerment.[10]

---

7. Mary Potter Engel speaks of sin as betrayal of trust. Mary Grey and Daniel Migliore speak of sin as the denial of relationship; see Grey, *Feminism, Redemption and the Christian Tradition*, 108–9, 113, 132–33; Migliore, *Faith Seeking Understanding*, 150–54. Ivone Gebara speaks of sin as disequilibrium or imbalance, rooted in idolatry of self or others; see *Out of the Depths*, 139, 142.

8. Like the invisible lines drawn down a high-school English classroom floor separating different ethnic groups at the beginning of the movie *Freedom Writers*.

9. Among this group of feminist and womanist authors, and for Drewermann as well, the charge that *patriarchy*, in which relational ties are hierarchical and based upon rigid and coerced patterns of domination and submission, is the root problem from which the world needs salvation is ubiquitous and definitive. See Parker and Brown, "For God So Loved the World?"; Brown, *Divine Child Abuse?*; Brock, *Journeys By Heart*, chap. 3 (esp. 50, 57); Bond, *Trouble with Jesus*, 33; Japinga, *Feminism and Christianity*, 89–92; Grey, *Feminism, Redemption, and the Christian Tradition*, 155; Ivone Gebara, *Out of the Depths*, 141, 161; and Rosemary Carbine, "Contextualizing the Cross for the Sake of Subjectivity," 94, 98, 100. On the relational distortion as kyriarchy, see Schüssler Fiorenza, *Jesus and the Politics of Interpretation*, 95; and *Jesus: Miriam's Child, Sophia's Prophet*, esp. part I. On a more general identification of the problem in structures of dominance and hierarchical power, which create unjust relations of gender, race, nation, and class, see Gebara, *Out of the Depths*, 41–42, 119, 134, 171; Grey, *Feminism, Redemption, and the Christian Tradition*, 113, 195, 202, 206, 208, 221; Smith, *Risking the Terror*, 42–44; Streufert, "Maternal Sacrifice as a Hermeneutics of the Cross," 68; Bond, *Trouble with Jesus*, 47, 92, 126–27; and Elizabeth Johnson, "Redeeming the Name of Christ," 123–27, 132.

10. Iris Marion Young identifies five specific elements of this kyriarchal web of systemic oppressions: exploitation, marginalization, powerlessness, cultural imperialism, and regularized and systematized violence (see *Justice and the Politics of Difference*). Social systems with these forms of hierarchies play on the powerlessness of the subordinated persons or groups. Ivone Gebara finds powerlessness rooted in lack of ownership, for lack of ownership entails a lack of control over the means of one's existence; it means poverty (*Out of the Depths*, 17–44).

By distorting the web of interdependent relationships, the perpetrators and beneficiaries of these kyriarchical systems *block the flow of
divine power by which all things are held in abundant life.* With systemic
violence the victim grows walls to protect the self from threats within
and beyond the self. He feels possessed by the internalized perpetrators'
voices of contempt—like Red and Brooks in Shawshank prison—or
possessed psychically, with ghosts floating in his dreams and subconscious. He lives within a self-made prison—like Brooks and Red. Stuck
in violent, distorted patterns because of disbelief that "anything can ever
change"; paralyzed when glancing ahead, fearing death; and complicit
with the present forces of death, he finds his movements blocked, like
breathing cut short.

With the self cut off from itself and from others, the recipient of
systemic violence loses her or his capacity for empathy and love—for the
self, or for another. Here, the link between lack of connection and loss of
life becomes obvious, for without love, we all die.

Along with being cut off from the God of life, God becomes
problematic for life. Or rather, as Drewermann, Bondi, and the others
in chapter 2 made so clear, *the distorted God-image within patriarchal
religions becomes a threat to life.* Humans thus need redemption from
this patriarchal God-image.

Most of the feminist and womanist theologians are satisfied with
the above description of humanity's problem. While the letting go of
power as dominating control will redeem everyone, the problem of the
dying persons is emphasized and differentiated from the problem of the
murderous and complicit. Attempts to describe the human predicament
with universalizing terms such as original sin, rebellion against God,
or guilt are seen as tactics to divert attention from the ways particular
unjust socio-political structures destroy the lives of particular oppressed
groups.

For the psychologically- and existentially-influenced theologians,
however, an existential, psychological, and spiritual condition that affects all humanity lies beneath the socio-political dynamics of power.
In a long, disturbing scene in *25th Hour*, Montgomery Brogan displays
this deeper condition.

Monty has one day before he enters prison for seven years for deal-
ing cocaine. Someone had snitched, the police raided his apartment, and
Monty sits with a dejected look on his face while they take the cocaine

out of his couch cushions. He had meant to get rid of the cocaine while he was sitting on top of the world, and end his drug-dealing.

That last night, while out to dinner with his father, Monty goes into the bathroom. Looking at the mirror, he sees both his own reflection, and the phrase "F[…] You!" scrawled into the mirror. His reflection begins to talk back at him: "F[…] you and this whole city and everyone in it." Then his reflection begins to blame and curse and condemn everyone he knows, from ethnic groups to Jesus to his own intimates, and finally to himself.

"No," he finally says back to his reflection in the mirror. "No. F[…] you, Montgomery Brogan. You had it all, and you threw it away, you dumb f[…]!"

The kyriarchal systems of dominance and submission; the violence; the isolation and exile from life-giving connections to true self and others and God; the distorted image of God as Ultimate Judge and Punisher who condemns all as unworthy to live—all ultimately lead, as they do here with Monty, to the spiritual attitude of *contempt*.

Beneath even contempt, however, these universalizing theologians find the deepest spiritual problem in the attitude of *fear*. Mistrust of the ambivalent, violent God is linked to mistrust of one's own true self. For Drewermann, the very desperate attempts to achieve what God gives freely—the justification of one's existence—lead to violence through funding the sacrificial mentality. That mentality guides the fearful self into self-justification, either through asceticism or moralism. With asceticism, parts of the self are excised to preserve a needed relationship. This sacrificial virtue uplifts obedience alone, and not the companion virtue of revolt against dehumanization. With moralism, one confuses the God-image with all the moralistic super-demands of the various fathers of kyriarchal systems. God, the ultimate sadist, demands the impossible. A person puts her entire valuation according to her agreement with external norms. By doing so in a fallen world, the person becomes enslaved to the collective and unconscious kyriarchal forces of death. The cost of trying to be perfect is that of leaving behind one's true self and one's humanity. As Red said of Brooks, and Hannah Arendt of Adolf Eichmann, you become "institutionalized."

THE MEANING OF SALVATION

In Tolkien's *The Lord of the Rings: Return of the King*, there is a scene toward the end of the saga in which the entire tone of the book changes. The last thing readers knew is that Frodo and Sam accomplished their feat of throwing the ring of power—the ring by which dominating, coercive power is used to control the world—into the fiery abyss from which it was forged. Sauron's power is broken, Frodo and Sam lie stranded on Sauron's crumbling mountain citadel. Eagles arrive and carry the delirious pair away.

In the next scene, Sam is in bed in Ithilien. Instead of being dead, he awakens. At the foot of his bed, he sees not a ghost or angel, but Gandolf, alive. After all the bad news, the many years under the power of Mordor and their forces of death, good news emerged before Sam's opening eyes—a good without a catch in it somewhere, as if heaven and earth were now working the way God intended. It was, as Tolkien coined, a *eucatastrophe*.

> "Is everything sad going to come untrue? What's happening to the world?" [asked Sam].
>
> "A great Shadow has departed," said Gandalf, and then he laughed, and the sound was like music, or like water in a parched land; and as he listened the thought came to him that he had not heard laughter, the pure sound of merriment, for days upon days without count. It fell upon his ears like the echo of all the joys he had ever known. But he himself burst into tears. Then, as a sweet rain will pass down a wind of spring and the sun will shine out the clearer, his tears ceased, and his laughter welled up, and laughing sprang from his bed.
>
> "How do I feel?" he cried. "Well, I don't know how to say it. I feel, I feel"—he waved his arms in the air—"I feel like spring after winter, and sun on the leaves; and like trumpets and harps and all the songs I have ever heard!"[11]

As he laughs, Frodo, Merry, and Pipin, also thought dead, enter and rejoice with him.

The human problem is oppression and the resulting dissipation of life. Salvation is the emergence of *abundant life* after bondage. It is quickening, the return of the powers of life which enable individuals and systems of mutuality to flourish. It is Sam coming to life in a world

---

11. Tolkien, *Lord of the Rings: Return of the King*, 283.

made whole. It is Andy Dufresne standing outside Shawshank's walls, arms grasping the rain-drenched sky. "The thief comes only to steal and kill and destroy," Jesus says. "I came that they may have life, and have it abundantly."[12]

While individually, salvation is abundant life, socially it is the appearance of *shalom*, the return of health and wholeness, pleasure and peace. Individuals are not sacrificed for group ideals. An enjoyment re-emerges in relationships, and wholeness reaches every dimension of existence: The spiritual, the psychological, the interpersonal, the socio-political, and the ecological. Spiritually, *shalom* replaces fear of God with trust in God. Individuals and communities open themselves to God, receiving from God energies for living, and giving back joy to God. Broken people come to life within the presence of God's soft heart.

On the psychological level, *shalom* brings healing to the damage done to the human heart caused by violence. For the fragmented self, with pain undigested and locked away and different parts of the self walled off from each other, God's *shalom* brings the reclamation of those wounded parts and the recovery of the lost, unified self. It enables the person to be profoundly present to self and to world, and all that is flowering within and around her or him. The integrity of the heart is restored, as norms, prejudices, and unconscious social forces of hatred that were internalized are let go.[13] One's humanity is also recovered. The person opens to all experiences and claims her power-in-relation. Capacities for empathy and love expand. The open heart now finds itself unwilling to compromise with inhumanity.[14]

---

12. John 10:10.

13. Several of our authors focus upon the psychological effect of God's quickening power, which brings a healing of the heart through a journey back to the true self. See Brock, *Journeys by Heart*, entire book, but esp. chaps. 1 and 2; Brock and Parker, *Proverbs of Ashes*, 59, 63, 249; Bondi, *Memories of God*, 34–35, 38, 135, 142–44, 170, 202; and Grey, *Feminism, Redemption, and the Christian Tradition*, chap. 4, "Redemption as Self-Affirmation." On the journey back to self and the healing of the fragmented self's renewing integrity, and allowing the purging of norms and exclusivisitc biases internalized from culture, see Brock and Parker, *Proverbs of Ashes*, 201–2; Brock's discussion of Job as paradigm for the heart with integrity, Brock and Parker, *Proverbs of Ashes*, 118–27; and Bondi, *Memories of God*, 76.

14. On the expanding of the heart leading to the refusal to accept inhumanity, and the return of humane impulses of empathy and compassion, see Drewermann in Beier, *Violent God-Image*, 225, 233.

On the interpersonal, socio-political, and ecological levels of human existence, God's *shalom* brings the restoration of right relation. Systemic oppressions are replaced by a community of equality, mutuality, and reciprocity, in which power is shared power. People are able to control the means of their existence, and eat the fruits of their labor.[15]

THE COMING OF SALVATION

In the generative model of salvation, redemption is *biophilic*; life flows out of life.[16] The metaphor is organic rather than militaristic. We come to life as we are held in being by a nurturing, creative center, a living and life-giving "other." The organic paradigm of life-generating-life is reflected in the model's saving images: God is like a strong woman beside a sheltering tree protecting all life. God is like a mother who births, breastfeeds, befriends, teaches to walk, guides. God's power is like the saving power of love between lovers, or friends.

In the penal substitutionary theory, God saves through the use of unidirectional power. God alone saves, by sending the Son to die, and by the Son's own heroic actions. In sharp contrast, in the generative model, divine love reclaims life *through a synergistic process*. God's loving power works through our capacity and willingness to participate in the healing of self and world. Just as a loving person works with and unleashes power found within the beloved, so God unleashes power within the creatures by creating non-hierarchical relations in which energy flows back and forth, empowering all.[17]

15. On *shalom* as entailing not only renewed trust in God and personal healing, but also the return of justice, and this justice identified as the kingdom of God, see Wolterstorff, *Until Justice and Peace Embrace*, Interlude I, "For Justice in Shalom," 69–72; Smith, *Risking the Terror*, 10, 23, 27, 34, 42, 68, 71–73, 101–3; Grey, *Feminism, Redemption, and the Christian Tradition*, chap. 5, "Redemption as Right Relation," and 205; Brock and Parker, *Proverbs of Ashes*, 37; Williams, "Black Women's Surrogacy," 30–32; and Elizabeth Johnson, "Redeeming the Name of Christ," 123, 131–32.

16. The term "biophilic" is Sheila Collins's, *A Different Heaven and Earth?* 203. On the saving process as biophilic, see Grey, *Feminism, Redemption, and the Christian Tradition*, 152; and Sally Purvis, on her contrast of power-as-control and power-as-life (or "power for life") in *Power of the Cross*.

17. On the saving process as synergistic, see, for example, Grey, *Feminism, Redemption, and the Christian Tradition*, 106–15, 130, 156–57, 170, 185. For detailed contrasts of unilateral versus synergistic conceptions of divine power, see Davaney, *Divine Power*; Case-Winters, *God's Power*; and Kyle Pasewark, *Theology of Power*.

Clearly, the means by which God saves is vastly different in the generative model, for *God saves through the power of love*, not through a violent and God-willed death. Compassion is not a mere sentiment, but a form of power, different from coercion, which heals broken hearts, minds, and social structures.

The focus on life's flowing out of life, on saving power as moving within and between creatures, and on compassion as a form of power is seen in the generative authors' choice of illustrative texts. Whereas the Suffering Servant of Isaiah 52–53 is a paradigmatic text for picturing how salvation occurs in the penal substitutionary theory of atonement, the generative model upholds the story of the hemorrhaging woman. She rises up when she listens to her true self, and when she acts to connect herself with the source of life flowing through Jesus. Her uprising in a fallen world necessitates nonviolent resistance to the keepers of purity laws and gender norms who seek to keep her down. When the generative model pictures salvation, it imagines this woman.[18]

GOD'S ROLE IN SALVATION

Who is the God who saves by bringing life out of life? The generative model employs a panentheistic model of God's relation to the world. All things exist within God's being (and God is in all things); yet God also transcends all things, in the sense of being "more than" the world. God is not located "above," but rather, "right here"—beneath, within, and between all beings.[19] God is related to the world like a heart is to a body, or a force field to those elements that thrive within its sphere of power.[20]

---

18. See Mark 5:21–43; Matt 9:18–26; Luke 8:40–56. While there are other iconic texts, this story of the hemorrhaging woman is used most frequently to describe the synergistic process of salvation. For example, see Brock, *Journeys*, 82–85; Brock, "And a Little Child Will Lead Us ," 55–57; Schüssler Fiorenza, *In Memory of Her*, 124; Motlmann and Moltmann-Wendel, *Passion For God*, 9–18; Grey, *Feminism, Redemption, and the Christian Tradition*, 123, 128.

19. Carter Heyward and Rita Brock are the authors who speak most frequently of God's power-in-relationship being found within the self, and in the connections between beings (see Heyward, *Redemption of God*; and Brock, *Journeys by Heart*). Moltmann-Wendel also speaks of God's healing powers as present everywhere, but also describes them as "under us" (*Passion for God*, 23).

20. On the use of the metaphor of matrix to describe the co-inherence of the life-giving Spirit with the whole of creation, see for example Grey, *Feminism, Redemption, and the Christian Tradition*, 97–98, 131; Smith, *Risking the Terror*, 11; Gebara, *Out of the Depths*, 149, 172. On imagining God as the heart of the universe, see Brock, *Journeys*

Like a wellspring, God is *the source of the power of life*.[21] Using natural metaphors, God is the *ground* under our being. God is the unquenchable *fire* in the heart of all things surrounded by cold and dark, providing light, warmth, and thus life-giving power. God is *a wide space for living* for those suffocating and bound in external and internal prisons. God is *the sea*, lifting us up, helping us overcome the burdens of kyriarchal powers. God is a large *oak tree* that shelters thousands of birds and beasts under its limbs.[22] As source of life, God is also described as *a loving, personal being*. God is *erotic power*, the power of a Being who passionately seeks a mutual relation of love with the world.[23] God is *the life-giving Spirit* who quickens all living things.[24] God is a *physician*, a *friend*, a *lover*, a *gentle grandfather* who provides a safe place for us to live; a *grandmother* who holds us daily in her thoughts; a *father* who helps us reclaim lost parts of ourselves; a *mother* who fights for our necessities; a *hospitable aunt* who receives our efforts of kindness with delight; a *child* who, without guile, opens to the gifts of people and the world.[25]

(for example, 42–49, 52–53, 103); as a field and a spider's web, see Gebara, *Out of the Depths*, 132–34.

21. On God as the inexhaustible ground or elemental source of the energy of mutuality-in-relatedness—the exchange of energy that creates, sustains, and redeems all life—see, for example, Grey, *Feminism, Redemption, and the Christian Tradition*, 110–18, 128, 130; Moltmann and Moltmann-Wendel, *Passion for God*, 18; and Heyward, *Our Passion for Justice*.

22. Brock and especially Parker describe God as an unquenchable fire at the core of life; see *Proverbs of Ashes*, 9–10, 233. Brock uses the image of the sea, which embraces all things, unites all shores, and buoys all things in existence; see *Journeys*, epilogue. On God as sheltering tree, see Bondi, *Memories of God*, 106–7.

23. Rita Brock and Carter Heyward especially describe God as erotic power, as do Wendy Farley and Mary Grey. See, for example, Brock, *Journeys by Heart*, 25–26, 33–42; and Brock and Parker, *Proverbs of Ashes*, 4, 158. Farley speaks of God as erotic love or power throughout *The Wounding and Healing of Desire*; see esp. 15–16, 77–78, 103, 164.

24. See for example Brock and Parker, *Proverbs of Ashes*, 4, 9, 136, 158, 233.

25. Elisabeth Moltmann-Wendel speaks of God, and of Jesus, as physician and friend; see Moltmann and Moltmann-Wendel, *Passion for God*, 21, 46, and chap. 2. Brock likens God to her grandfather and grandmother (Brock and Parker, *Proverbs of Ashes*, 56–58, 228–33). She also likens a lover and friend, Pritchy, to God (ibid., 220–22), as do Heyward and Farley (*Wounding and Healing of Desire*). Bondi likens God to a nun named Mother Jane, to her own mother, and to the tall woman under the tree; to the father of the prodigal son, and to her hospitable Auntie Ree (*Memories of God*, 75–78, 81–105, 93, 139–42, 177–87, respectively). Brock speaks of God as like a child in "And a Little Child Will Lead Us."

How does the God who is quickening Spirit save us from death's grip? The Redeemer God acts in three ways: as mediator, as presence, and as guide. God acts as Go-Between, reconnecting us to the powers of life—within the self, within relationships, and within God. Rather than constricting, divine erotic power increases breathing space and relational connections, allowing life-giving energy to flow in non-coercive ways.

God also acts as loving Presence and Guide, luring us toward life-enhancing possibilities. When these possibilities come before us in circumstances or our mind's eye, we experience God as hope. As quickening power, loving presence, and beckoning guide, God rebuilds earthly structures of distinction-in-unity which embody fecundity, intimacy, and beauty.

To break death's grip on God's beleaguered creatures, God must act in specific ways toward the multiple enslaving bonds found in the spiritual, psychological, interpersonal, socio-political and ecological dimensions of existence.

On the spiritual level of existence, God acts to free us from the fear and contempt which fuel violence by ending its root—our distorted image of God. God acts to show us who God truly is—unconditionally for human life, nonviolent, and generous with power.

God communicates that God is not ambivalent toward humanity. God does not discard people into outer darkness. God's love, mercy, and forgiveness are unconditionally given, and God will never withhold these from us. God loves concrete, imperfect persons rather than ideals, and God's holiness does not prevent God from loving us.

Alongside God's unconditional regard, clearly God is not violent. God does not use violence to draw humanity closer to Godself. Nor does God sanctify human violence. God uses God's powers of life to midwife others' powers. God is a birthing God, a God with breasts who nurtures, nurses, and guides her children. This nonviolent image is maternal (though not solely) in the sense that love brings life. If there is a life-giving "sacrifice," it is that of life springing from within another's life, not from within death.[26]

By communicating God's unconditional love, God enables us to move spiritually from fear to trust. Though imperfect, we are no longer

---

26. Distinguishing maternal sacrifice from militaristic or martyr sacrifice within patriarchal societies marks the heart of Streufert's argument in "Maternal Sacrifice"; see, for example, 73–75.

afraid of God, but are able to trust ourselves with God within a life-giving mutual love. We base our life's work upon the divine embrace. The sacrificial mentality, and the asceticism and moralism which fund violence against self and others, are no longer necessary.

On the psychological level of existence, God quickens us by luring us toward both integrity and connectivity. God reconnects us to life-giving powers found within the self, within communities, and within God.

As we have seen, victims of violence lack an internal spaciousness within which they can be present to themselves. Protective internal walls, separating parts of the self, keep the self fragmented. God re-creates a breathing space within the self in which a person can become present to her- or himself again.[27] God then graciously comes to be present with the person in that space, inviting the person to face hidden parts of her- or himself. Like a quilter, God helps the person see beauty in lost or discarded parts, and collect, repair, and sew them together into a coherent whole. By reclaiming the lost pieces, she begins to recover her deepest self hidden amidst disjointed pieces. Along the way, God provides her with experiences of such wholeness, which give her hope.

The discovery or rediscovery of the unified true self empowers the person for creativity, self-protection, and self-definition, for the true self is a wellspring of generative power. And beneath or alongside the true self, God is perceived as the One who dwells within the self, providing the original energies for living. God encourages us to open our hearts to others.

The empathy that God encourages within the new self acts in the service of life. An ethic for life affirms both obedience to authorities and revolt against forces of death; both connection and letting-go; both giving of the self to protect other people's right to life, and claiming the right to life for oneself. This skill of maintaining equilibrium in protecting the life of self and others is essential if one is to maintain the integrity of self, rather than "give the self away" or lose oneself in dissipation or violation.[28]

27. Brock and Parker speak at length about God's reintroduction of breathing space within the self. See *Proverbs of Ashes*, 115–16, 156–58, 220–22, 251–52.

28. On God's creating an ethic which balances empathy for self with empathy for others, see Brock and Parker, *Proverbs of Ashes*, 4, 21, 31, 36, 158, 201; Grey, *Feminism, Redemption, and the Christian Tradition*, 101, 117–18; and Smith, *Risking the Terror*, 12–13, 33–34.

On the interpersonal, socio-political and ecological levels of existence, God elicits an uprising within us in its second sense. In order to gain and keep the lost whole self, a person must be ready to resist the perpetrators of kyriarchal systems who do not want the reintegration of one's self. Tasting a form of community rooted in equality emboldens the person to stand up to structures—and persons—of unjust relations. It was not only Andy Dufresne's determined attempts to remember who he was by gaining access to a cool beer on a sunny morning, or the beauty of "Duettino—Sull 'Aria'" from Mozart's *The Marriage of Figaro*, which led to his uprising. It was also his friendships with Red and other compatriots locked away in Shawshank Prison.

JESUS'S ROLE IN SALVATION

The author of Luke describes Jesus as "a Savior," as one who rescues others from harm or threat of extinction.[29] Three premises of the generative model of salvation, however, make it impossible for Jesus to play the role of savior. First, as power is conceived in this model, it is not a quality that can be possessed by an individual—even by Jesus or God. Power by nature is synergistic: shared between beings, and located in the movement between beings-in-relationship—including the dynamic movement between God and creatures. Second, the generative model presupposes that God is continuously acting in creative and redemptive ways in history, through countless events and personalities; it would be odd to single out Jesus for a qualitatively different saving role. Third, the generative model advocates a non-exclusivistic view of Jesus's saving role amidst religious pluralism. To describe a qualitatively distinct role for Jesus as savior sets Jesus above the God of creation, makes Jesus a superior mediator of grace, and particularizes pietistic focus in him.

Further, imaging salvation through a savior is problematic, for it disempowers victims of violence—the very opposite of its intended goal! When victims of kyriarchal forces are told to rely on an all-powerful male hero, they leave such an encounter without having asked themselves the crucial questions: Who am I, truly? And is there a source of power within me that is my own, from which my life may spring up in fecundity, and from which I can draw to resist violation? The savior

29. See, for example, Luke 2:10–11.

model of redemption is thus not only inconceivable; it is also unhelpful for disempowered persons and communities.[30]

So in the generative model of salvation, Jesus does not play the role of heroic savior, nor is he the object of trust. God, who as erotic power is located within and between all things, is the object of trust.

Nor is Jesus the incarnate second person of the Trinity. Once again, three premises of the generative model make it impossible to single out Jesus as "Emmanuel." First, because divine erotic power—likened to a field of force, or a mind in a cosmic body—is everywhere by its very nature, it cannot be reduced to a certain historical person. Second, in the penal substitutionary model of atonement, sin creates a barrier between guilty humans and a holy God, which Jesus then overcomes. In the generative model, sin does not alienate God from impure humans. God is unconditionally available, negating the need for one specially incarnate person who acts as mediator. Third, because the theory rejects exclusivistic notions of Jesus's saving role, the generative model concludes that Jesus cannot be the only incarnation of God.

In contrast to the tradition, "incarnation" becomes conflated with "divine omnipresence" in the generative model, acting as a metaphor for the general incarnation of God in the world, particularly in new forms of liberative communities.[31] Rather than Jesus alone revealing the divine erotic power or life-giving Spirit, Jesus participates in its revelation as he

---

30. As Carter Heyward warns, victims of violence and the marginalized "participate in the perpetuation of our own oppression insofar as we allow our visions and energies to be drawn toward a heavenly man and away from our human situation as sisters and brothers, by fixing our attention on the spiritual accomplishments of a divine Savior rather than on the spiritual possibilities of a concerted human commitment that can be inspired by the Jesus story as a human story: a story of human faith, human love, and human possibility as the agency of divine movement in history" (Heyward, *Our Passion for Justice*, 216).

31. On "incarnation" as referring to God's universal embodiment in the world and its web of relational connections, see Brock, "And a Little Child Shall Lead Us"; *Journeys by Heart*, Introduction; and "Cross of Resurrection and Communal Redemption", 250. See also Bond, *Trouble with Jesus*, 91–94. It is Bond who uses the terms "general incarnation" to describe that to which Jesus's activity points. She rejects the notion of a "special incarnation," in Jesus or any historical individual. See Bond, *Trouble with Jesus*, 34, 46, 52, 113–15, 134. Elizabeth Johnson does believe in an incarnation of the second person of the Trinity in the person of Jesus, though she also believes divine Sophia "indwells" broadly and beyond Jesus; see Johnson, *She Who Is*, chap. 8: "Jesus-Sophia." Trelstad ("Lavish Love") never addresses the issue. She never denies that Jesus is the second person of the Trinity incarnate, nor does she describe him as such. Regardless, it is not clear how the incarnation would be necessary to her model.

opens himself to its flow. He may do so with more openness than we do, but his participation is not qualitatively different than ours.[32]

Who, then, is Jesus? To portray him, metaphors are not taken from the military or political spheres (which often represent kyriarchy and its dominance-submission), but from communities of coequality and mutuality. So instead of heroic savior, Jesus is *a friend*, the friend of life who saves by befriending others.[33] Jesus is *a lover*, open to the other and desiring the reciprocity of love. He is *a physician* who uses his powers-for-life to free others from death's grip. Jesus is *a strong mother*, self-possessed and graceful, calmly conveying the unconditional regard of God, and displaying an extravagant valuing of beauty. He mothers people into their own autonomy.[34] He shows the possibilities for a rising up into new life that are open to human beings. He shows what is possible through his example, his words, his compassion, and his formation of a new type of community.

One of the most common themes of advocates of the generative model is that it is Jesus's life that saves us, not his death.[35] Through the way that he lives, Jesus becomes a conduit of God's saving, erotic power. Jesus dared to trust God absolutely, and such intimacy gave him a corresponding trust in himself. He lived with integrity, overcoming fear of what humans can do to him.[36]

32. Brock is especially direct on this point; see *Journeys by Heart*, 52–53; and Brock and Parker, *Proverbs of Ashes*, 53, 156.

33. Moltmann-Wendel, Bondi, and Deanna Thompson in particular emphasize what Moltmann-Wendel calls "a friendship Christology." See Moltmann and Moltmann-Wendel, *Passion for God*, 7, 12; Bondi, *Memories of God.*, 38–49, 184; and Thompson, "Becoming a Feminist Theologian of the Cross," 87–90.

34. See Bondi, *Memories of God*, 108. Julian of Norwich, like other medieval women mystics, speaks of Christ as our Mother, giving us birth, feeding us, "mothering us." See the Fourteenth Revelation of the Long Text, particularly chaps. 57–63, in *Julian of Norwich: Showings*. For other women theologians (medieval and contemporary) who use female imagery for Jesus's saving work, see Bynum, *Jesus as Mother*, esp. chaps. 4 and 5; Elizabeth Johnson, *She Who Is*, 86–100, and chap. 8; and Kwok, "God Weeps with Our Pain."

35. See for example Bondi, *Memories of God*, 38; Moltmann and Moltmann-Wendel, *Passion for God*, 4, 7, 22–23, and esp. 29, 42, 37–38; Williams, "Black Women's Surrogacy," 30; Terrell, "Our Mothers' Gardens," 44; Streufert, "Maternal Sacrifice," 64, and esp. 73–75; Trelstad, "Lavish Love," 110; Smith, *Risking the Terror*, 61, 82; and Gebara, *Out of the Depths*, 180.

36. It is Drewermann who above all presents this existential, philosophical, and psychological interpretation of the saving significance of the way Jesus lived. The claim

In a kyriarchal world of empire, Jesus challenged coercive power
and offered an alternative—divine power, which is a relational form of
power held in communities of equality, reciprocity, and mutual empowerment. He broke with kyriarchy's ethic of domination and submission.[37]
Jesus resisted religiosity rooted in fear, opposing both an ambivalent,
violent portrait of God and the sacrificial mentality that comes with it.
He affirmed the inalienable worth of every human being as God's beloved creatures. He valued the individual[38] and exhibited confidence in
the individual's freedom. He took joy in people, respecting their difference from himself, giving them space to breathe, displaying the eros and
tenderness found between equals.

By his own uprising, Jesus provides others with an example which
inspires, as Andy Dufresne did for Red. Jesus demonstrates to us the possibilities of our own rising up; of having an immediate, intimate relation
with God; of becoming open to the flow of divine erotic power and living within it rather than by dominating force; of acting in saving ways
toward the world. He shows us our own capacities.[39]

By his words, Jesus similarly connected those around him with
God. He taught people new ideas: the absolute regard of God, and the
coming reign of God which ends kyriarchy. Through such ideas, people
"regained their senses" and were able to see the world as it really is—
held in death's grip by kyriarchal forces and an ambivalent, violent God-

---

that Jesus dared to live by a nonambivalent, nonviolent God-image is the heart of
Drewermann's theory; see Beier, *Violent God-Image*, 6–7, 239–41. On Jesus as daring to
live with an attitude of absolute trust in this nonambivalent, nonviolent God, and this
trust leading to a trust in his true self, see Beier, *A Violent God-Image*, 6–7, 224, 226,
233–35.

37. Jesus's unconditional affirmation of life implying a necessary resistance to kyriarchal forms of power and social ethics is a universal theme for advocates of the generative model. See for example Beier, *Violent God-Image*, 122; Brock and Parker, *Proverbs of
Ashes*, 31, 48, 158; Brown and Parker, "For God So Loved the World?"; Japinga, *Feminism
and Christianity*, 103; Terrell, "Our Mothers' Gardens," 44; Streufert, "Maternal Sacrifice,"
73–75; Carbine, "Contextualizing the Cross for the Sake of Subjectivity," 95–96; and
Trelstad, "Lavish Love," 116–17.

38. His parables of the shepherd searching for the one sheep, the woman searching
for the lost coin, and the prodigal father waiting patiently and passionately for the one
son (Luke 15) are three such examples.

39. On Jesus as exemplar, see for example Brown and Parker, "For God So Loved
the World?"; Brown, "Divine Child Abuse?"; Terrell, "Our Mothers' Gardens," 39, 42,
45; Japinga, *Feminism and Christianity*, 97, 123–25; Bond, *Trouble with Jesus*, 109; and
Smith, *Risking the Terror*, 11.

image, yet also suffused with the in-breaking of God's alternative forces of life—and themselves as they really are: God's beloveds and royalty in God's kingdom.

Jesus saves by his compassion, which connects people to the flow of divine, life-giving energy. Jesus's compassion is seen in the way he treats people, befriending and casting his lot with those whom the world shames and reduces to nothing: women, outcasts, "sinners," tax collectors, and the poor. He is a cheerful receiver, allowing for a reciprocity and mutuality of respect, support, comfort, challenge, and love. Mary, Martha, and Lazarus, for example, are his adult friends, whom he trusts and needs. Further, through healings, exorcisms, and raising the dead, he restores bodily and psychic integrity. Through an extension of his essence—through spit, breath, and blood as life forces—Jesus carries healing power to victims of violence by opening the blockages to the normal flow of erotic power, as when he healed with mud the man born blind (John 9).

While Jesus acts to open up whatever blocks those whom he loves from life-giving energies, he does not do so as a solo figure. It is the divine relational web of connections which saves, and this web takes its strongest form in new forms of just communities. Jesus's ability to heal is connected to his relation with such a community. He gained strength from his community of disciples and adult friends, and he helped direct the brokenhearted to such communities by which they found their own strength. In this sense, it is not just Jesus's life that is saving, but also God's act of Pentecost, which symbolizes the formation and unleashing of these Spirit-filled communities of life based upon equality and reciprocity.

While Jesus's life-giving contact with people redeems, as does people's experiences of a new form of community, there is nothing salvific in Jesus's death. The reason the cross cannot save is because it does not end the kyriarchal structures of domination and submission—the *sin qua non* of God's reign of *shalom*. Further, pain cannot be a basis for love, and violence cannot save.

Nor did Jesus have to die for us to know that God is present with us in our pain, for the Jews, among others, already knew that.[40] The panentheistic conception of God's omnipresence confirms it.

---

40. Parker makes this point in Brock and Parker, *Proverbs of Ashes*, 212–13.

God did not will or involve Godself in bringing about Jesus's suffering and death.[41] It was not an act of divine atonement or divine justice. Nor did Jesus choose the cross. It was not an act of self-sacrifice, nor did Jesus preach a sacrificial theology. For Drewermann, Jesus's attitude toward his death is revealed in the Markan version of the crucifixion, in which Jesus does not see it as a cultic event or as God's will. He never thought to declare the endurance of inhumanity and torture to be signs of a true trust in God (Mark 15:20b–41).[42] Indeed, many like Finlan would say that plenty of parables and remarks by Jesus show that he did not think it was God's will that he should be murdered, especially the parable of the vineyard owner, in which the owner is enraged when the tenants kill his son.[43]

If Jesus did not want to die, nor God ordain it, then why did it happen? His death is attributable not to Jesus's acts of self-sacrifice, but to his acts of righteous rage. As we have seen, Jesus nonviolently resisted the death-dealing forces of kyriarchy, and was committed to the formation of a new type of community based in shared, generative power. Such impassioned behavior is seen in his cleansing of the Temple. He died as an enemy of socio-political figures who saw him as a threat to their self-interest. He died because he refused to leave the side of his oppressed friends, as Gandhi, King, and Romero died in the twentieth century.[44]

Jesus also died because God was unable to prevent it. God's love was present to Jesus through human agents while he suffered and died—such

---

41. God's opposition to Jesus's crucifixion is stated with clarity and unanimity. See, for example, Brock and Parker, *Proverbs of Ashes*, 157–58; Brown, "Divine Child Abuse?"; Carbine, "Contextualizing the Cross," 97–99; Finlan, *Problems with Atonement*, 110; and Drewermann's thought in Beier, *Violent God-Image*, 218, 252, 258.

42. See Beier, *Violent God-Image*, 220–24.

43. Matt 21:33–41; Luke 10:9–19; Mark 12:1–12. See Finlan, *Problems with Atonement*, 109–10.

44. On Jesus's death as due to his commitment to the reign of God and his solidarity with the victims of kyriarchy, see Streufert, "Maternal Sacrifice," 68, 75; Carbine, "Contextualizing," 101–5; Trelstad, "Lavish Love," 115; Brock, "Cross of Resurrection and Communal Redemption," 249; Moltmann and Moltmann-Wendel, *Passion for God*, 7, 37–38; Japinga, *Feminism and Christianity*, 123–25; and Elizabeth Johnson, "Redeeming the Name of Christ," 124, 126. For Jesus's death as that of a martyr, see Grey, *Feminism, Redemption, and the Christian Tradition*, 131, 157, 170, 187–88, 190; and Trelstad, "Lavish Love," 116–17. Brock (*Journeys by Heart*, 94–96) ties the temple cleansing to the interpretation that Jesus's commitment to justice rather than to self-sacrifice led to his death.

as the women at the cross and tomb.[45] But God was unable to intervene to save Jesus from his death, for power is not unilateral and coercive, but shared and persuasive.

The generative model shifts the locus of salvation off the cross and onto both Jesus's life and Pentecost (as symbol for God raising up new communities). There is also a role for the resurrection of Jesus as a locus of salvation, although it is ambiguous.

The resurrection of Jesus points toward a broader event—God's gift of resurrection life that occurs whenever a person or community becomes open to the flow of divine energy that is omnipresent, and experiences new energies for living which come with that increased flow of energy.

Beyond this general definition of resurrection, things get fuzzy. Some advocates at least suggest that the term also refers to something that happens to Jesus after Good Friday and Holy Saturday—i.e., to the raising of a dead person to a qualitatively different form of bodily-spiritual life in relation to which death no longer has power, and in which God's *shalom* is established in purity and perpetuity.[46] Elizabeth Johnson, for example, describes God the Mother/Father gathering "her child and prophet into new transformed life, promise of a future for all the dead and the whole cosmos itself."[47] The problem, however, in connecting the resurrection of the dead with the general definition of resurrection above is that Jesus is dead. His life is not merely dissipating; it has expired. Since resurrection as "resurrection life" within a synergistic framework necessarily entails a human response—one which the dead cannot give—interpreting Jesus's resurrection as involving the resurrection of a dead person has coherence problems within the generative model of salvation. Some theologians within the model avoid this problem by asserting agnosticism on the issue of whether Jesus was raised from the dead.

Even for those who do give a nod to Jesus's resurrection from the dead, it is not clear that whatever occurs to Jesus on Easter Sunday is interpreted as a new saving act of God. His resurrection may simply re-

45. See Grey, *Feminism, Redemption, and the Christian Tradition*, 133; Brock, *Journeys by Heart*, 96–100; Johnson, "Redeeming the Name of Jesus," 125.

46. See 1 Corinthians 15, esp. vv. 35–58, and the discussion of the "spiritual body" of the resurrected person (v. 44).

47. Johnson, "Redeeming the Name of Christ," 125. See also Smith, "Risking the Terror," 2; Gebara, *Out of the Depths*, 121–25, 129, 131.

fer to the divine embrace of one's life after death which occurs to every human who dies. Parker says that Jesus "didn't have to rise from the dead for us to know that God's creative power is greater than death. Judaism already affirmed all this, knew all this."[48]

While ambiguity remains, the generative model clearly claims that resurrection is something that happens to humans who respond to God's offer of erotic power, divine presence, and divine lure toward possibilities of life. Here, resurrection refers to experiences which occur to Jesus *before* his death, and to other persons in general during their lives.[49] With this more specific interpretation, Jesus's resurrection symbolizes the *uprising* which occurs broadly, and which is the redemptive experience which dominates this model. Resurrection occurs whenever individuals and communities choose life, and refuse to live according to the power structures and threats of the forces of death. For Jesus, his resurrection occurs during his final week—in his cleansing of the temple, in the Garden of Gethsemane, and on his final day—when he refused to abandon his commitment to the truth even though his enemies threatened him with death. "On Good Friday," say Parker and Brown, "the Resurrected One was Crucified."[50]

The saving role of Jesus's resurrection, in conclusion, remains ambiguous overall. Beyond the ambiguity concerning whether he was raised from the dead, his resurrection merges as a theme into the more-predominant loci of salvation in the generative model—God's general saving activity, Jesus's life and ministry, and Pentecost. In terms of its role in salvation, Jesus's resurrection may thus be superfluous.

THE HOLY SPIRIT'S ROLE IN SALVATION

While Jesus's resurrection may be superfluous in the generative model of salvation, a distinct discussion of the role of the Holy Spirit is clearly redundant. That this is so is evidenced by the fact that in the works by the model's advocates, the words "Spirit" or "Divine Spirit" are frequently used, but the phrase "the Holy Spirit," as a reference to the third person of the Trinity, is noticeable by its almost-complete absence, for it is unnecessary to the model of salvation. The superfluity occurs because the ways

48. Brock and Parker, *Proverbs of Ashes*, 212–13.

49. I.e., to persons in contact with Jesus both during his life and after his death; and to persons unrelated to Jesus, in other religious traditions and cultures.

50. Brown and Parker, "For God So Loved the World?" 28.

God acts to save in the generative model are those divine acts usually attributed to God the Holy Spirit within the Christian tradition. In the Biblical and Christian theological traditions, the Holy Spirit is identified as "the Spirit of Life," the source of creative and new energies for living for all creatures. This Spirit is omnipresent, and constantly at work to sustain and vivify. The Spirit also is the divine person who brings about relations of distinction-in-unity, relations that reflect the fecundity of God's own trinitarian life.[51] The Holy Spirit descends upon Jesus and fills him with God's life-giving power, enabling him to heal, cast out demons, resist oppressive forces, and remain faithful to Abba. Jesus's openness to the Holy Spirit enables him to transfer the Spirit's power to others in healing and empowering ways. Finally, the Holy Spirit is breathed by Jesus onto believers, and descends upon the members of the early church at Pentecost, forming an ongoing community that embodies relations of reciprocity and mutual empowerment.

Since in the generative model, these various distinctive works of God the Holy Spirit are already attributed to the singular divine being described as the milieu of erotic power, as presence, and as lure, it would be repetitive to describe the same divine acts twice. Thus, the Holy Spirit has no unique role in bringing about creaturely salvation.[52]

OUR ROLE IN SALVATION

As we have seen above, violence creates a downward spiral in which persons and communities are increasingly closed-off from the sources of life-giving power located within the self, and in the web of connections between all beings.

Our task is *to rise up*, as Jesus stood up. We are to rise up, both in the sense of grasping abundant life, and resisting those forces which seek to keep us imprisoned in death's grip. We are to open ourselves to the flow of divine power moving both within us, and in the relational connections among all beings.

---

51. The title chosen by Jürgen Moltmann for his book on the person and work of the Holy Spirit exemplifies the first point: *Der Geist des Lebens*. See *Spirit of Life*. The second point, while clear in Moltmann, is especially emphasized in Michael Welker's *God the Spirit*.

52. The problem of Christian exclusivism presents a second reason. While "Spirit" is a religiously inclusive term, "the Holy Spirit" is religiously specific. Like the concept of the incarnation, the Holy Spirit as one of three divine persons is a Christian notion.

We are, in other words, to seek erotic power by our own action. Our courage and willingness to act opens links and generates power.[53]

Flowing against the downward pull of violence, erotic power creates an upward spiral. The act of rising up connects us to resources that increase our capacity to rise up.

1. *Intimate relationships and communities* based on the equality, reciprocity, mutuality and self-determination found in friendship.

2. *Acts of resistance to kyriarchal forces.* As was true for Andy Dufresne when he locked out the guards and turned up the volume on the two Italian ladies singing Mozart, and for Jesus when he took the whip and cleared the money-changing tables from the Temple, such acts put the self in touch with that part of the self that rightly rebels against such repression.[54]

3. *Experiences of beauty and attending wholeness.* They are moments in which, at least for a time, the fragmented self experiences itself as whole, and the isolated self experiences a natural union-in-differentiation with others. As Red suggested, alongside the voices of those two amazing singers, their own hearts soared.

4. *The act of remembering.* When we bury wounding experiences, our strength dissipates: we still feel their impact, but we cannot remember the context in which the events occurred, who perpetrated the violence, the reasons they happened, or why they impacted us so much at the time. Remembering those past events of violation helps the victim stitch the self together again.

5. *Trusting the self again.* "He is able to be present to himself again, and discovers that the powers of his own life that were buried alive early on are set free again."[55]

The upward spiral of increased capacities for presence to self and openness to the world is fueled by uprising, which connects the self to

53. On this succinct understanding of our agential role in salvation, see for example Brock in *Journeys by Heart*, 104, and especially the Epilogue.

54. Acting to retrieve the voice of the true self requires one to "quit playing cards with the jailor" (Smith, *Risking the Terror*, 100–103).

55. Drewermann quoted in Beier, *Violent God-Image*, 250.

the five experiences where erotic power flows. In his uprising, Jesus lived from these five rivers of erotic power. Ultimately, however, Jesus allowed the streams to connect him to the wellspring: God, the divine source of life. However, the "obedience" demanded by this God is obedience to one's true self, the inner law and unique destiny to follow which is placed within each self by God. Obeying God and obeying one's heart are mutually supportive.[56]

None of God's efforts to save us can become effective without our willingness to participate, to stand up and act. In every case in which people encounter Jesus, his effectiveness is contingent upon persons taking up their own role—becoming open, acting to stand up, claiming their right to the erotic powers of life. Along with Jesus's encounter with the hemorrhaging woman, other key texts revealing this essential human role include Jesus's raising of Jairus's daughter; Jesus's encounter with the Syrophoenician woman; and Jesus's inability to do miracles in Nazareth (yet the disciples' ability to do them).[57] In each case of encounter with Jesus, the believer's courage to rise up and claim her or his right to life-giving power is constitutive to the event of healing.

THE PROMISE, AND FRAGILITY, OF GOD'S SAVING ACTS

This nature of divine power as nonviolent and co-created means that the victorious realization of salvation is not guaranteed. God's powers for life are "stronger than forces of death" in the sense that they can outlast them, and their breadth is wider than them. Yet they are fragile. Even God cannot stop perpetrators of violence if they refuse to respond to God's presence and lure toward the way of life. God is dependent upon that human response. And so is the realization of God's salvation.[58]

At the end of *The Shawshank Redemption*, one last thread remains to be tied in the narrative. After decades of denials, the Board of Probation finally grants Red's request. He lands at the same boarding

---

56. On Drewermann's notion of obedience to God entailing obedience to one's true self, see Beier, *Violent God-Image*, 224, 267–71, 332.

57. Mark 5:21–24, 35–43; 7:24–30; and 6:1–13, respectively.

58. This theme of the eschaton's fulfillment being unknown and contingent upon human responsiveness to God's lure and efforts to save the world is a common theme in process theology, as well as in the work of Sallie McFague and Gordon Kaufman. In *Tragic Vision and Divine Compassion*, Wendy Farley also describes the fragility of God's efforts to save, and the uncertainty of a comprehensive eschatological fulfillment; see esp. chaps. 4–5.

house at which Brooks landed. He works at the same grocery store. He finds Brooks' initials carved in the beam where Brooks hung himself. As the days "outside" the prison go by, Red himself seems to be wavering, his demeanor listless. Whether he finds new energies for living depends upon whether or not he will believe the words Andy Dufresne told him in the yard: there are places not made of stone, and an imagined life worthy of hope, and within reach. Does he believe that?

Red breaks his parole and catches the bus north to find something Andy said he would leave for him: a coffee can, buried in the dirt under an oak tree, with an invitation to join Andy on the Pacific coast of Mexico, and a map to guide him.

5

Jesus, the Light and Guide

Enlightenment

FARAMIR

IN PETER JACKSON'S 2003 movie of J. R. R. Tolkien's *The Lord of the Rings—The Two Towers*, Faramir, one of the leaders of the human realm of Gondor, has captured the two hobbits, Frodo and Sam, who are attempting to take the ring of power and destroy it in the fire from which it was forged. The battle has begun between Sauron's forces and the soldiers of Gondor, for whom the prospect of victory looks dim.

"Men, who are so easily seduced by its power," notes the voice of Galadriel from beyond the scene, one of the elves who has the power to see things from afar. "The young captain of Gondor has but to extend his hand, take the ring for his own, and the world will fall."

Faramir is told that they do not have the strength to repel Sauron. He questions Frodo, and when he learns of the ring's nature, tells him: "The ring of power within my grasp. A chance for Faramir, captain of Gondor, to show his quality." Sam insists the ring must be destroyed. Faramir instead tells his men to prepare to leave, with the hobbits. "The ring will go to Gondor."

When they are close to the sentry town of Osgiliath, they find it burning. This time, Frodo pleads with Faramir. "The ring will not save Gondor. It has only the power to destroy. Please . . . let me go." Faramir is unpersuaded.

Upon reaching the city, they find that Orcs—monstrous soldiers in Sauron's army—have taken the eastern shore. "Their numbers are too great. By nightfall we will be overrun," says the town's military leader. When Faramir directs his aides to take Frodo and Sam to his father, with news of "a weapon that will change our fortunes in this war," Sam tries to warn him, shouting that it was the ring that killed Faramir's own brother by driving him mad, but Faramir is undeterred.

During this conversation, the terrifying Nazguls come overhead—riders atop winged dragons, Sauron's main agents of power. Faramir hides Frodo and Sam. Frodo, however, under the sway of the ring, walks out onto a clearing, lifts the ring up toward the Nazgul, and then begins to place the ring on his own finger. Faramir sees all of this take place, then shoots the Nazgul, as Sam rescues Frodo.

Faramir also observes the conversation between Sam and Frodo minutes later. Frodo, feeling their task of taking the ring to its destruction is impossible, says, "What are we holding on to, Sam?" "That there's some good in this world, Mr. Frodo, and it's worth fighting for," Sam responds.

At this point, Faramir walks up to Frodo, kneels, so that they see one another eye to eye, and says, "I think at last we understand one another, Frodo Baggins."

Faramir indicates that he will let the hobbits go on their way. "You know the laws of our country, the laws of your father," interjects Faramir's lieutenant. "You let them go, your life will be forfeit."

"Then it is forfeit," responds Faramir. "Release them."

ILLUMINATION AND POWER

In the scene from *The Lord of the Rings—The Two Towers*, Faramir believes that the power of the ring will be Gondor's and his own deliverance, when in fact it shall destroy them all if attempts are made to wield it. Three times Faramir rejects suggestions that he misperceives the situation. Only when he oversees Frodo lifting the ring to the Nazgul, against Frodo's own wishes, and overhears the pure purpose behind Frodo's and Sam's intent to destroy the ring does Faramir's perception of reality change.

The problem for humankind in the generative model resides in experiences of powerlessness. People are enervated and in bondage to forces that bind their strength. Salvation is found in empowerment, experiences that bring new energy for living, and liberation from the forces that bind.

In this chapter's model, one's powerlessness resides in the deeper experiences of *blindness*. Like Faramir, individuals, groups, and nations are steeped in ignorance, and living in a fantasy world which does not cohere with reality. Salvation is brought by *illumination*, by seeing reality and one's connections to it. Illumination brings liberation, and thus I term this new model *the enlightenment model of salvation*, with Jesus as a leading light and guide.

Apart from one exception concerning the saving meaning of the cross,[1] there is nothing in the generative model of atonement with which the enlightenment model disagrees. They are extremely similar models, and cohere together well. Like the advocates of the generative model, advocates of the enlightenment model sharply criticize the penal sub-stitutionary theory of atonement. Like the previous model, they correct the faulty Christian praxis of violence by making a fundamental shift from an ambivalent, violent God-image to a nonambivalent, nonviolent image of God. Further, both models share the six traits common to their alternative soteriologies.[2]

What distinguishes the enlightenment model from the generative one is a shift in emphasis. This shift in emphasis is enough to create a new model with a fresh perspective on how God saves the world that God loves. Salvation comes from seeing the world aright.

Salvation, however, does not come merely from seeing "what is" in general. What must be perceived are the nature and dynamics of power. In the generative model, salvation occurs when, like the hemorrhaging woman, we reach out to claim our rightful access to the divine, life-giv-ing powers which flow abundantly. In the enlightenment model, salva-tion occurs when, like Faramir, we perceive the difference between true and false forms of power, and our participation in each. Seeing enables emancipation.

New Testament scholar Marcus Borg shall be our main guide for the enlightenment model, along with Dorothee Soelle in her book *The Silent Cry: Mysticism and Resistance*. Borg and Soelle share in common the belief that mystical experiences are powerful in leading to the trans-formed cognition which emancipates. Borg adds a rationalist strain to his mystical model as well. Common elements of both rationalist and mystical approaches to reality are the beliefs that correct information about 'the way things really are' is available to the human mind, and that

---

1. This we shall discuss below on Jesus's saving role.

2. See chapter 3 for the predominant shift in God-images and the six traits shared by these two soteriologies.

we humans have the capacities to see the structure of reality, if we are aided by the divine spark or Spirit that resides within us.

THEOLOGICAL METHOD

In their approach to knowledge of how God saves us, advocates of the enlightenment model are solid modernists, with a dash of postmodernism thrown in. The modern turns to experience and to reason are taken seriously, but also the postmodern recognition of the plurality of perspectives. "What I come to know in my own experience can be trusted to be true in a way that what we learned secondhand from tradition cannot be trusted," writes Borg.[3] Yet a description of God's salvific ways must speak not only to our experiences of God, but also to our minds, its credibility enhanced by the reasonableness of its picture of God and the world.[4] Further, affirming a postmodern sensibility, advocates of the enlightenment model reject religious exclusivism. Certainly no one religion contains all the truth, or could be the exclusive route to salvation. The Christian view of salvation is best understood when seen within the broader context of the world's manifold religions and their common traits.[5]

However, this postmodern openness to pluralism conceals beneath it a very modernist—and European/North American—understanding of the content of those multiple religions. The advocates presuppose that the great religious traditions share a "primordial tradition," a core experience of the sacred which crosses religions, cultures, and time periods. They presuppose a *panentheistic* view of God and the world—that all things exist within God's own being—for God must not be so transcendent that God cannot be experienced. And they presuppose an optimistic view of the human capacity to experience and know God: access to God is immediate. This view that God can be known directly through reason or self-transcending experiences, that God is present and closely identified with nature and humanity, and that different cultural-linguistic forms are used in the world's religions to describe this one God, is a modern European/American view of the world's religions.[6]

---

3. Borg, *God We Never Knew*, 4.

4. See ibid.

5. Ibid., 4. On the rejection of an exclusivistic framework for understanding Christian salvation, see esp. Borg, *Heart of Christianity*, preface, 81, 111, 118–19, 207–8, 218.

6. On the major world religions sharing a common core religious experience, see Borg, *Heart of Christianity*, esp. chap. 11. On the advocates presupposing a panentheis-

Given this embrace of human experience and reason, and of the immediacy and universality of experiences of the sacred and of its liberating power, the choice of a *theological norm* makes sense. "The data of religious experience" is the theological norm.[7] More precisely, *mystical experiences* are the norm, experiences which range from altered states of consciousness occasioned by particular encounters with the sacred dimension of reality, to less dramatic experiences in which one is simply aware of the divine reality's presence in one's everyday life.[8] A unity is experienced beneath all multiplicities. These mystical moments are unmediated, even by the Bible, and exhibit universality, crossing history and culture.[9] When one stands in the presence of the sacred, one perceives both "the way things really are," and "the path one must take toward life" in light of ultimate reality.[10]

As we have seen, advocates of the generative model ask: Does a view of salvation function to save life, enabling the oppressed to rise up and affirm their own agency and resist the forces of death? In contrast, advocates of the enlightenment model ask: Does a view of salvation cohere with the core experience of the sacred described by the world's religious traditions?[11] While different, this latter norm connects to the former. In mystical experience, knowledge of God comes directly to one's own life, and is rooted in the Spirit's work, which is independent from hierarchical, institutional control of knowledge. The norm is thus friendly to the dispossessed. Further, advocates of the enlightenment model also qualify their norm functionally. A true mystical experience must lead one to af-

tic model of God's relation to the world, see Borg, *God We Never Knew*, 5 and chap. 2; Borg and Wright, *Meaning of Jesus*, 61, 233. On epistemological access to God as immediate, see Borg, *God We Never Knew*, chap. 2, esp. 36–37, 46. On this perspective being a modern liberal European/North American one, see Masuzawa, *Invention of World Religions*. See also Lindbeck, *Nature of Doctrine*, esp. chaps. 2–3; and Heim, *Salvations*, esp. part 1, "Pluralisms."

7. Borg, *Heart of Christianity*, 64.

8. On immediate experiences of the sacred as the theological norm, see Borg, ibid, 64, and Ch. 11; Borg and Wright, *Meaning*, 60–61, 230–31; Borg, *God We Never Knew*, 1, 37–46; and Soelle, *Silent Cry*, 16–17.

9. Soelle, ibid, 12, 15, 19. A more extensive discussion of the nature of these normative experiences of the sacred follows below.

10. See Borg, *Heart of Christianity*, 47, 214, 216.

11. On the role of comparative religions scholars in delineating the theological norm, see Borg, *Heart of Christianity*, 213–19; Borg and Wright, *Meaning*, 9, 60, and esp. 230–31; Borg, *God We Never Knew*, 89.

firm the right of the biologically inferior and economically expendable to have life. This ethic rests in the affirmation that we are all creatures, a commonness experienced in the mystical encounter with God.

Finally, similar to the generative model, the enlightenment model places weight on the same criteria to judge the adequacy of a view of salvation. Theologies must cohere with lived human experience: experiences of hunger for life and meaning, of oppressions, and of liberation from hunger and oppression, all related to the mystical experience of oneness and of the goodness of God, world, and self.[12] Further, portrayals of salvation must make sense, presenting a rationally-coherent faith.[13] Finally, scripture and tradition are given a historical-metaphorical reading. The bible is a human product, containing voices of both oppression and protest against oppression, of conventional wisdom and subversion to that wisdom. Yet the divine voice is found in, with, and under these human voices.[14]

THE PROBLEM WITHIN THE HUMAN CONDITION

In the generative model, the problem is that people are dying because they are cut off from the sources of life. In the enlightenment model, there is a similar problem of being "cut off"—only in this case people are cut off from the truth about reality. Individuals do not perceive the crucial piece of information that makes one's life lucid. They are deluded.

This delusion occurs on two levels, the individual and the communal. For the individual, the delusion is experienced as exile, closed-heartedness, and captivity. At the communal level, it is experienced most often as systems of domination and injustice.[15] "Domination systems," writes Borg, "are hierarchical social orders marked by economic exploitation and political oppressions in which a few persons (almost always men) rule over everybody else."[16] As on the individual level, so also on

12. Soelle, *Silent Cry*, 46–49.

13. See Borg, *Heart of Christianity*, preface; Borg and Wright, *Meaning*, 231; Borg, *God We Never Knew*, 11.

14. See Borg, *Heart of Christianity*, chap. 3; Borg and Wright, *Meaning*, 234–40.

15. These are similar to what the generative model identifies as kyriarchal structures.

16. Borg, *God We Never Knew*, 69. On the domination systems at the corporate level of the fallen human condition, see Borg, *Heart of Christianity*, chap. 7, and 90; and Borg, *God We Never Knew*, 166.

the communal, both the beneficiaries and victims of the systems are *deluded*. Like Faramir and Sauron, they think that this coercive power is genuine power, when it is not.

As miserable persons squatting in a prison, asleep from being overwhelmed, we live in exile from our true home, with hearts closed to the outside world and the self split and held captive by the preoccupations of the ego and requirements of the culture. And yet, the deepest element of our lost human condition is this: the cell door is open; we simply do not notice the fact. We are blind to the truths all around us.[17] God is all around us. We live within God, and God has always been in relationship to us, journeying with us, yearning to be known by us, yet we do not know or experience this. Further, what we knew as children, we have forgotten: though we are earth and ashes, we are royal children, for whose sake the world was made. This world, and the God who gives it and dwells within it, is gracious, generous, and life-giving, not hostile or indifferent. This God loves us and accepts us, unconditionally. In addition to being blind to God's compassionate presence, we are blind to true power as shared power which moves through egalitarian structures. Saddest and most problematic of all, we are blind to our own ignorance. We do not see that we are squatting in a prison cell whose door is open.[18]

Why are we blind? As Borg says, things happen to us that weaken our ability to perceive truths around us, and as we grow, we deepen the effects.[19] In the process of growing up, we inevitably forget the closeness of God and oneness of all things which we knew as children. Though we are capable of perceiving God's presence in day-to-day flesh, our five senses are geared to knowing the world of matter and energy, time and space, while missing the divine. Because we are finite creatures, we live with a basic insecurity which pulls our attention toward the self. The

---

17. Beneath the multitude of human problems lies limited vision. See Borg, *Heart of Christianity*, chaps. 6 and 8; Borg, *God We Never Knew*, 160–61; and Soelle, *The Silent Cry*, 20.

18. On our sensory malfunction and intellectual incomprehension leading us to miss God's all-encompassing and constant presence, see Borg, *Heart of Christianity*, chap. 8; Borg, *God We Never Knew*, 77, 111–15; and Soelle, *Silent Cry*, 17–18, 37–38, 78. On our forgetting what we knew as children—that God is always with us and loves us unconditionally, for we are God's beloved and royal children—see Borg, *Heart of Christianity*, 25, 76–78, 114; Borg, *God We Never Knew*, 111–15; and Soelle, *Silent Cry*, 37–44.

19. See Borg, *God We Never Knew*, 158–59.

learning of language brings with it a movement from the *I–Thou* encounters with God and other creatures we experience as children to the *I–It* relations of subjects to objects. The words and categories of culture, while giving us wisdom to perceive certain things, also screen out the reality known in *I–Thou* moments.[20] The act of naming also may serve the creation of relations of dominance and possession rather than co-equal forms of unity.

Beyond the biological, existential, and linguistic reasons, the deeper reason we begin to forget the primary truths of our lives is a developmental one. The birth of self-consciousness brings the knowledge of oneself as a separated self. But the natural and inevitable result of that knowledge is self-concern, a turning of one's focus inward to protect the self. Increasingly, we forget the One from whom we came and in whom we live each moment, and stop seeing the oneness of all creatures beneath the wonder of their diversity. In a poem revealing a nine-year-old's musings at turning ten, Billy Collins describes this forgetting, and its sad, inevitable loss:

> The whole idea of it makes me feel
> like I'm coming down with something,
> something worse than any stomach ache
> or the headaches I get from reading in bad light—
> a kind of measles of the spirit,
> a mumps of the psyche,
> a disfiguring chickenpox of the soul.
>
> You tell me it is too early to be looking back,
> but that is because you have forgotten
> the perfect simplicity of being one
> and the beautiful complexity introduced by two.
> But I can lie on my bed and remember every digit.
> At four I was an Arabian wizard.
> I could make myself invisible
> By drinking a glass of milk a certain way.
> At seven I was a soldier, at nine a prince.
>
> But now I am mostly at the window
> watching the late afternoon light.
> Back then it never fell so solemnly

---

20. For the difference between *I-Thou* and *I-It* encounters, Borg is drawing from the famous work by Jewish theologian Martin Buber, *I and Thou*.

against the side of my tree house,
and my bicycle never leaned against the garage
as it does today,
all the dark blue speed drained out of it.

This is the beginning of sadness, I say to myself,
as I walk through the universe in my sneakers.
It is time to say good-bye to my imaginary friends,
time to turn the first big number.

It seems only yesterday I used to believe
there was nothing under my skin but light.
If you cut me I would shine.
But now when I fall upon the sidewalks of life,
I skin my knees. I bleed.[21]

The beautiful, distinctive self becomes a self separated from God and other creatures, and eventually from one's own truest self as well. Culture's messages about who we should be and how we should act become internalized. The self splits, and as Soelle says, we hold back. We live from the outside in rather than the inside out. We compare ourselves with others, and bring harsh judgment upon others, or oneself, or most despairingly, both, like Montgomery Brogan cursing into the mirror. When we finish our psychological development, we've forgotten the way home. We need a guide.[22]

While all are affected by the development of self-consciousness and its attendant self-focus, the loss of awareness of God's presence is compounded for many by their social environments. As we have seen, abuse during childhood makes the self build a protective wall which also diminishes the capacity to perceive God. The spirit of industrial production and consumption in modern Western culture encourages us to live our lives on the surface of reality, seeking satisfaction in the finite, and missing the sacred which dwells in the depths of reality. As we have noted, with its focus on possessions, Western culture also encourages us to approach relationships with a utilitarian, objectifying attitude, while wielding coercive power to control the other. Preoccupied by the com-

21. Collins, "On Turning Ten," in *Art of Drowning*, 48–49.

22. On language acquisition's bringing a concomitant loss of capacity to perceive God's presence and the oneness of all beings, see Borg, *God We Never Knew*, 112–13; and Soelle, *Silent Cry*, 62–63. On psychological development inevitably leading to egotism, see Borg, *Heart of Christianity*, 113–17, 153.

motion of modern life, which lets in everything—all light, music, tricks of thought, variations of pain and memory and expectation—we are closed to the one thing beneath the commotion, the unity of all things. We perceive neither God's presence in all things, beckoning with love, nor the integrity of our own buried self or of other selves and creatures we meet. We see nothing beyond the bundle of the things we "have." Through their attempts to control us, systems of injustice further hem our innate capacities to see, and of course that is their intent. Finally, religion portrays God as a patriarch who dominates our lives and demands dependence, the portrait binding our psyche and spirit to legalistic conceptions of our relation to God.[23]

The world batters us. Over the course of our lives, our hearts gradually become closed, and we become disconnected from God. This hardening of our hearts and fading of our sight, however, also involves our free will. We devote ourselves to some thing in the world, rather than God who is the underlying oneness. We submit to the powers of this world which bring spiritual death to our souls and real death to our neighbors, particularly the three powers of *ego*, *possessions*, and *violence*. We indulge in self-centeredness. We can do terrible acts of violence, to others and ourselves. Not only are we deceived, but we deceive ourselves, for we do not want to see with clear eyes our own acts of violence, capitulation, and callousness.[24]

While the advocates of the enlightenment model acknowledge that we sin against God, neighbor, and self, and thus bear guilt, this nod toward sin and guilt is qualified in three ways. Like the generative model, the enlightenment model denies that the deepest human problem is sin and guilt from rebellious acts against God's law. Though we commit these acts, we do them more due to our suffering under our ignorance, alienation, and bondage under the powers of the domination systems than due to our own willfulness.[25] Our hearts are surrounded like eggs

23. On our blindness due to preoccupation in our busy, consumption-oriented Western lives, see Borg, *Heart of Christianity*, 118, 154; Borg, *God We Never Knew*, 113. On the disenchanting of the world in the West, and Buber's motif of commotion, which blocks our sensitivity to God, see Soelle, *Silent Cry*, 17, 30–33.

24. Borg and Soelle are clear that our hard hearts and blindness are not merely the result of things done to us. We deepen the effects. For our sin as surrender to the powers, see Soelle, *Silent Cry*, chap. 2, esp. 27, 33; and 192, 213. On the role of self-deception, see Borg, *Heart of Christianity*, 152, 168; Borg, *God We Never Knew*, 158.

25. On personal responsibility for sin playing a relatively small role compared to

in their shells. We contribute to that shell, but we do not put ourselves inside those walls. Moreover, the original capacity to give and receive God's love and the love of others is never lost; it is merely covered over.[26] Finally, while some hearts are more deeply hardened due to childhood abuse or unjust oppression, others are only somewhat hardened by the natural effects of linguistic and psychological development.[27]

We need to be awakened, or to rouse ourselves.[28]

But we are not dead, needing to be resurrected by another.

THE MEANING OF SALVATION

We are asleep in our fantasies—and yet deluded about our true state. In that delusion, we are disconnected from every aspect of reality.

Salvation is sobriety. It is our being awakened from our delusion, and thus our restoration to reality. It is Faramir—finally perceiving the nature of the ring of power, and seeing Frodo and Sam, his brother Boromir and himself rightly for the first time—bending down to talk with Frodo eye to eye, and taking risks for his benefit. In salvation, one begins to live in what is real rather than in the delusions of a fantasy world. This return to reality reconnects us to what is genuine: deep knowledge of self, intimacy with others, joyful participation in life, and honest relationship with God.

In salvation, we encounter two realities unfamiliar yet strangely buried within as a memory of something we knew long ago. Primarily the experience is social and political: We experience a form of communal unity that is not based upon patterns of domination and submission. This non-hierarchical and non-exploitative social order—one radically different from that of Egypt—is described in the Bible as the "Promised Land" in which every family is allocated a portion of land in perpetuity, and political and economic engagements are egalitarian. The commu-

---

social sin and suffering, see Borg, *Heart of Christianity*, chap. 9, esp. 167–71; Borg, *Meeting Jesus Again*, 127–33; Borg, *God We Never Knew*, 77–78.

26. Both Borg and Soelle speak of our problem as the covering-over of an original capacity to participate in the love of God. This mystical capacity of childhood—expressed so well in the Billy Collins poem—is buried, but not fundamentally distorted or lost. See Soelle, *Silent Cry*, chap. 1, esp. 10–12, 22–26, 85–86.

27. On not all hearts being equally hard, see Borg, *Heart of Christianity*, 153–54.

28. On the imagery of being asleep in the prison of the ego and needing an awakening, see Soelle, *Silent Cry*, 34, 81–84.

nity represents "God's *shalom*" and "the kingdom of God," symbols not of a different place, but of this earth as ruled by God.

In salvation, one experiences not only a different kind of community, but also a different type of self, one that is whole again. Other-inflicted or self-inflicted wounds are healed. Such healing is portrayed in multiple ways. Salvation is like what happens to the heart when it comes home after years of absence. It is like being born a second time, for a new soft heart replaces an old closed and grasping heart. The eyes see freshly. Like Ebeneezer Scrooge when he awakes in his own bed on Christmas morning after three ghosts rid him of his delusions, the new heart is now fully open to reality, taking in all the wonders and sufferings of the world and moving back out into it with an exuberant desire for encounter and union. Salvation is like moving from solitary confinement into a broad place in which there is room to breathe. One is emancipated from the shackles of the domination systems, and the internal chains of one's own jealousy, envy, fear, self-hatred, depression, guilt, and constant concerns about ego.[29]

All the metaphors describe salvation as an awakening of human capacities that lie dormant, a growth from less activation of capacities to more activation, of restoration of sight and genuine interaction with the world.

THE COMING OF SALVATION

Religious salvation comes like the solving of a puzzle—with a moment of insight in which a person sees a pattern in a collection of details that was not seen previously, but that had been there all along. Salvation is "perceiving truths not known before that make life's mysteries lucid."[30] However, a catalyst is needed to activate the slumbering internal eyes.

29. On salvation as healing, see Borg, *Heart of Christianity*, 175; Borg, *God We Never Knew*, 157; as return from exile, see Borg, *Heart of Christianity*, 169, 175; Borg, *God We Never Knew*, 159–60; Borg, *Meeting Jesus Again*, 128–29; as being born again or as the "hatching of the heart," see Borg, *Heart of Christianity*, chaps. 6 and 8; and Borg, *God We Never Knew*, chap. 5; as unleashing in the heart an "erotic exuberance" for connections with life, Borg, *God We Never Knew*, 167; and as an exodus from slavery to a space of external and internal freedom, see Borg, *Heart of Christianity*, chap. 6; and Borg, *Meeting Jesus Again*, 128.

30. Soelle, *Silent Cry*, 21. Other religions put forth the idea that knowledge of reality is the key to liberation. For Buddhism, see, for example, Burton, *Buddhism, Knowledge and Liberation*.

The catalyst is an experience of the sacred: one sees and encounters within the daily earthly reality another layer of reality, a sacred one—like Moses encountering Yahweh in a burning bush, and the Buddha becoming enlightened under the Bodhi tree. The recipient discovers that "the other is like you," a *thou* and not an *it*, and all things are part of one great living whole. She simultaneously finds herself within a form of unity not based on domination.

These insights may be atheistic in form. In panentheistic and theistic forms of the epiphany, the recipient also sees that all things are valued as ends in themselves and that all things are one because God—the principle of being—values, indwells, and quickens all things without qualification.

Instead of hostile or indifferent, the cosmos is experienced as gracious and life-giving, leading to a feeling of "coming home." The recipient remembers that, while being of dust and ashes, she is nevertheless a "royal child." This experience of the world as welcoming and unified provides the foundation for the recipient's later nonviolence.[31]

The experience of God's presence includes within it an epiphany of the socio-political and ecological dream of God. The world as God's reality and under God's direction is a world ruled by gracious, generative power, and the domination systems have ceased. God's reality is kyriarchy's end.

The moment of saving insight may come through such a direct experience of God. It may also come through the study and following of wise teachings from those who have had such experiences.[32]

The encounter with the divine shows what is real, and how we should live in response to that reality. As catalyst, it opens the eyes. But a moment of sight, while necessary for salvation, is insufficient to save because salvation entails the transformation of one's life and of the world. Humans whose actions are inspired by the enlightened knowledge redeem the world. Such wise action entails a "yes" to the reality perceived in the ecstatic experience and to the nondominative community of all

31. On experiencing the cosmos as gracious, leading to a feeling of "coming home," see Borg, *Heart of Christianity*, 25; *God We Never Knew*, 41–44; Soelle, *Silent Cry*, 37–44, 97, 101.

32. On wisdom traditions leading to transformation, see Borg, *Heart of Christianity*, 47; Borg, *God We Never Knew*, 115.

things. It also involves resistance to fraudulent orders of death claiming to be real.[33]

Finally, paradoxically, the way toward salvation is the way of return, to truths we experienced in our moments of amazement as children, but forgot long ago. The world is our home, and God is here. We remember what we once knew.

We just need to be reminded.

GOD'S ROLE IN SALVATION

> Come, Spirit.
> Help us sing the story of our land.
> You are our mother;
> we, your field of corn.
> We rise from out of the soul of you.[34]

In the movie *The New World*, John Smith and the English sail up the James River in 1607, bringing with them the cravings and ethos of what Soelle calls the three powers of death: ego, possessions, and violence. John is seeking the desired but elusive Northwest Passage to the East; its discovery would bring him fame and wealth. The colonists, while starving for lack of effort in husbandry, paw the ground feverishly in search of gold. They want to return to England as rich men. They also see the land, seemingly empty of peoples, and certainly depopulated by the waves of European-born diseases that swept North American tribes in the previous century. They want to grab it for themselves and fence it off; they will shoot those who trespass.

John Smith also has an experience with the land, but one more mixed. He too thinks the land is vacant for the taking, and he wants to possess it. When he is sent up the James River to meet Chief Powhatan and barter for food, he carries with him two Algonquians bound and forced to serve as guides. In his use of violence to gain possessions, in his inability to transcend his own ego and have a genuine encounter with the Other, he differs not a wit from his fellow colonists. Yet he also imagines a social world different than the one he left, one in which none

---

33. Soelle describes salvation as the twofold consciousness of the oneness of all things, with actions governed by "radiant intelligence," i.e., knowledge of that oneness and goodness (38), which includes resistance to forces of death. See, for example, Soelle, *Silent Cry*, 5–6, 10, as representative of the book's thesis.

34. Pocahontas, *New World*.

are dispossessed of the means of subsistence, and rapacious greed does not lead to warfare. One that is more just. "We shall make a new start. A fresh beginning," he thinks as he paddles upriver.

> Here the blessings of the earth are bestowed upon all. None need grow poor. Here there is good ground for all, and no cost but one's labor. We shall build a true commonwealth … We shall have no landlords to rack us with high rents or extort the fruit of our labor. None shall eat up carelessly what his friends got worthily or steal away that which virtue has stored up. Men shall not make each other their spoil.

There is ground for all, if it is shared in a community of reciprocity and equality, but he does not yet imagine that.

Along with his mixed experience of nature, however, John Smith also has two unanticipated mystical experiences after he is taken captive by the Algonquians, then surprisingly set free after Pocahontas pleads with her father Powhatan to spare his life. He experiences a form of community not based upon domination—one of reciprocity and mutuality. The Algonquians accept him into their community. One day as he has been playing and laughing with a family group, a baby crawls upon his chest, kissing him upon the lips. He reflects: "They are gentle, loving, faithful, lacking in all guile and trickery. The words denoting lying, deceit, greed, envy, slander and forgiveness have never been heard. They have no jealousy, no sense of possession. Real, what I thought a dream."

He not only experiences a form of communal unity not based upon patterns of domination and submission, but also a form of interpersonal unity in which the individuality and wonder of each are heightened through reciprocity. Pocahontas and Smith gradually come to love one another. In one scene, they are playfully trying to trip one another in a field. Pocahontas stops. She cups her hand at his mouth, takes his breath in her hand, brings her hand to her mouth, and breathes in his breath. Then she does the same from her mouth back to his. Then back to hers again, as she thinks, "My life in you, your life in me." Later they rest beside one another in the grass. The rain falls, he strokes her forearm, and thinks, "Love. There is only this. All else is unreal."

In both his communal and interpersonal experiences of oneness not based upon domination, he has extended experiences of self-transcendence. He sees, with an experiential knowing, that the way of ego-driven greed and violence is not the only way to live, not the most real. There is something more real, and his encounter with this ultimate reality heals him.

Pocahontas has always lived within her awareness of the oneness of all things. Smith has forgotten it, but is now reminded of it. This is how God saves us, and through us the world: by reminding us of truths we knew once as children, but have since forgotten. God reveals God's unabashed love, and gives a taste of communal life without domination. We taste "the good beginning" of all things, the world as originally blessed—which politically points to the original equality of all humans and to creation as not private property.[35]

In one sense, God achieves this saving revelation simply by existing as God, like the sun that warms and enlightens and nourishes life simply by being itself, and shining upon all things. We are like corn, and we rise from out of God's soul. What is this God like? God is "the far-near one,"[36] a view of God almost identical to that found in the generative model. Both models share a panentheistic model of God's relation to the world. The visible world of ordinary experience is surrounded and indwelled by a formless nonmaterial divine reality. The Spirit, like the wind and our breath, moves outside of us and within us. God and creatures are one organic whole, with the material layer of reality often described as God's "body."[37]

As with the generative model, for Borg and Soelle, this panentheistic God is not Trinitarian.[38] Nor is it clear that the Ultimate Reality is an agent, since it can be encountered in atheistic frameworks and imagined with transpersonal metaphors. The model also rejects the ambivalent, violent God-image. God is not a distant king with omnipotent dominating force; God is a lover who desires mutuality and reciprocity.[39] God

35. On the Spirit's revealing the "good beginning" and its egalitarian, compassionate community, see Soelle, *Silent Cry*, 88–91; and Borg, *Meeting Jesus Again*, 61.

36. The phrase is Soelle's (*Silent Cry*, 119), used by troubadours for the beloved, and by mystics for God.

37. For Borg's panentheistic model, see *Heart of Christianity*, chap. 4 and 155; Borg, *Meeting Jesus Again*, 14; *Meaning*, 61; *God*, 3, 12, 26–27, 48, 72. On divine-creaturely interdependence, see Soelle, *Silent Cry*, 106–11.

38. That doctrine simply refers to God wearing different masks and playing different roles in relation to creation. See Borg and Wright, *Meaning of Jesus*, 153–55; Borg, *God We Never Knew*, 98; and 107 n. 49.

39. On rejection of royal and patriarchal imagery for God, as well as divine omnipotence, see Borg, *God We Never Knew*, 62–71; Soelle, *Silent Cry*, 6, 63, 100. On God as lover, see ibid., 36; and Borg, *God We Never Knew*, 74–75.

does not visit transgressors with wrath; rather, God is like the father of the prodigal son, full of compassion and mercy, or a mother bending down to feed her toddler.[40] God does not demand sacrifices in order to forgive. God's forgiveness is simply given freely, without the conditions of either Jesus's death or our belief in him.[41]

This loving presence, when perceived, can change us. Whether God saves by simply existing, like the sun, or by consciously acting to disclose Godself to humans, God's role in salvation is to show up.

While God may reveal Godself anywhere, certain places—which the Celts call "thin places"—more naturally become permeable, allowing the divine layer to shine through the material layer.[42] As Pocahontas does continuously, and Smith intermittently, a person may experience nature as an "other," a "thou," and feel intensity, presence, and light. In erotic love, in which relations of domination and submission are transcended and subverted, one may experience a oneness similar to that shared with God: the "other" is like you, and the "other" is not like you. Pocahontas and Smith felt this gradually, through daily interactions. The desire for union with one who cannot be possessed or encompassed displays for the participants the fact that love, like all reality, is interdependent. When love is sustained even in suffering, we may hear "the silent cry" of God who suffers within all broken creatures. In egalitarian community, we find our desire for true fellowship. In experiences of beauty, we live as "transcendently immanent," with a pure attentiveness that brings a joy unattached to any object. We stop asking, "and then what?" The mystical eye also perceives the beauty of God at work in liberating movements in history, present in beaten-down life to revive.[43]

---

40. Biblical texts describing such wrath represent the views of the redactors; in reality, "judgment" comes as a historical effect of one's sinful acts. On rejection of divine punishment and the alternative images of intimate father and mother, see Borg, *Heart of Christianity*, 75–78; Borg, *Meeting Jesus Again*, 84–85; Borg, *God We Never Knew*, 17, 73.

41. See, for example, Borg, *Meeting Jesus Again*, 129–31; *Heart of Christianity*, chap. 4, and esp. 74–78.

42. God operates in and through the "thin places" to encounter us, opening our hearts. See Borg, *Heart of Christianity*, chap. 8; Borg and Wright, *Meaning of Jesus*, 250. On different types of experiences of the sacred, see Borg, *God We Never Knew*, 3, 37–44.

43. See Soelle, *Silent Cry*, part 2.

All of these mystical encounters describe one experience: the transcendence of the self into the whole of reality, a whole composed of distinction-in-unity. The union of harmony and intensity is what is most real, as well as the structure of love, the wellspring of life, and the luminosity of beauty.[44]

JESUS'S ROLE IN SALVATION

Jesus is no more essential to an experience of salvation in the enlightenment model than the Buddha is to an experience of awakening, or Lao Tzu is to a discovery of the *Tao*. Nonetheless, his role in salvation is not insignificant.

Jesus is a piece of creation that has become luminescent, allowing us to see dimensions of ourselves and the world we overlooked before. He is a human being whose feet are grounded firmly in the nonmaterial sacred dimension that indwells and surrounds all things, giving life, and so he shines. He is a "thin place," one of many at which the boundary between the material and sacred dimensions of reality becomes open. Like a crystal scattering light, Jesus discloses that sacred dimension, and what a life filled with it looks like, and the way home to it.

While a luminescent one, Jesus was not divine, nor a divine savior or Messiah. Rather, he was a Jewish mystic. As in the generative model, in which he was a human being open to the flow of divine energy, so here, Jesus is a human being open to and able to mediate the divine presence, light, and love. He takes in, then breathes out, the sacred. While in the generative model he quickened, here he illuminates, acting as himself both the light, and a lamp to guide the way to the divine. He is the saving catalyst ignited by God, helping eyes see God either by acting as a medium through which recipients encounter the sacred, or through his wise teachings.

Jesus was a peasant who was exceptionally intelligent and who had a zest for life. What did he do? He preached of the Kingdom of God, which Borg identifies as life in God's presence now, and social life under God's lordship rather than that of the domination systems. "The Kingdom of God is spread out upon the earth, only people do not see it."[45] Jesus re-

---

44. While Borg and Soelle use studies in comparative religions and anthropology to describe experiences of an ultimate oneness of reality, neurologist Jill Bolte Taylor explains the neurological basis to such experiences. See Taylor, *My Stroke of Insight*.

45. *Gospel of Thomas* 113, quoted in Borg and Wright, *Meaning of Jesus*, 75. Borg also points to Luke 17:21.

vealed God's and the Kingdom's presence through five roles: He was a spirit person; a healer and exorcist; a subversive sage; a social prophet; and a founder of a renewal movement.[46]

Through these five activities, Jesus opens the eyes of those he encounters to the presence of God within and around them, and to a domination-free form of community. He is one whose lens is clean, thus allowing him to see God clearly and reflect God to others. But in these capacities, he is neither unique nor different in kind from us. He was simply a human whose psyche was unusually open to the Spirit, allowing the Spirit to flow through him, like light through glass. In this, he actualized possibilities open to all persons. Rather than being "the Father's only-begotten Son," Jesus is "our eldest brother." He shows us of what we are capable, once we allow our dormant abilities to be awakened.

In the enlightenment model as in the generative, it is Jesus's life that saves, not his death. His role as social prophet alone killed him, with his scattering of the moneychangers the likely trigger. By revealing God's nearness and immediacy of access, he broke the Jerusalem temple's hold on access to God, and his social vision challenged native and Roman dominations systems. So the rulers of the domination systems killed him.[47]

Nevertheless, the cross has saving power through its symbolism. It symbolizes the death of the old basis of life in possessions, achievements, and dominative power, an internal "dying of self" necessary if one is to be born into a new way of life without delusions, rooted in reality. The way home is the way of dying and rising.[48] (Only with this schema do the enlightenment and generative models part ways, for advocates of the generative model would see the twofold dangers—the sacrificial

46. In each of his books, Borg describes this five-point portrait of the historical Jesus, which he bases upon a religious personality type known in many religious traditions (see *God We Never Knew*, 89). His most extensive discussion is in *Meeting Jesus Again*, 29–111.

47. On the nonnecessity of his death, see Borg and Wright, *Meaning of Jesus*, chap. 5. Jesus was also not likely killed for blasphemy (91). On his death a consequence of his politics, see *Heart of Christianity*, 91–92, 138; Borg and Wright, *Meaning of Jesus*, 88–91; Borg, *God We Never Knew*, 142.

48. On the religious meaning of the cross and resurrection as pointing to the way of transformation, see Borg, *Heart of Christianity*, 93, 105–13; Borg and Wright, *Meaning of Jesus*, 139.

mentality and the myth of life flowing out of death—embodied in such a spiritualization of the cross.)

The resurrection symbolically allows Jesus to play his role as catalyst for new insight for those living today. While the empty tomb and resurrection appearances are not likely historical, people experienced Jesus as a living reality after his death, and have ever since. They experience him through apparitions, visions, or a spiritually-felt presence. Jesus, like God, is a spiritual reality able to be experienced anywhere. Further, the resurrection points to God's affirmation of Jesus's way of life, countering the cross's negation.[49]

Like Gautama Buddha and Lao Tzu, Jesus reveals a path—the way of dying to an old identity and rising up to a new identity—that is the truth seen in Jesus and in all world religions. He is the subjectively decisive disclosure of God and of this way of salvation for Christians, but he is not the only expression of this way. Jews find it in Moses and the Torah, Muslims in Mohammed and the Quran. And everything Jesus discloses of God and of the way is found in the Israelite tradition before him. All major religions know the sacred. Though Jesus is a light and guide, he is not the only one.[50] This is why he is not necessary for salvation.

THE HOLY SPIRIT'S ROLE IN SALVATION

Since the enlightenment model, like the generative, imagines God's relation to the world using a unitarian rather than Trinitarian model of panentheism, it is no surprise that the enlightenment model has no more of a unique saving role for the Holy Spirit than did the generative model. Neither Borg nor Soelle mentions the Holy Spirit, save on one page where Borg explains that his term "Spirit" for God is not the Holy Spirit. While the Holy Spirit is seen "as one aspect of God" and as

49. On Borg's rejection of the historicity of the empty tomb and resurrection appearances, and on resurrection's symbolizing experiences of Jesus as living spiritually after his death, see Borg and Wright, *Meaning of Jesus*, 129–39, 148; Borg, *God We Never Knew*, 92–4; Borg, *Heart of Christianity*, 138; Borg, *Meeting Jesus Again*, 16. In a recent book, Borg admits in relation to the afterlife, "I don't have a clue about what happens after death." But he thinks the evidence from those who have had near-death experiences points to continued spiritual existence beyond the grave (Borg, *Heart of Christianity*, 181).

50. On Jesus's saving role within religious pluralism, see Borg, *Heart of Christianity*, 118–19, and chap. 11; Borg and Wright, *Meaning of Jesus*, 54, 156, 241, 256 n. 2; Borg, *God We Never Knew*, 25–26, 84–85.

a specifically Christian doctrine, Spirit "evokes a universal perspective and signifies divine activity in its widest reaches," describing God's broad transcendent engagement with the world.[51]

OUR ROLE IN SALVATION

Jesus reminds us of the home we knew long ago as children, but have forgotten. He opens our eyes to the God who loves us, has always accepted us, and is present with us, and to the deepest form of union brought about by compassion and generosity rather than domination. When we encounter Jesus, we perceive these truths which make our lives lucid and our selves whole again. We find ourselves home.

Yet it is not that simple, just as it was not that simple for John Smith after his mystical experiences with the Algonquian. Since it entails our own and the world's transformation, salvation demands our own effort, risk, and a journey undertaken toward the home we have already experienced as present and real. We must act according to the enlightened knowledge our experience of the sacred has given us.

Soelle and Borg find that Christian orthodoxy leaves little room for this role for human wise action. It focuses upon a negative anthropology: the "I am earth and ashes" and its attendant weakness, misery, and dependence upon God. In contrast, mysticism focuses on the companion truth: "For my sake was the world created" and the greatness of the human soul in its capacity for love. The illuminating experience of oneness substantiates the dignity and beauty of being human. "I am loved by the One who is not of this world; and thus, I love." The enlightenment model affirms that all humans have this capacity to respond to and love God, even if it lies dormant. It simply needs to be awakened by the profound intimacy of love.[52]

Protestant theology in particular focuses upon salvation by God alone. God loves, protects, and renews us. Yet Soelle argues that the only love that exists is mutual love. And so it is also our love *for* God that saves. We love God personally in our longing for God. Or, in a Buddhist framework, we love all things when we attend to them, when we live with mindfulness. So we also love, protect, renew, and save God through our longing and attentiveness. We love God socially in our political and

51. Borg, *God We Never Knew*, 72. Borg is quoting from Johnson, *She Who Is*, 83.
52. See Soelle, *Silent Cry*, 42–44.

praxis-oriented actualization of God's dream of a domination-free order within the world. Love for God involves a "No!" to the world as it exists now, ruled by forces of kyriarchy.[53]

To love is to do all things without calculation of *quid pro quo*, without the ego being held by craving dominance. Such love, or pure attending, brings about a form of unity with the "other" that is not based upon dominance. It brings the end of kyriarchy.[54]

Though the mystical experiences which re-awaken such human capacities for love cannot be learned or taught, we can prepare ourselves so that we are ready when such experiences occur. Intention, awareness, and practice all play a role. Our longing for transformation spurs us toward becoming attentive and toward practice. Christian practices, both individual and corporate, can reveal "thin places" and train our eyesight for the presence of God. Individual practices may include prayer, meditation, contemplation, journaling, dream work or spiritual direction. They also include daily things in life: honoring the body; learning how to say no; practicing hospitality; singing; keeping the Sabbath; performing acts of compassion; joining a church community. Corporate practices may include sacred worship, silence, music, story, rituals, and honoring the seasons.[55]

These practices may themselves become windows to the divine. They also gradually soften hard hearts. At a deeper level, these practices lead us along the one path to salvation known by all religions, and toward which Jesus guides us: the path of dying to the false basis for the self in delusions, and rising to a new basis of identity in God. The path brings us through four experiences necessary for salvation.

Through what Soelle terms the *via positiva*, we experience wonderment, the oneness and beauty which lead us to rise up in self-forgetfulness and joy.

Such joy leads simultaneously to the *via negativa*, a call to let go of our delusions about self and world and God. Such dying of the old self means ultimately letting go of our submission to the three powers

---

53. On our love for God as saving God—the opposite of the Protestant salvation motto!—see ibid., 1–4.

54. See ibid., 60–63.

55. On individual practices, see Borg, *Heart of Christianity*, 119–21, 157–63, and chap. 10; Borg, *God We Never Knew*, 122–28. On corporate practices, see Borg, *God We Never Knew*, 116–22.

which rule this deluded world: ego, possessions, and violence. While there needs to be an ego first, preparing for God involves detaching the self from its ego and the bondage it wields. Avarice and the mentality of the possessors must also be put aside, for possessions involve the use of domination to protect them, and domination destroys relations with neighbor, nature, and the self. The possessor sees all in terms of use-value, and worries about social status differentiations based upon property. And as Gandhi and King realized, the desire to kill must be given up.

The third experience is resistance, the *via unitiva* or *via transformativa*. The healing of the self is reflected in a move outward in desire to heal others in acts of compassion and justice. Love of God makes one resist becoming habituated to the forces of death rooted in corporate avarice, hierarchies of dominance and submission, and violence. Because one knows that life-giving forces are ultimate, the penultimate forces of death are resisted. One demands communities of just relations.[56]

The final experience is that of *increasing sensitivity*. One becomes aware of God in ever deeper ways. That includes joy in the beauty of experiencing God's love, presence, and the oneness of all things. It also includes grief. One suffers more for the neighbor, feeling anguish at unliberated life. Jesus the light and guide leads us into darker places of the world, and opens our eyes to the presence of God in the suffering of the innocent and the losers of history. Our re-awakened capacities for love make the darkness deeper and more unbearable.[57]

On our journey home, love for God and inconsolability move together, hand in hand, for God's silent cry from the midst of the creatures can now be heard. Nevertheless, though trembling at times, we walk forward with confidence and hope, because we have tasted great joy, and know that such joy cannot be overcome. "The light shines in the darkness, and the darkness did not overcome it" (John 1:5).

Yet the road is precarious, and our choices matter. The mystical encounter must lead to wise action based upon the ultimate reality one now sees clearly. It must lead to personal transformation and resistance to the social forces of death rooted in delusions. When Powhatan asks John to return to Jamestown, he finds there the colonists' mistrust of the Alqonguians, their "rancor, thievery, jealousy, envy, lying, violence, pride."

---

56. On these first three experiences, see Soelle, *Silent Cry*, 84–93, and part 3.

57. On the journey to new life entailing an increase in capacity to suffer and an engagement with dark forces in the world, see Soelle, *Silent Cry*, chap. 8.

Here is his fork in the road: Will he believe that his experiences with the Alqonguian community are more real than life within Jamestown? While deliberating, Pocahontas visits him. "There's something I know when I'm with you that I forget when I'm away," he tells her—his own experience of freedom, of true light, of love which cannot lie. "That fort is not the world," he says to himself. "The river leads back there [to the fort]. It leads onward, too. Deeper. Into the wild. Start over. Exchange this false life for a true one. Give up the name of Smith."

But back at the fort, he is told the king of England wants him to search for the Northwest Passage to the Indies. "Shall you be a discoverer of passages?" the commander of Jamestown asks, appealing to his ambition. His mind jumps to her, running ahead through the grass, turning back toward him, beckoning. "The king has great hopes for you. Plans." Thoughts invade:

> Tell her.
> Tell her what?
> It was a dream.
> Now I am awake.
> Damnation is like this.

Smith abandons her without that truthful reckoning, returns to England, and commences his search for the Northwest Passage.[58]

---

58. He is lost, but perhaps not eternally. Years later, Smith sees Pocahontas again in England. He had been unable to take the risk needed to continue his relationship with her, or his new identity within an alternate, life-giving form of community. Upon seeing her, he reconsiders his earlier choice: "I thought it was a dream, what we knew in the forest," he tells her. "It's the only truth. It seems as if I were speaking to you for the first time," and they look directly in each other's eyes.

PART THREE

Traditions and Alternatives

A Salvific Death Effected by a Nonviolent God

6

Jesus the Savior

THE REJECTION OF THE AMBIVALENT, VIOLENT GOD

The sharp critics are correct in their assessment of lethal weaknesses of the penal substitutionary theory of atonement. Chapter 2 above explained those deadly problems—basically that it leaves its hearers with an ambivalent, violent God-image and a distorted gospel that is no longer unambiguously "good news." By portraying God as using violence to save, it supports violence in personal and social life. For those whose dominant problem is shame rather than guilt, it often deepens their shame and increases self-shaming, making them complicit in their own destruction.

By promulgating the myth of redemptive violence, the theory reinforces the violence of perpetrators while blocking attempts by victims to get out of abusive relationships, for it portrays in words and graphic icons the twin falsehoods that the suffering of the innocent is redemptive and that God supports the sacrifice of the innocent.

Penal substitutionary theory undergirds the ambivalent picture of God's character and intent toward humankind by presenting a form of religion rooted in fear and self-abasement; employing the logic of mimetic exchange, in which violence is responded to with equal violence; deleting the role of 'the Devil' from atonement models, making God the one who desires the death of Jesus; and conceiving an ahistorical account of atonement which strips the event of its sociopolitical contexts, both past and present. When combined with the myth of redemptive violence and the iconic role of the innocent substitute, that ambivalent, violent God-image functions to sanctify human violence against others on the national and international levels, for it provides a metaphysical framework that sanctions violence. It says that good comes out of violence against the innocent.

Alongside these devastating problems, the penal substitutionary theory of atonement also fails methodologically, ethically, and evangelistically.

The heart of the solution lies in a shift from an ambivalent, violent God-image to a nonambivalent, nonviolent image of God. Religion must no longer be founded in fear and its attendant sacrificial mentality. All other changes in soteriology come in relation to this fundamental shift.

For this shift to occur, the ground must first be cleared. Like its sharp critics, I counter the premises of penal substitutionary theory which lead to a violent God-image with the following claims:

- Guilt is one, but not the only, problem of the human condition from which we need saving. The others include suffering and tragedy, shame and meaninglessness.

- God is just, but divine justice is not to be equated with retributive justice and its logic of mimetic exchange.

- The notion that an innocent substitute may justly pay the price of punishment for someone else's guilt is rejected as nonsensical and unjust.

- God is holy, but God's holiness does not mean God cannot abide sin or have fellowship with the unholy. God's history with Israel and Jesus's table fellowship with "publicans and sinners" bears this out.

- Forgiveness, by its nature, is a gift. God does not need a guilty party's punishment "paid in full" before God forgives. Among other things, such a view would go against the doctrine of divine sovereignty and freedom.

Further, I counter the qualifications of the divine love which lead to the portrayal of God's character and intent toward us as ambivalent:

- God loves us as the very people we are, not in spite of who we are.

- God cares for particular individuals, and does not have greater concern for abstract principle over such individuals.

- The divine love is not surrounded by the divine "father's" rage and his threat of condemnation, violence, and death. God does not want to kill humans for their sinful disobedience, an urge which leads him to kill Jesus, or leads Jesus to offer his life in our stead and for our protection.

GOD MAKES ALL THINGS NEW

Many of the theological moves common to the generative and enlightenment models of salvation are strong and can guide us toward a soteriology based upon a nonambivalent, nonviolent God-image.

- *Theological Method.* The context in which the theological meaning of the cross is discussed matters. When the context is one of militarism, colonialism, or environmental abuse, the cross may act to counter human pride and arrogance. To Jews and Muslims throughout Western history, the cross may terrify, reminding them viscerally of Christian pogroms and crusades under its sign. For a child abused by her or his parent, the cross's punitive image may block the road to healing by suggesting they should suffer to redeem either the perpetrator or themselves. For oppressed groups, such as Christians before they were dragged into the Roman Coliseum, African Americans under slavery and Jim Crow ordinances, peasant groups during the Latin American wars of the 1970s and '80s, jailed Christians during the student movements for democracy in South Korea, or Palestinians being walled off in their land, the cross conveys that Jesus is on the side of the oppressed in their struggles against kyriarchal forces.

- *The Problem within the Human Condition.* The generative and enlightenment models rightly lift up the suffering caused by kyriarchal forces as a central problem that the redeeming God is determined to overcome. People are dying, their capacities for life are dissipating, and much of this is caused by violence. Further, in our attachments to ego, possessions and violence, we act with complicity as benefactors of kyriarchy.

- *The Meaning of Salvation.* God saves by countering the forces of death with God's own superior forces of life. On the individual level, divine salvation is the salve that heals broken bodies, psyches, and hearts. On the communal level, God "makes all things new" by introducing forms of communal unity not based upon domination and submission. Kyriarchy ends.

- *God's Role in Salvation.* The central move for soteriology is the shift from an ambivalent, violent God-image to a nonambivalent, nonviolent image of God. Countering the serpent's questions which made Eve wonder if God were trustworthy, we assert that God gives us unconditional acknowledgment, acceptance, and love. Our life is precious to God. The gift of relationship is offered freely, and without regard for the moral or spiritual nature of the recipient.

- *Jesus's Role in Salvation.* Jesus does not play the role of innocent substitute who "pays the price" of punishment and death for our sins. Rather, he acts as our representative, going before us toward new life and the new community.

SAVED BY ONE OUTSIDE OURSELVES:
THE HUMAN NEED FOR A SAVIOR

In the generative and enlightenment models, Jesus acts as a strong mother, friend, and physician, connecting us to God's powers of life. Jesus illuminates our minds and transforms us at the very seat of agency; he thus is our light and guide toward the new creation that is breaking into our midst in him. These portrayals of Jesus are true and need to be affirmed. But they are also insufficient and therefore devastatingly inaccurate. In the alternative soteriologies of the sharp critics, Jesus ceases to be who he is in the gospels and New Testament letters: the savior of the world.

With the alternative soteriologies' misportrayals of the person and work of Jesus come distortions of the God-image and of the gospel. God, like Jesus, becomes a helper and not a savior. God discloses possibilities for salvation but does not offer salvation itself. The good news of God's saving act in Christ—the realization of salvation in him—disappears.

The criticisms of penal substitution are compelling and powerful. But with the loss of accurate portrayals of Jesus, of God, and of the gospel, their alternative soteriologies are as fatally flawed as penal substitution. While the penal substitutionary theory of atonement contributes to violence, the sharp critics' soteriologies likewise cease to be Christian, for they lose the good news about Jesus's saving act.

The critics' alternative soteriologies are not viable because their central premise concerning the human condition—that we have innate capacities through which we can return to God and the good—is not true. Such an optimistic portrayal does not fit the final assessments of the Old Testament and the New Testament, the dominant thread of the Christian theological tradition, or our own experience. We are not sleeping; we are dead in our sins, our sufferings, and our tragic patterns of existence. We have capacities; yet all are distorted, such that not one of them can enable us to rise up and to see the truth around us.

Because the sharp critics' central premise concerning the human condition is not true, their central argument concerning the process and means of salvation cannot be viable. As we have seen, in the alternative soteriologies, the prime source of agency for salvation shifts from Jesus to a combination of God and the believer. The salvation process is *synergistic*, a model which imagines a reciprocal relation of being and power between God and the world, and which heightens the role of the believer in her or his salvation and that of the world. For example, in the generative model, Jesus provides us with an example through his own uprising and openness to the flow of divine erotic power, demonstrating possibilities for uprising inherent in ourselves. But without our willingness to rise up and act, none of God's efforts to save us can become effective.

In the enlightenment model, though a mystical experience of unity may clear our eyes, such a catalyst is not essential; saving insight may also come through studying the wise teachings of the world's religious traditions. Further, though a moment of insight is essential it is insufficient to save, for it must be followed by a spiritual journey of wise actions which lead to the transformation of self and world. As Soelle says, since all love is mutual, it is not only God's love that saves, but also our love *for* God. We also love, protect, renew, and save God. Through our longing, attentiveness, and actions of resistance to kyriarchy, we actualize God's dream of a domination-free order within the world.

Such agency on our part is possible, according to the enlightenment model, since all humans have this capacity to respond to and love God, even if it lies dormant. In both the generative and enlightenment models, the road to the self's and the world's healing is precarious, and the fulfillment of God's *shalom* is not guaranteed, for its victorious realization is dependent upon that human response of uprising and wise action.

But if all of our capacities to respond to God—to open ourselves to the flow of divine erotic power, and to accept a mystical moment, shed our life of delusions and begin a life guided by our enlightened knowledge—are in fact dead, not merely diminished, then anyone's efforts to enhance them, God's or a religious guru's or one's own, are for naught. If all of our faculties by which we may return to God and the good are distorted, then the possibilities Jesus exhibits are not our possibilities.

We need not a helper, but a savior.

Despite its multiple and profound weaknesses and its lack of viability, penal substitutionary theory has one great strength: In its narrative, Jesus actualizes salvation. Saving healing and the new domination-free community then come from God to beleaguered creatures as gift, as grace, and as power for new life. On this one point, the penal substitutionary model understands the nature of the gospel, of God's will and intent toward us, and of Jesus's saving act.

"We are beggars," said Luther, while William Munny, grasping his friend Ned in the middle of the night, and Montgomery Brogan, staring out the window as his father drove him upstate to prison, knew this truth from their own experience.[1] Face to face with a deserved coming destruction, each longed for mercy with a hope they could imagine but could not believe was possible. If they were to rise up to newness of life within a new community not based upon domination, they knew that the actualization of such a hope would have to come from outside of themselves.

It comes from God the Mother/Father, through Jesus the Son, by the power of the Holy Spirit.

THE NONVIOLENT GOD WHO SAVES US THROUGH THE CROSS OF CHRIST

Both sets of theologians—those promoting the penal substitutionary theory of atonement, and the sharp critics who advance the generative and enlightenment models of salvation—develop unviable soteriologies and misunderstand the relation of divine love and violence to the saving significance of the cross of Christ. Both sets do so because they understand those relations using linear, univocal modes of reflection when the only way to understand it is through paradoxical forms of thought.

---

1. In the movies *Unforgiven* and *25th Hour*, respectively. See above.

Advocates of penal substitutionary theory understand divine love and violence conjoined mysteriously at the cross, and the cross as the apex of God's saving work. God brings about redemption through violent means, and the torture and death of Jesus is seen straightforwardly as the will of God. Advocates of the generative and enlightenment models take an opposing, but equally straightforward and linear stance. "There is nothing of God in the blood of the cross," as Delores Williams says.[2] God saves through the power of love, not through Jesus's torture. The locus of salvation is moved off the cross to what occurs before and after it.

In Part Three, I present a soteriology that represents a third way to answer the question of the relation of divine love, violence, and the cross: *God acts through Christ and the Spirit to save the world, and the cross is a constitutive moment in that salvific act. Yet the triune God saves us through nonviolent means.* This third view of the cross's saving significance retains the central strengths of the penal substitution and alternative soteriologies of its critics while avoiding their mortal weaknesses.

The success of such a jarring connection of statements—*God is nonviolent*; and *reconciliation occurs in the work of Christ, and the cross plays a role in that divine work*—depends upon the use of paradoxical forms of thought. For example, this third response moves from a simple to a complex view of the divine will in relation to Jesus's narrative. The cross both is, and is not, the will of God for salvation.

Instead of saying there is nothing of God in the blood of the cross, the gospel narratives of Jesus describe a saving act by the nonviolent God. This truth can be gained only through the narratives of the New Testament themselves. God's salvific acts as witnessed in the Old and New Testaments reveal the way that God saves.[3] Logical formulations based upon human forms of justice—such as retributive justice—cannot discover it, nor can the wisdom traditions rooted in the cumulative evidence of general religious experiences as collected by (mostly European and North American) scholars of comparative religions. Rather, the Hebrew and Christian scriptures, the Christian theological traditions, and our own experiences with sinfulness and grace are all sources for the third soteriological way, for in them we find divine mysteries. Such

2. Williams, "Black Women's Surrogacy," 32.

3. The three criteria for evaluating the strength of a theological model are these: (1) external coherence with Scripture and tradition; (2) internal coherence; (3) external coherence with lived experience (cf. 63 above).

mysteries can only be spoken of with paradoxical forms of expression, or the movement of art. Further, in a sinful world we do not see anything clearly, including ourselves. In our delusions, we swing from inordinate optimism to despair concerning our capacities to save ourselves and this world. Christians believe that we see ourselves truly only in the biblical narratives, as these find resonance in our own paradoxical lives.

While coherence with Scriptures, traditions, and lived experiences is crucial, internal coherence is also significant for the third soteriological way. When grace meets a fallen world, the effects are mysterious to the human eye. That does not mean the salvation described in the gospel narratives is a problem to be solved, or a puzzle to be figured out, for these would suggest that linear thought can grasp the event of salvation. Rather, the salvation brought by God in Jesus Christ through the Spirit's power is a mystery, and as such it often demands saying multiple things at once, things that are paradoxical, seemingly contradictory, or that at the very least retain a tension.

TENSIONS WITHIN THE CHRISTIAN NARRATIVE OF SALVATION

The penal substitution, generative, and enlightenment models seek to reduce the tensions found in the gospel narratives of salvation, creating a univocal understanding of the relation between the divine love, violence, and the saving significance of the cross. This third way does the opposite. It keeps the tensions intact, for this is the only way to speak accurately about a divine mystery. This third way is possible through the use of complex descriptions of human existence and of God's saving act not found in the first two responses elaborated in Parts I and II above. Some are paradoxical. All tensively hold together seemingly contradictory claims in order to describe the divine mystery of salvation.

A Complex View of the Human Condition
under Sin, Suffering, and Tragedy

The penal substitutionary, generative, and enlightenment portrayals of the human condition lack the required complexity to correspond with human experience and scriptural traditions. The biblical portrayal of the fallen human condition entails three problems: sin, suffering, and tragedy. While the penal substitutionary theory acknowledges only sin, the generative and enlightenment models underplay sin in favor of suffering and tragedy in human experience. For example, while Borg says we participate in clinging to our hard-heartedness, our hearts grow hard mainly from the sufferings we undergo, from socialization within sinful social contexts, and from natural psychological development. Human responsibility, however, is more deeply interrelated with suffering and tragedy than is acknowledged by the models of either Part I or II, creating a more complex and dire view of the human condition.

To speak of God redeeming us is to speak of God "buying us back" from the overwhelming, downward-spiral effects of all three of these powers—sin, suffering, and tragedy—so that God may bring us, as communities and individuals, toward our God-intended destiny as reflections of the trinitarian beauty. "See, I am making all things new." Redemption thus has three meanings that, while related, cannot be dissolved into one overarching signification.

Individuals and groups need to be redeemed from *the evil that they do*. Sin is active violation of relationship with God, one's neighbors, nature, and one's own self. The actions incur guilt in relation to God and concrete persons, and bring a resulting estrangement from these others and the self. Redemption is *atonement*, and involves divine judgment, forgiveness, and reconciliation with God despite the sin. God extricates and rescues individuals and communities from the dire consequences of sin, guilt, and estrangement.

Persons and communities also need to be redeemed from *the evil that befalls them*. Redemption is the destruction of the evil powers that break these lives. God recreates those lives within new communities whose unity is based upon equality, reciprocity, and mutuality, God's *shalom*. Redemption is *healing*, the making whole of broken bodies, psyches, social bonds and natural ecosystems. It is eschatological in form, the new creation in which God will dwell with the creatures, and evil forces are finally ended.

But neither sin nor suffering fully explains our human condition of brutal immorality and catastrophic woundedness. We also experience our brokenness in a third form, that of *tragedy*. In our sin and out of our suffering, we act in ways that unleash forces of evil that we can then no longer control, and that destroy ourselves, others, and our social and natural worlds far beyond whatever suffering might be deserved by the culpability of the original act.

Such tragedy is experienced in three ways. First, the human agent experiences it in the captivity of her or his freedom, what Luther and Calvin identified as "the bondage of the will" and Paul Ricoeur paradoxically called *the servile will*.[4] Seemingly incompatible ideas—those of the free will and of the unavailability of that freedom to itself—are brought together. We sin in responsibility, defiling ourselves; and we exist as slaves to our own sinning. The paradox of the bound-free will is cogent if several theological moves are followed. To begin with, it is possible if I am both the subject and the object of the enslavement: I use my freedom to enslave my freedom. "I do not understand my own actions. For I do not do what I want, but I do the very thing that I hate" (Rom 7:15). Next, the enslaving of the self involves a movement from act to state. As with addiction, it is difficult not to continue the actions. Further, the action that enslaves is an act of "yielding," an act in which I use my agency to make myself a slave to another power beyond my own agency. Finally, the element of time must be added. The concept of the bound-free will makes no sense in static "substance" language, but does when we see it telling a story, a narrative of a person's or group's fall over time from the heights to the depths, from glory to misery, from freedom to a prison's cell. Through these acts, humans take their desire and distort it; and once distorted, it can no longer bring us back to where we were.[5]

Ebenezer Scrooge exemplifies this state of lostness, including a lack of recognition that he is lost and of the steps that made him so. In Charles Dickens's *A Christmas Carol*, ghostly and enchained Jacob Marley visits his old business partner Ebenezer late one night and explains that Scrooge has forged an identical chain, with studied acts so gradual he does not see that it now secures him tightly:

> "You are fettered," said Scrooge, trembling. "Tell me why?"
>
> "I wear the chain I forged in life," replied the Ghost. "I made it link by link, and yard by yard; I girded it on of my own free will, and of my own free will I wore it. Is its pattern strange to *you*?"
>
> Scrooge trembled more and more.
>
> "Or would you know," pursued the Ghost, "the weight and length of the strong coil you bear yourself? It was full as heavy

---

4. For the following progression of theological moves explaining the coherence of the paradoxical concept of the servile will, see Ricoeur, *Symbolism of Evil*, 151–55.

5. On human acts leading to the distortion of desire and its self-captivity, see Farley, *Wounding and Healing of Desire*, esp. chaps. 3–5.

and as long as this, seven Christmas Eves ago. You have laboured on it, since. It is a ponderous chain!"

Scrooge glanced about him on the floor, in the expectation of finding himself surrounded by some fifty or sixty fathoms of iron cable: but he could see nothing.[6]

The Christian symbol of "original sin" points toward this first tragic experience of the self that binds itself and brings about its own condition of slavery. Like the hostile act of the prodigal son who demands his inheritance before his father's death, the act of violating others or oneself in the long run turns the sinner away from God, neighbor, nature, and self. This estrangement is a change each person causes in herself or himself.

Yet the symbol of "original sin" points as well to *corporate sin* as the second tragic dimension of life. Before we act sinfully, we are all born into distorted situations of violence that shape us. As communities, our joint actions unleash forces of destruction that break free of our grasp, turn, and threaten us. In their face, we find ourselves overwhelmed and paralyzed. Despite the threat of global warming, for example, communities find themselves impotent to change consumptive habits. Such communal sin is attributable to individuals' actions, yet also greater than their sum.

The third tragic dimension of human existence is that *the good and evil in us, while distinct, are conjoined in a way beyond our ability to separate.* The good traits are infused with elements of evil; our sin is often inspired by lofty intentions and carried out with glorious skills. We are not partly good and partly evil, each element separated and intact, with the good accessible to us in a pure form. Rather, as Bruce Cockburn sings, we are paradoxically two wholes, angel and beast.[7] Through our own capacities, we cannot pull the evil off of the good in us without also destroying the good.

These tragic experiences of self-captivity and of every moment, good or bad, being tainted by the distorted element of the self are portrayed in a scene in the movie *Before Sunrise*. A young American, Jesse, has met a young French woman in Paris, and they have decided to spend one day together. In the middle of the night, Jesse and Celine are lying on

6. Dickens, *Christmas Carol*, 11.
7. "Burden of the Angel/Beast," *Dart to the Heart* (Columbia Records, 1994).

the grass in a park. As they look up at the sky, Celine says: "So often in my life I've been with people and shared beautiful moments like traveling or staying up all night and watching the sunrise. And I knew those were special moments. But something was always wrong. I wished I'd been with someone else. I knew that what I was feeling, exactly what was so important to me, they didn't understand. But I'm happy to be with you . . ."

Jesse, quiet for a moment, eventually responds.

> I know what you mean about wishing that somebody wasn't there. It's just, usually, it's myself that I wish I could get away from. Seriously, think about this. I have never been anywhere that I haven't been. I've never had a kiss when I wasn't one of the kissers . . . I've never been out bowling if I wasn't there, making some stupid joke. I think that's why so many people hate themselves. Seriously, it's just, they are sick to death of being around themselves.
>
> Let's say that you and I were together all the time. You'd start to hate all of my mannerisms. The way every time that we would have people over, I'd be insecure, and I'd get a little too drunk. Or the way I tell the same stupid, pseudo-intellectual story again and again. You see, I've heard all those stories, so of course I'm sick of myself.
>
> But being with you, it's made me feel like I was somebody else.

Celine thinks that her happiness problems are peripheral to herself, in the people she chooses to be with. Jesse knows his problem is not peripheral to who he is: it is not in those he is with, or in particular daily circumstances, or even in his choice of actions. The problem is himself, the person who is the source of his own agency and freedom, charm and insecurity. Nothing he does can get him away from himself, who is the real source of his lostness.

In response to our violating acts of sin, God extricates us from the consequential guilt, estrangement, and self-isolation that would destroy us. In relation to our suffering, God heals us and renews the world. In response to this third dimension of a fallen world—the tragic intermixing of our sins and our sufferings, and our incapacity to separate the good in us from the tainting vines of evil—God the savior brings a third form of redemption, *disentanglement*. God separates the strands of evil from the good God created, both within the human heart and in our relational bonds and communal structures. This separation brings liberation, release, and empowerment.[8]

When we sin, we often cannot undo the damage we have done. We cannot control the forces of violence that wound us—forces individual and corporate. We cannot disentangle the "me" from which we want to be freed. The problems of sin, suffering, and tragedy run straight through human hearts and communities rather than between them, and humans are in a state of captivity rather than mere weakness. They need, not a guru, but a savior, one able to *constitute* a new divine-human relation and a new human condition, not merely entice humans toward an actuality for which they already have the potential.

Rethinking a Paradoxical View of Divine Justice and Mercy

The Christian story of salvation involves the divine traits of justice and mercy, and both penal substitutionary theory's advocates and its sharp critics misunderstand the relationship between these two traits. The strength of penal substitutionary theory is that it rightly acknowledges the differentiated presence of both traits in God. God is love, but God is not merely love, for God is also the Just One. God is loving justice, and just love. Penal substitutionary theory's fault lies in its failure to clearly explicate the unity of the divine mercy and justice, leaving the appearance that these are conflicted within God. As we saw in chapter 2, the result is the ambivalent, violent God-image portrayed in the theory and the sanctioning of human violence that attends it. Roberta Bondi's image of a patriarchal father with rage simmering just below the supposed love, ready to burst its dam when the child's insolence and misbehavior reaches a threshold, aptly applies.

In opposing this disastrous view of God, the sharp critics rightly lift up the divine simplicity. God is not divided or conflicted within Godself—one part wanting to save us, one part wanting to kill us. The generative and enlightenment models portray a God who embraces us without condition, wants us to flourish, and acts always toward that end. However, the critics create that unambivalent portrait of God by simply reacting to the dangerous portrait of God given by penal substitutionary theory. Like the Protestant liberals of the nineteenth and twentieth centuries, they drop the biblical concept of divine wrath in order to focus

8. David Kelsey presents this complex view of the human problem in *Imagining Redemption*, 11–15.

upon divine love. God is unconditionally gentle, merciful, forgiving. But without the notions of the divine holiness, righteousness, justice, and judgment, the God of the sharp critics ceases to be the Yahweh of the Hebrew Scriptures, or the God of Jesus Christ.

The solution is neither to pit divine justice against divine mercy, nor to drop the former in favor of the latter, but to see the relation rightly. God's holiness is inseparable from God's love, an inseparability perceived in two ways. First, the traits exist in an asymmetrical, differentiated unity: *the divine holiness is always in service to the divine love; yet the divine love is never without the divine holiness.* As we saw in chapters 1 and 2, this relation becomes difficult to perceive when the framework imagines individual sinners before a divine Judge within a legal context. But when we examine two other contexts, the relation becomes clear.

The first framework for reflection is Jesus. In his encounters with others, it becomes clear that grace comes free of charge, and that like the father of the prodigal son, God seeks us out for fellowship even after we have turned away. There is nothing we can do to make God love us more than God does; there is nothing we can do to make God love us less. Yet it is also clear in Jesus's encounter with others that God is opposed to the violence of the world, the suffering that it causes, and the escalating forces of death which human sin unleashes and abets. Like the conditional Mosaic covenant that is situated within the broader Adamic, Noahic, and Abrahamic unconditional covenants, God's opposition to human acts of violation—against others, nature, and oneself—is situated within God's unconditional choosing of the world for fellowship with God. Because God loves us, God is against our self-destructive and other-destructive ways of being.

The second place to envision the right relation of justice and mercy is within the critics' understanding of the human problem. Instead of focusing on the sins of individuals within a legal framework, they focus on kyriarchy. The elites who support kyriarchy understand power as invulnerability. The loving God who is just challenges such forces of invulnerable coercion, but not with an omnipotence of dominating force. God does not gain victory over the forces of nothingness by using a stronger hand of invulnerable force. Rather, God opposes such nihilistic force, but without using its form of power. God uses a form of power that exists outside the world of domination and submission. God's justice and judgment and opposition include God's love, and thus God leaves us our freedom and our humanity in God's engagement with us. The righteous God is not a God of sheer power. Nor is God's righteousness the awe-inspiring grandeur of a worldly ruler. God is holy because *God is different than we are*—One who, without having to do so, descends to dwell with the humble and meek. Through such means, God seeks a triumph over kyriarchal forces that incorporate the salvation of God's beloveds.

Though they reject the concept of divine wrath, the generative and enlightenment models do portray the interrelation of God's love and justice. For as Jesus rises up to nonviolently oppose the kyriarchal forces of death which seek to deny him and the weak their rightful claims to erotic power, so God opposes such forces. And while they declare clearly that God's forgiveness and embrace are unconditional, they also understand forgiveness within a covenantal framework in which reconciliation depends upon a perpetrator's truth-telling and acts of restitution toward the one he or she has violated.[9]

Upholding this differentiated and paradoxical unity of divine judgment and mercy is essential for conceiving the Christian story of salvation rightly.

A Multilayered Portrayal of the Divine Will in Relation to the Cross

The penal substitutionary, generative, and enlightenment models all give a simple portrayal of the divine will in relation to the cross. As we have seen, for penal substitution, Jesus's death on the cross is the very center of the divine will for salvation. For the sharp critics, his death is in no way the divine will, and is not salvific at all.

But the New Testament gives a complex portrayal. As S. Mark Heim points out, there is a tension to the New Testament's presentation of the theological meaning of the cross. The crucifixion of Jesus is God's plan—and an evil act; Jesus sets his face to Jerusalem—and his killing is the unjust murder of an innocent person by those who have no concern for truth or for God's ways; his death saves the world—and it ought not to have happened. Jesus himself reflects both views of the cross. In Gethsemane, he indicates that his journey to the cross is out of obedience to God (Mark 14:36; Luke 22:42). Yet at the Last Supper before they all head to the Garden of Gethsemane, Jesus asserts it is wrong for him to be betrayed and delivered up: "For the Son of Man goes as it is written of

9. See above, 37.

him, but woe to that one by whom the Son of Man is betrayed! It would have been better for that one not to have been born" (Mark 14:21).[10]

In light of this New Testament witness and against the theological tradition as seen in the penal substitutionary theory, I argue that God the Mother/Father does not will, intend, plan, send, or cause Jesus to be killed. The act of torture and murder is an outrage to the triune God.

However, to move to a position that states—as do the generative and enlightenment models—that the cross has no salvific role, and is thus completely outside the sovereign plan and will of God, is to reduce the tension found in the New Testament witness in a fashion similar to that done by penal substitutionary theory.

The way to respect the tension is to conceive God's will in a more complex fashion. God the Mother/Father sent the Son to act as the Messiah, inaugurating "the Day of the Lord," the day in which kyriarchy ends and communities form with a unity not based upon domination. The triune God's *intentional will* in sending the Second Person was to transform the world, breaking its bonds of sin through the actions and ministry of the Incarnate One and the Holy Spirit. This is why Jesus, the Jewish Messiah, offers divine judgment and mercy during his lifetime through his acts of healing and exorcism, table fellowship and teaching. He embodies the divine form of power not based upon domination and submission.

God did not send Jesus to die as a sacrifice. Far from it, God sent Jesus to re-create life. However, in sending the Son, the three divine persons knew his murder, while not necessary by some ontology of sin or of mimetic exchange, was likely, if not inevitable. Because of this knowledge, God was absolutely opposed to Jesus's murder, but also prepared to enact the salvation of creation through it. If the circumstances should dictate it—as seems inevitable—the triune God determined to save the world through Jesus's death rather than through God's intended route of the Messiah bringing in the reign of God through the power of his life and ministry. The journey to Golgotha reflects God's *circumstantial will* for Jesus in a world that resists God's saving presence, and not God's *intentional will* in the sending of the Son. Yet as the upcoming constructive models show, the divine judgment and mercy which Jesus enacts in

---

10. See Heim, "Saved by What Shouldn't Happen," 213–14, 221; and Heim, *Saved from Sacrifice*, chap. 4.

his life and ministry become heightened in power and effectiveness on Good Friday, Holy Saturday, and Easter Sunday.

While the triune God intended to re-create the world and bring life through the sending of the Son, each of the three persons was willing to re-create the world, if necessary, through a confrontation with the forces of sin, kyriarchy, and death that would bring mortal violence upon the Son, and each took up that task with resolute agency. This complex view of the divine will explains the tension found in the New Testament: The cross both is, and is not, the will of God.

Salvation as a Finished Act that Engages Human Responsibility

One of the criticisms of the penal substitutionary model of atonement is that salvation seems to involve an intra-trinitarian drama that happens "over our heads." Its narrative never situates itself within socio-political contexts, and the Son's death effects a salvation that can be gained without any personal or social transformation.

The critics counter with a synergistic model of salvation. Salvation means transformation, and this transformation is brought about by the combined efforts of God and human beings. Such a view prioritizes potentiality over actuality. Humans already have the capacity to open themselves up to the flow of erotic power, to follow practices that increase the likelihood of encountering God in "thin places," and to respond to God's love with their own love. But these capacities are weakened and inactive. Jesus acts as catalyst to awaken us to our powers. Through their wise actions, the new domination-free communities and awakened individuals realize the reconciliation only begun in Jesus. Through their love, they also save God and God's dream for creation.

But when the human problem is seen as more dire, when humans are perceived to be in bondage to sin and forces of death, the models that prioritize potentiality over actuality become both nonsensical and hopeless. If Jesus acts only as an instantiation or cipher or incitement for a new creation we are to fulfill, we are without hope.

I reject such a moralization of the gospel.[11] I argue that in Jesus's ministry, death, and resurrection, the reconciliation of God and humanity is *a finished act*. Jesus does not merely envision a new creation and point the way for us to fulfill it. He actualizes the new creation and gives

---

11. The phrase is Webster's in "Ethics of Reconciliation," 116, 123.

it to us as gift. This asymmetrical relation of divine and human agency contrasts sharply with the synergistic model of salvation, for salvation comes from God alone, from the future, and as grace. As Paul writes, the church looks retrospectively at a new creation already accomplished in Christ: "So if anyone is in Christ, there is a new creation: everything old has passed away; see, everything has become new! All this is from God, who reconciled us to himself through Christ, and has given us the ministry of reconciliation; that is, in Christ God was reconciling the world to himself, not counting their trespasses against them, and entrusting the message of reconciliation to us" (2 Cor 5:17–19; see also Col 1:20–22 and Eph 2:14ff.).

The power of the new life "belongs to God and does not come from us" (2 Cor 4:7), a view expressed not only by Paul but also by the saints throughout the ages, who consistently point to God's work in them rather than their own contributions. This priority of actuality over potentiality is present throughout the New Testament witness and Christian traditions, a prioritizing of Jesus's actions over ecclesiology.[12] In chapters 7 through 11 we shall investigate the various dimensions of Jesus's saving accomplishment, but *that* salvation is accomplished is a premise of my third way of seeing the cross.

God in Christ through the Spirit has already accomplished a saving alteration of the human situation. A definitive and objective change has occurred irrespective of any subsequent actions by humans. Yet the effecting of salvation in Christ does not happen "over our heads," without our participation in it, for the risen Christ and the Holy Spirit also continue to act graciously, inspiring a human response to and incorporation into the new life made real in Jesus. And Christ and the Spirit always engage us in a way that leaves our freedom intact. Nevertheless, our human actions in relation to salvation are consequential, not constitutive (or even co-constitutive). Through faith and obedience, we acknowledge and participate in a new reality that already exists. Such actions matter, for they expand the portions of earthly life that conform to God's reign, bringing healing to the world and resistance to kyriarchal forces. We do indeed rise up. But our actions do not create the divine reign itself.

12. For this argument I am indebted to Webster's essay "The Ethics of Reconciliation."

Jesus as Savior, the Necessity of Incarnation, and the Scandal of Particularity

In Christ through the power of the Spirit, the triune God constitutes a new divine-human relation and new creaturely reality. This saving change accomplished in Jesus is both unique and decisive.

There is a scandalous particularity in this view of how salvation comes about. Salvation is wrought for all through the representative action of one. Salvation is not predicated upon some universal human capacity or some truth discoverable from human reason or observation, spiritual openness or moral conscience, as was true in the generative and enlightenment models. The events that happened need not have happened. That God came among us in Jesus to fulfill God's purposes and reconcile the world to Godself is a contingent truth, not a universal one. The route of reconciliation is through a person—through the singular and vicarious faithfulness of Jesus Christ—and not through learning a teaching or assimilating a philosophy funded by universally available knowledge.[13]

While in the generative and enlightenment models, the divine redemptive power is separate from Jesus's identity (he is a medium, but not a "savior"), in this third way, that power is inseparable from his identity. Jesus is the savior. Similarly, Jesus is the gospel. Christians have faith in what he accomplishes, not only in teachings or a social vision he proclaims.[14]

As we shall see in the following models of salvation, external consistency with Christian Scriptures, traditions, and experiences of redemption as well as the internal coherence of each model move soteriology toward an embrace of divine incarnation. If only God can save, yet Jesus saves the world from its sin, suffering, and tragedy in a comprehensive way, then Jesus must be both God and human, paradoxically present in one center of personal identity and agency.

Expanding the Locus of Salvation beyond the Cross

The advocates of the penal substitutionary theory place the entire weight of the Trinity's saving work upon Jesus's last six hours of life. This approach entails all the problems described in chapter 2.

13. See Rae, "Remnant People"; and White, *Atonement and Incarnation*.
14. See Reno, *Redemptive Change*, 213–16.

The advocates of the generative and enlightenment models respond to the problems of penal substitutionary theory by shifting the locus of salvation away from the cross entirely. Salvation occurs before the cross in Jesus's ministry, and after the cross in the church's formation of domination-free communities in response to Jesus's ministry. Such a view eclipses the full reality of Jesus as savior and salvation as a finished act.

The appropriate counter to penal substitution's failures, however, is to expand the locus of the triune God's saving activity to include the full narrative of Jesus's work: the incarnation; Jesus's ministry of healing and proclamation; his death; his being raised from the dead by God; his ascension; and Pentecost, which signifies the continuing activities of the risen Jesus and the Holy Spirit. It is Jesus's life that saves us, not merely his death. But the new way that he lives as a human being involves the full progression of his story.

The Two Hands of God: A Trinitarian View of God's Saving Work within a Religiously Pluralistic World

The portrayal of Jesus as savior, and his accomplishments for salvation as unique and decisive, run smack into the sharp critics' presuppositional insistence that Jesus cannot be the unique savior because this would undermine their claims that knowledge of the sacred and routes to salvation are present in all the major religions.

My third way refuses to shift saving agency off Jesus and onto a combination of God and the believer. It does, however, affirm that the God known in Jesus Christ is at work in other religions and cultures outside of Christianity, moving persons within those spheres toward salvation. Christ and the Holy Spirit as known in the gospel stories are also cosmic, at work broadly, revealing the way of grace in a world lacking grace. The living, risen Christ attempts to reveal himself in other cultures, and the Spirit is at work broadly, pointing to Christ's presence, vivifying all things, and enabling experiences of grace and responses of gratitude. Evangelists and missionaries thus should approach those of other religions and cultures with a combination of boldness and humility, ready to witness to the good news of the gospel of Jesus Christ, but also ready to listen for Christ's voice and the Spirit's vivifying movements present in these other arenas before the missionaries ever arrived. Furthermore, other religions have insights of God and of grace we do not have, but need. For example, Buddhists may teach Christians about non-attachment to ego, possessions, and violence, and developing attentiveness, in ways beyond what churches in the ego- and possession-fixated Western cultures may do. Other religions may also offer penultimate paths to the salvation accomplished in Christ: the dwelling of the triune God with all creatures in a healed universe.

Such an openness to the triune God's presence in other religions still includes the scandal of particularity. Christ saves, and we participate in that salvation through union with Christ in faith. It is conceivable, however, that some persons embracing other religions will, after death, recognize the cosmic Christ and embrace him as the One who has accomplished salvation in Judea for the entire world, the risen, living One working in their midst *incognito*, and the embodiment of the way of grace they have already experienced.

Such a Trinitarian approach to the relation of Christ's saving work and the world's religions will not satisfy the exclusivists of Part I, nor the relativizing pluralists of Part II. But it offers an approach beyond the narrowing of the triune God's saving work to six hours of Jesus's tortured death, and beyond the vague view of salvation through an erotic power or mystical encounter that has shed any necessary connection to the concrete particularities of the saving work of God the Mother/Father, Jesus, and the Holy Spirit in the biblical witness and Christian traditions.[15]

THE NECESSITY OF FIVE MODELS OF SALVATION

Saving faith requires a Christian to believe *the fact of salvation* in and through Jesus's work. Those who were far off have been brought close. Those who were in bondage, have been set free. Those who were broken have been healed. Those who were dirty have been cleansed. The demonic forces of evil have been definitively defeated. *The means by which*

15. For this Trinitarian approach to a theology of religions, see especially Migliore, *Faith Seeking Understanding*, 316–23; Dupuis, *Toward a Christian Theology of Religious Pluralism*; Heim, *Depth of the Riches*, and (though less directly helpful) *Salvations*, part 2. See also Moltmann, *Way of Jesus Christ*, and *Spirit of Life*; and Welker, *God the Spirit*. On the presence of the living, risen Christ and the Spirit in other religious and cultural movements, see Migliore, *Faith Seeking Understanding*, 312–13, 326–29; and Barth, *Church Dogmatics*, IV/3.1:114–35. On Christians allowing truths from other religions to challenge their own understandings and praxis, see Migliore, *Faith Seeking Understanding*, 313–14; and Lindbeck, *Nature of Doctrine*, chap. 3.

this comes about in the events surrounding Jesus and the Holy Spirit involves the mysterious coming together of sovereign divine and free human agencies in such a way that all human models, including the five coming immediately, point the way toward explication while failing to capture the rich event in its entirety.

Thus five models together are more capable of capturing the diversity and plenitude of grace in the event of salvation than is one model alone or some "grand theory." They are also more able to speak to readers' differing autobiographical and social contexts.

Five models are helpful for the same reason those who put together the New Testament canon included four gospel stories instead of just one, or an amalgamation of the multiple stories. Each gospel telling picks up different elements of the one manifold story of salvation. It sees it from a different angle. Together, the five models display the breadth and depth of the ways in which the nonviolent God saves us through the cross of Christ, making all things new.

7

Jesus, the Power of Life over Death

Emancipation

*Much of Atlantic civilization in the nineteenth century
was built on the back of the enslaved field hand.*[1]

THE RISE OF "THE COTTON KINGDOM"
AND THE "SECOND MIDDLE PASSAGE"

A NDREW JACKSON'S VICTORY IN New Orleans over the British at
the end of the War of 1812 and his subsequent invasion of Florida
sealed American control of the Old Southwest, encouraging one of the
most rapid migrations in human history. Land-hungry thousands rushed
into Louisiana, Mississippi, and Alabama. Land was $2 an acre, but the
choicest property near water transport could command $50 an acre.
These territories were violent, even by American standards, as whites
were determined to maintain racial supremacy over Native Americans
and free Negroes through lynchings.

What made migration into dangerous territory attractive was the
high price of cotton. The "saw" cotton engine solved processing difficul-
ties, and with the end of the Napoleonic and 1812 wars, the price of cotton doubled on the New Orleans market. The "virgin" earth (gained by
forcing the Creek, Cherokee, and Chickasaw to cede it) of the Alabama
black belt could yield three times the yield of South Carolina's soil. The
Old Southwest became the most favored location for the production of
a raw material of global demand, as did the Caribbean sugar islands and
the oil-rich Middle East in their own day. The settlers came with short-

---

1. Howe, *What Hath God Wrought*, 132. On the importance of cotton to the American
economy, see North, *Economic Growth of the United States, 1790–1860.*

term advantage in mind, as their environmentally-destructive practices revealed. They wanted quick profits.

Thousands of former semi-subsistence farmers became cotton producers. But the rapid rise of "the Cotton Kingdom" also transformed the economies of the world, for the manufacture of cotton textiles in New England and Great Britain fueled the industrial revolution on both sides of the Atlantic. By 1840, cotton comprised 59 percent of American exports, exports that enabled the country to buy manufactured goods, pay interest on its foreign debt, and import further capital.[2]

But cotton cultivation required use of intensive labor. While slavery was being phased out in many Northern states and Southern leaders prior to this period had expressed a desire for its eventual end, the spread of cotton cultivation changed the minds of all Southern politicians, including Thomas Jefferson. Because of cotton's demand, slave-plantation agriculture spread far beyond the areas that would have sustained it with traditional export crops: tobacco, rice, and indigo. Slaves from the Southeast coast were forcibly marched into the newly acquired lands in a way that shamed and disgusted even contemporary observers. One farmer wrote of a slave coffle in 1815: "A wretched cavalcade . . . marching half naked women, and men loaded with chains, without being charged with any crime but that of being black, from one section of the United States to another, hundreds of miles."[3]

Migrating slaves would likely never communicate again with spouses and children left behind. This second giant disruption in the generation following the end of the trans-Atlantic slave trade constituted a "Second Middle Passage."[4]

The rise of the Cotton Kingdom meant that money was to be made not only in cotton, but also in slaves. The vast new demand for slave labor doubled the price of a prime fieldhand between 1814 and 1819. As tobacco became less profitable, Chesapeake planters were determined

---

2. "'Whoever says the industrial revolution says cotton,' observed the great economic historian Eric Hobsbawm. The same short-staple cotton that spread plantation agriculture all over the South gave rise to textile mills" (Howe, *What Hath God Wrought*, 132.) As in Europe, so in America the textile industry proved central to industrialization. "In 1832, textile companies comprised 88 of the 106 largest corporations in America" (ibid., 136).

3. James K. Paulding, quoted in Forbes, "Slavery and the Meaning of America," 23; see Howe, *What Hath God Wrought*, 129.

4. The term is historian Ira Berlin's (Howe, *What Hath God Wrought*, 130).

to make up that loss with the sale of humans. Slave children were capital gains. So Thomas Jefferson advised his son-in-law: "A woman who brings a child every two years [is] more valuable than the best man on the farm."[5] When Representative James Tallmadge Jr., of New York proposed in 1819 the prohibition of the further introduction of slaves into Missouri as a condition of its admission to the Union, plus the emancipation of all twenty-five-year-olds born to slaves after such admission, the Southern Senators acted as one to block the proposal. For restricting the expansion of slavery into the West threatened to permanently end this lucrative market.

And so the raising of capital and the industrialization of Europe and America was built on the backs of an enslaved population.[6]

CINQUE AND THE AMISTAD REVOLT

As Joseph Cinque sat with the thirty-seven other defendants before their second trial for piracy and murder in Hartford, Connecticut, January 1840, he told what had happened to him and the others to U.S. District Judge Andrew Judson. Through an interpreter, he explained that he had been born around 1813 as Sengbe Pieh in Upper Mende, ten days' march from the coast. He was married with a son and two daughters. Going to his fields in January 1839, he was captured by four men who took him to Mayagilalo, their boss. Mayagilalo, indebted to the son of Vai king Manna Siaka, gave Sengbe over as settlement. He was marched to Lomboko Slave Fortress on the coast and sold to the Spaniard Pedro Blanco, whose activities had made King Siaka wealthy.

In March, the Portuguese slave ship *Tecora* illegally departed for Cuba with five to six hundred purchased slaves. On board, they were whipped. The slavers, having underestimated the amount of provisions, threw fifty overboard. They attached the slaves to a long line of chains weighted by rocks. When they reached Havana in June, two plantation owners, Jose Ruiz and Pedro Montez, purchased Sengbe and fifty-two others for $450 each to work on their sugar planation further down in Cuba. Ruiz changed Sengbe's name to Joseph Cinque in order to pretend he had been born in Cuba as a slave, and thus could be legally purchased

5. Jefferson to John W. Eppes, June 30, 1820, quoted in Deyle, "Origins of the Domestic Slave Trade," 51; see Howe, *What Hath God Wrought*, 148.

6. For this section, see Howe, *What Hath God Wrought*, chapter 4, "The World that Cotton Made," esp. 125–36, 148–50.

and enslaved. They created similar false records for the other fifty-two as well, and put them on the chartered Spanish schooner *La Amistad* for the journey.

Three days out at sea, Cinque freed a loosened nail and unshackled himself and his fellow captives. Armed with cane knives, they rose up against their captors. They killed the captain and cook, but spared Ruiz and Montez, insisting the men take them back to Africa. Ruiz and Montez, deceptively sailing east by day but west by night, brought the ship eventually to Long Island where it, and the Mendians, were captured.

After Cinque's tale, District Attorney William Holabird asked Cinque if the Mende owned slaves, and for what purposes they were obtained. Cinque hesitated, then said slaves were gained through wars or debt payment. Turning toward the audience with a cynical but satisfied look, Holabird said, "It's all about money."

As he sat with his fellow captives, the words of the judge and Holabird and his own defense attorneys began to blur, and the memories of his home, of his wife and children, of the sufferings he'd endured, flooded his thoughts. Then he rose, held out his shackled wrist to the judge, and shouted in English, over and over again, "Give us ... free! Give us ... free! Give us, us free!" Everyone in the courtroom, black and white, became silent.[7]

WILLIAM WILBERFORCE AND THE STRUGGLE TO ABOLISH THE SLAVE TRADE

He tossed in bed, delirious from dreams of slaves in shackles, then woke. His cousin, Henry Thornton, came in, poured a dose of opium. At Thornton's encouragement of sleep, the man demurred. "It shows me things I should have done, but didn't. I accomplished nothing ... And the worst thing—I can't sing anymore."[8]

William Wilberforce had come to his cousin's house to recoup from ill health and exhaustion. He had once gloried in God's presence, but now felt left in the lurch.[9] A committed abolitionist, he had put bills before the House of Commons almost yearly since 1789; all had failed.

---

7. The scene is depicted in the movie *Amistad*. The events, including the courtroom scene above, are historically corroborated in Arthur Abraham's *Amistad Revolt*. Arthur Abraham is one of Sierra Leone's foremost historians.

8. From the movie *Amazing Grace*.

9. In 1786, Wilberforce had undergone a spiritual rebirth.

When he met Barbara Spooner that early spring in 1797, he told her brusquely that he came to Bath to be cured of politics. But whenever he looked in a mirror, he saw ghostly slaves in chains.

During an all-night conversation a few weeks later, Barbara asked to hear his activist story. He told of the day Olaudah Equiano—a freed slave and abolitionist—visited him in the early 1780s and described the Middle Passage: "They lie in a space 4 feet by 18 inches. They have no sanitation. Very little food. Stagnant water. Their waste and blood fills the holds within three days, and is never emptied. These irons and chains are to keep them from throwing themselves overboard. Half die. When you reach the plantation, they put the iron to the fire and do this [he opens his shirt to show the branding scar], to let you know that you no longer belong to God, but to a man."

William told Barbara of Lord Tarleton's reaction the first time he put his bill to the House of Commons in 1789: "I can hardly believe my ears. It seems my young friend opposite has a long-term strategy to destroy the very nation that spawned him ... Now he would hand over the riches of the Indies to the bloody French. If we didn't have slaves, there would be no plantations. And with no plantations, how would we fill the coffers of the king? And does my honorable friend really believe that if we left off the trade, the French wouldn't immediately step into our place and reap the rewards?"

The vote lost, only sixteen Ministers of Parliament joining Wilberforce. When France went to war against Britain in 1792, he was mocked as traitorous by almost everyone. He collected three million signatures to abolish the slave trade. Nearly every autumn, he had presented his bill. "And still, after all the petitions, all the speeches and the bills," he yelled at Barbara, "ships full of human souls in chains sail around the world as cargo!"

"Is that the end of your story?" she finally said in response.[10]

---

10. Abolitionists like Equiano, Granville Sharp, and Thomas Clarkson probably did more to effect the abolition of the slave trade and, eventually, slavery in the British Empire, though Wilberforce played a key role as well. For an excellent history of resistance to slavery by both blacks and whites during this period, see Schama, *Rough Crossings*.

BRINGING LIFE TO THE DEAD

For those like the Chesapeake slaves marched hundreds of miles to create cotton fecundity in Alabama, Mississippi, and Louisiana; or like Cinque, shackled arms outstretched; or like those who endured the 4 feet by 18 inch space of the Middle Passage—those who are enslaved by powers and pushed to death's edge—Jesus redeems or "buys them back" into freedom. Cinque rises up, claims his own right to life and resists in every way possible those forces arrayed to keep him chained or send him to the gallows.

This saving image shows that this theory, which I call *the emancipation model*, shares much with the generative model described in chapter 4, but holds differences that, finally, make it vastly different. It is more pessimistic concerning the depth of the human problem, believing suffering to be so intertwined with sin and self-captivity that all three reach to the very core of our identities. There is thus no resource without or within we can access by which to rise up to claim life.

The emancipation model is also more optimistic than the generative model, for Jesus does not merely resist the forces of death as a martyred hero, and show us we can do the same. Rather, Jesus defeats the powers of death and constitutes a new form of life.

Finally, compared to the linear, logical—indeed, "common sense"— view of the relation of divine to human agency in the generative model, the relation in the emancipation model is paradoxical. Given the incapacity of human beings to access resources by which to free themselves from their captors, and yet the optimism concerning the extent of new human capacities for free action accomplished by Jesus, a paradoxical description of the relation of divine and human freedom is necessary. Rather than a *synergistic* model by which humans and God each partially and jointly bring about the interior power by which we arise, the emancipation model upholds a *double agency* model, a model which smacks of "bad math." God does the act of rising up wholly, and we do the act wholly, yet it is one act. The power to rise is not possessed by us at all, but solely by God. We arise like those brought to life from the dead, like Lazarus from his tomb; we do not merely rouse ourselves and our innate capacities, even if spurred by an outside catalyst. And yet, like Joseph Cinque, we do rise, by powers constantly given to us by God the Mother/Father, through the Word by the power of the Holy Spirit.

Despite the stark similarities with the generative model, in light of these three features in the emancipation model, everyone's role in salvation looks different—God the Mother/Father's, Jesus's, the Holy Spirit's, and our own.

THE PROBLEM WITHIN THE HUMAN CONDITION

The way the penal substitutionary theory of atonement is told, there are only two players in the narrative. Humans have sinned, bringing guilt upon themselves and alienation in all their relationships, most especially the one with God. God acts with an atonement on the cross that removes the guilt and bridges the relational gulf, allowing divine forgiveness and reconciliation to sinners.

The emancipation model does not deny the problematic realities of sin, guilt and alienation, or the importance of God's act to bring forgiveness and reconciliation. But it tells a different story, for alongside God and human beings, it perceives something beyond these two players, a "third factor," which complicates the entire narrative. This "third factor" is malevolent. It seeks to destroy all life, and threatens God's beleaguered creatures. This destructive force is found outside the individual, suffused within social structures, communal ethics, and even nature. But it is also present deep within the human being, a corruption of the human springs of action in a person's mind, will, and volition. As with the generative model, the problem is the suffering of creatures, but the experience is deepened to include the experience of possession, of captivity under this "third factor" to such an extent that individuals and whole communities experience themselves as beyond hope of release.[11]

In the New Testament, the third factor in the narrative engaging God and human beings is "the demonic." The early Church Fathers had an increasing tendency to personify the Devil as an individual, imagining a battle fought between God and the Devil outside the concrete relations humans experience on earth. Modern theologians reinterpreted the demonic as merely psychological or social forces lacking any objective reality beyond mere human motives.

---

11. While divine solidarity resolves a story with one element, human suffering, and reconciliation involves two characters, humans and God, redemption has three characters in the narrative: "ourselves, our redeemer, and the master or jailer in whose grip we live" (Placher, "Cross of Jesus Christ," 156).

This modernist interpretation underplays the objective force of evil. While the emancipation model can function with personified understandings of evil—a personal Devil, and spiritual demons at work in the world—it does not need such personification. "The demonic" points to the human experience of helplessness and possession before powers that hold an individual or a society in bondage. Such forces are earthly, yet go beyond mere human motive and agency, being present in psychological, social, and cosmic forces. For example, not only did the Southern Senators who blocked James Tallmadge's attempt to prevent the spread of slavery to Missouri; or the Tecora's commander, who chained fifty slaves to rock weights and threw them overboard; or Lord Tarleton, who argued vociferously against Wilberforce's bill to end the slave trade, have demonic characters. So did corporate structures beyond mere individual motives and actions: the British Parliament; the U.S. Congress; the slavery-protecting laws on the books; the textile manufacturers, all dependent upon slave labor for their exploding profits. There is rationality to evil, but also irrationality. Like the gang violence of the *Tecora's* crew who dispatched slaves overboard with an energy of personal hatred while pretending the objects were simply excess cargo, evil generates a momentum that sweeps up humans in its power. As social historian Hannah Arendt eventually concluded from her study of acts of genocide, evil is both very real and banal. Its occurrence in hundreds of daily acts by thousands of persons working within social structures hides its malevolence. Once the evil and erroneous premises that fund the social systems are accepted, its commonness makes it seem "normal," even "reasonable."[12]

The origin of the demonic is a mystery; even the Bible states only the fact of its existence, and not its origin.[13] Yet it is possible to explain how it appears in human existence. It appears when humans worship an element of creation rather than God, and as both testaments and human experiences such as those displayed in the previous paragraph make clear, such worship occurs at both the individual and societal levels. God created humans to experience not only joy, but also certain

---

12. See, for example, her classic study, *Eichmann in Jerusalem*. Not only did Hitler have a demonic character; but so did his regime, and it swept up people like Adolf Eichmann.

13. Partly because its existence is irrational. It erupts in a good world sustained and loved by a good God, a world in which there is no reason for it to erupt.

forms of suffering that enhance life, forms which even Adam and Eve in Paradise and Jesus in Galilee and Judea experienced.[14] The experience of loneliness and of otherness clarifies that love given by another is gracious. Limits to our capacities—our knowledge or strength or relational abilities—make possible a contingency of experience that brings us moments of surprise, novelty, and grace. We do not control everything. Temptations toward evil make acts of truth-telling, love, and goodness possible. Even death can serve life by providing a gracious boundary to our existence, so that our choices within our limited span of time matter. We cannot redo everything.

But this openness of our future, when combined with our limits and possible failure, brings an anxiety that, while not evil, opens the door to it. With our anxiety, individuals and societies face a choice: They can either trust in God and in their neighbors to secure their existence, or they trust in something other than God, some creaturely element which they believe more capable of securing their existence. Nothing is innately demonic, but any part of the good creation can be distorted into the demonic. When we treat any part of the good creation as if it were a god—the center of our existence and power and meaning—we corrupt it, and it begins to behave toward us like a god, but for destructive rather than creative ends.

As Paul Ricoeur explained, idolatry tells the story of free human agents handing over their freedom to an idol, one whose forces they eventually will be unable to control. Anything can become the object of worship and addiction and the enslaving idol of a community or individual: from the most base, such as substance addictions and sex, to the sublime, such as beauty or justice. A common one, however, is coercive power, an idol whose use brings an ironic downfall eventually. For to use power in dominating ways is to become possessed by it, as happened to Sauron and Smeagol, and very nearly to Faramir, in Tolkien's *Lord of the*

14. I interpret Genesis 1–11, including the Garden of Eden and fall stories, existentially rather than historically. We all follow the same pattern of behavior and tragic loss as Adam and Eve, falling from the heights to the depths during our life journey. For a related approach, see Brueggemann's analysis comparing the characters and conflicts in Genesis 1–11 to the David stories in "David and His Theologian."

Rings.[15] Whole societies can be possessed by dominating power, as by a demon.[16]

Further, idols gain demonic power over us because such worship demands our submission to a lie. The finite object, of course, is not God, no matter how lofty, and it does not have the power we think it has. It will fail us in the end. Tragically, our submission to the falsehood that it can secure our existence soon brings with it the inability to tell truth from falsehood, good from evil, a capacity essential as guide to our moral agency and freedom. Such delusions are seen, for example, in Cambodian dictator Pol Pot, architect of "the killing fields" genocide who, when finally captured and imprisoned for trial, told a reporter, "I am the victim. I have suffered." Pol Pot's inability to tell truth from falsehood disables his moral guidance, a capacity necessary for the freedom to choose between good and evil. Without such freedom of volition, our faculties of body, mind, and will are in the grip of something finite turned demonic, the little god we worship. But as all such descents into captivity show, our 'enemies' are self-inflicted.[17]

Sin—the worship of a created good as if it were a god—opens the door for the demonic in an all-good world. But the demonic is found not only within our hearts, but above and all around us as forces of death which hound us, like Chesapeake traders whipping slaves in the coffle. As Soelle points out, the demonic resides in social structures and attitudes based upon ego, possessions, and violence. Violence is harm or damage done to another. This can include killing (in murder, war, or capital punishment); physical injury to bodily integrity; or damage to a person's dignity and self-esteem, such as occurs in the belittling of a spouse or child, or the dehumanizing practices found in the systemic violence of kyriarchal structures (patriarchy, racism, systemic poverty).[18] The examples of demonic societal attachments to ego, possessions and violence tumble over themselves. Communal violence is present in societies that uphold the principle of mimetic exchange, or insist upon honor killings,

15. Faramir's near fall occurs only in the movie version. In the book, he remains free of such temptation.

16. On the worship of the finite corrupting good elements of creaturely life into the demonic, see especially Gunton, *Actuality of Atonement*, 62–74.

17. Paul links idolatry with submission to the lie and resulting captivity to sin; see Rom 1:18–32.

18. For this definition of *violence*, see Weaver, *Nonviolent Atonement*, 8.

or defend millennia-old caste systems—as when John Calhoun defends slavery, gender oppression, war, and violence as "natural," "inevitable," and "not sinful." Demonic attachments to possessions and violence are seen in societies in which economic growth is dependent upon slave labor, and the perpetrators and beneficiaries are unwilling to give up the profits required to end the immoral practice. Societal demons rear their heads whenever a unity is sought that solidifies relations of domination and subjugation, as when Southern senators only agree to support Northerners' bills if slavery is allowed to expand into the West below the 36-30N latitude. The worship of ego, wealth, and the controlling effects of coercive power occurs whenever a person or group uses power demonically—that is, when they objectify fellow subjects and creatures, turning them into means for their own purposes, as when once-free Africans are transformed into property through branding on the other side of the hellacious transport called the Middle Passage.

Paul identifies these demonic tyrants that crush us as existing on the individual, corporate, and cosmic levels: sin, the Law, the principalities and powers, distorted regularities in the natural world, and death itself. Though the Bible mostly speaks of *sin* in connection with human freedom as the willful turning away from God and refusal of grace, Paul also describes it as having a type of objective existence, "reigning" in our bodies, making us slaves, dissipating our energies for living.[19]

Beyond sin as a power, structures created for social good by God, when worshipped as divine, begin to exercise power demonically. For example, *the Law* was given by God for ethical guidance. However, the Law only points provisionally to the spirit of God's character and intentions; only a human life, such as Jesus's life, can reveal it fully. But when its provisional character is lost, and the letter of the Law is upheld as absolute, it exercises demonic power. For it is used by certain groups or persons to ease insecurities; as with the purity system in Jesus's day, humans use the law to judge others as less worthy of divine regard, and themselves as more worthy. Legalism kills, because it aids the human act of objectifying subjects—either the "other," or the self.[20]

---

19. For sin's acting as a slaveholder, imprisoning us, see Rom 6:6–7, 16–18, 20; 7:11, 14; and Gal 3:22.

20. On the law as provisional, as "promise" looking toward fulfillment, see Rom 4:1–17; 10:4; Gal 3:15–29. On the superiority of the law's spirit over its letter, see Rom 2:14–15.

Similarly, the *principalities and powers*, when worshipped, become demonic. In the Jewish worldview, God gave the angelic 'powers' that lie behind the visible fabric of the world the role of administering the nations.[21] But while still partially performing this function, they also are in rebellion against God. For example, the organized state of the Roman Empire—which is the visible face of an angelic power—legitimately keeps the peace in society. But when it shifts to regard itself and its survival as ultimate, it becomes demonic and a force for lawless terror and violent oppression.[22]

The sinful turning to created goods to secure existence has also distorted *regularities in nature*. Similar to the state, the New Testament describes the angels behind the fabric of nature as rebelling against God, creating "wildernesses" outside God's dominion. We may understand it today as natural forces out-of-kilter. Evolutionary processes driving biology forward are violent, indifferent to the fate of countless 'losers' of evolutionary history. Creation groans.

Even *death*, created by God as a gracious boundary for the living of our lives in a narrative form, has become an enemy of humankind due to the worship of the finite. It destroys achievements and spoils life. Death seals in the alienation of oneself from God, others and oneself; time runs out before reconciliation is possible. Lurking on the horizon, our approaching end increases the anxiety that throws us into the arms of our little gods who already enslave us. Death is "the last enemy" (1 Cor 15:26).[23]

Thus the problem within the human condition is suffering. We suffer under the violent domination of these tyrants: sin within our bodies, minds, and wills; legalisms enforced by those who benefit from them; kyriarchal forces bent upon maintaining the privileges of an elite; chaotic forces in nature; and beyond them all, death.

Beyond the problems of human sin and human suffering, however, we also groan under the tragic weight of our own lives. Like addicts, the sin, the painful wounds, and the self-destructive behaviors reach all the way down to our identity's root. And while Jesse lying next to Celine in *Before Sunrise* could perceive the intermixing, most cannot.

21. In contrast, Yahweh ruled over Israel directly; see Deut 32:8–9.

22. Rome's legitimate authority (Rom 13:1–2) becomes a "mystery of lawlessness" through demonic worship (2 Thess 2:6–7).

23. The fear of death holds us in slavery to the demonic (Heb 2:14–15).

We suffer under violent, kyriarchal, enslaving forces that seek to reduce us to objects for their own ends. Yet like Ebeneezer Scrooge, or the
Chesapeake planters and subsistence farmers swarming into Alabama's
best land, or any addict, we are also collaborators in the making of our
own chains. Further, like Jose Ruiz and Pedro Montez buying slaves in
Havana, we are blind to the tragic twining of good and evil, truth and
falsehood within us. We cannot escape the tyrants' grasp, for we have no
untainted resources by which to release the clasp.

Like the creation itself, like Israel when threatened with annihilation, like Paul, we cry out for one who can redeem: "Wretched man that
I am! Who will rescue me . . . ?"[24]

THE MEANING OF SALVATION

Despite the unlikelihood of winning re-election, President Martin Van
Buren appealed Judge Judson's decision to the Supreme Court to shore-
up his Southern base. Seven of nine justices were Southern slave owners.
The defense attorneys got death threats. Joseph Cinque questioned his
attorneys in an attempt to bolster his case.

On March 9, 1841, the Supreme Court delivered its verdict. Cinque
and the other Africans on the *Amistad* were "not slaves, and therefore
cannot be considered merchandise. But are, rather, free individuals, with
certain moral and legal rights, including the right to engage in insur-
rection against those who would deny them their rights. And therefore,
over one dissent, it is the Court's judgment that the defendants are to be
released from custody at once, and if they so choose, to be returned to
their homes in Africa."[25]

Immediately, guards took the shackles off the hands of Cinque and
the rest.

Salvation is emancipation. The God who sees our sufferings has
compassion upon us, and acts with loving determination to free us from
captivity to the kyriarchal forces that cause our sufferings. In arguably
the paradigmatic text of the Hebrew Bible, God hears the cries of the oppressed Israelites. "Then the Lord said [to Moses, from out of the burning
bush], 'I have observed the misery of my people who are in Egypt; I have
heard their cry on account of their taskmasters. Indeed, I know their

---

24. Rom 7:24. The verse finishes, ". . . from this body of death?"
25. From the movie *Amistad*.

sufferings, and I have come down to deliver them from the Egyptians'"
(Exod 3:7–8a; see also 2:23–25).

In a New Testament text outlining Jesus's ministry, he quotes from
Isaiah to proclaim the same divine intention and determined action:

> The Spirit of the Lord is upon me,
>   because he has anointed me
>   to bring good news to the poor.
> He has sent me to proclaim release to the captives
>   and recovery of sight to the blind,
>   to let the oppressed go free,
>   to proclaim the year of the Lord's favor."
>   (Luke 4:18–19, quoting from Isa 61:1–2; 58:6)

Salvation is release from the captivity under the demonic tyrants:
sin reigning within us; the societal use of the law to bind; the principalities and powers which enforce oppressions; the distorted forces of
nature; the death which steals even the life of the living.

Salvation also means freedom from the demons within. When we
cry out with Paul, "Wretched man that I am! Who will rescue me?" Jesus
responds, "Come to me, all you that are weary and are carrying heavy
burdens, and I will give you rest" (Matt 11:28).

In releasing humans from bondage to enemies without and enemies
within, God's act of salvation brings the restoration of capacities for a
truly human life. Like Jesus healing those out of whom he casts demons,
the God who saves heals broken bodies and spirits. God restores new
energies by which we rise up to grasp our claims to life, and resist forces
of death which seek to block that uprising. God restores our capacity for
moral agency by returning our ability to discern truth from falsehood,
good from evil.

As the exodus story reveals, God restores to humans the ability to
live in a humane way by bringing them into a "land," one "flowing with
milk and honey" (Exod 3:8b). In other words, God creates an alternative
form of community based on forms of unity rooted in equality, mutuality, and reciprocity rather than domination.

THE COMING OF SALVATION

In the penal substitutionary theory, a sacrificial death brings life. In the
generative model, new life is generated not from death, but from the life
of nurturing others, such as a mother giving birth, or a gardener nurtur-

ing a plant. In the enlightenment model, salvation comes with a moment of insight into the true nature of reality, particularly its power structures, and from the wise actions which follow.

In the emancipation model, salvation comes with a victory over the demonic tyrants who hold human beings and other creatures under their sway, and the opening up of a new community of freedom in which the humane life which God intended may grow.

In perhaps the earliest Christian theory of salvation called "Christ the Victor," Christ is the victor over these demonic forces. He defeats the demons and the Devil. He also defeats death and the Law with its death-dealing guilt. The emancipation model continues this classic picture of salvation through battle, but with counter-intuitive changes. The victory Christ achieves is gained through nonviolent means. Despite appearances, the victory is definitive. Instead of defeating the forces of evil by using overwhelming force from outside the creaturely sphere of time, space and matter, of physicality, joys and temptations, God defeats evil from within the creaturely sphere (a bit like Frodo and Sam in Tolkien's *Lord of the Rings* defeating Sauron from inside the gates of Mordor). Most surprising of all, God's definitive victory in Christ from within the creaturely sphere involves the seemingly utter defeat of the forces of good at Golgotha. "We proclaim Christ crucified," Paul writes to the Corinthian Christians, "a stumbling block to Jews and foolishness to Gentiles." But despite appearances, "God's foolishness is wiser than human wisdom, and God's weakness is stronger than human strength" (1 Cor 1:23, 25).

GOD'S ROLE IN SALVATION

In the penal substitutionary theory, the holy God approaches guilty sinners with righteous anger. God also has righteous anger in the emancipation model. But the real object of God's wrath is not the human being, but rather the demonic forces which hold human life captive.

In ancient Israel, when a person falls into slavery under foreigners, the closest relative—the *go'el*—is obligated to buy back the person's liberty so they may rejoin the clan in freedom. In the Hebrew Bible, Yahweh comes to be called Israel's *go'el*. When Israel is threatened, Yahweh comes to her defense, as Yahweh did in liberating the Hebrew slaves from Egypt.[26]

---

26. *Ga'al* means "to liberate," and a *go'el* is "one who liberates or ransoms"; a "redeemer" and "protector"; see Lev 25:47–49, and Num 35:18–19. On Yahweh as Israel's *go'el*, see Isa 44:6, 24; and on the poor being brought into God's own clan, see Ps 68:6–7.

Now, in the person of Christ, Yahweh again sets God's face against the forces of death which threaten God's beloved creatures. What is new is that God's opposing actions in Jesus involve increasing levels of divine risk and vulnerability. While previously God sent the prophets, now God sends God's own beloved One, the Son, like the vineyard owner who began by sending his slaves but eventually sent his own son to confront malevolent usurpers of his property (Matt 21:33–46).

We know that God acts as redeemer of the enslaved because this is how Yahweh acts in relation to the enslaved Hebrews in Egypt, and this is how Jesus acts when he performs saving miracles. In each account of healing, Jesus takes the side of the suffering person, and places himself against the destructive forces arrayed against her or him. It becomes clear that God does not will the suffering; rather, God negates its source, and reveals a sorrow which suggests that God's own self is being violated in the attack against God's beloved creature. As Karl Barth points out, in the accounts, Jesus never asks a question about the sufferer's sin. Jesus goes right past the person's sins and tragic entanglements, straight toward the demonic forces causing her or him to suffer: "speaking and acting in His [sic] own cause, [God] takes the side of man [sic] and enters the field against this power of destruction in all its forms. That is why the activity of the Son of Man, as an actualisation of His Word and commentary on it, necessarily has the crucial and decisive form of liberation, redemption, restoration, normalization . . ."[27]

Jesus cares about their sin, and he will deal with that with judgment and forgiveness; but more fundamentally, he cares about the human being who is God's creature. God's wrath is against "the enemy who does not let man breathe and live."[28] In Jesus, God acts to create for the weary, imprisoned, beleaguered humans a new future.

The battle is difficult, even for God, not only because the enemy is strong, but also because human beings are implicated in its presence on earth. The situation is tragic, since the sufferer has evil intertwined with good all the way to her or his core. Coercive power used directly against the evil might destroy it, but will kill the person in the process.

In *Aikido*, a Japanese form of martial arts, the practitioner attempts to disarm rather than destroy evil, thereby protecting all life—both hers, and that of her attacker. Instead of meeting sheer force with opposing

27. Barth, *Church Dogmatics* IV/2, 225.
28. Ibid.

counterforce, the practitioner moves with the flow of the attacking energy and uses its own momentum to disarm the violent thrust. Similarly, God definitively defeats evil in a nonviolent fashion, without using dominating force, ending the destructive force and leaving life intact.

The way that God accomplishes this "conquest from within" is through incarnation and indwelling. Instead of sending the heavenly hosts, God the Mother/Father sends the Son to oppose and disarm the principalities and powers, and sends the Holy Spirit as his companion and co-agent.

JESUS'S ROLE IN SALVATION

Adolf Eichmann organized the mass extermination of the Jews throughout Germany and Poland. In an act of passive resistance, Eichmann initially disobeyed orders and sent his Jewish captives to labor rather than death camps. Only after he was hauled in and reprimanded by a superior SS officer did he do as he was told, and with efficiency.

Evil wins if it either gets you to join its ways, or it kills you. As Eichmann's superiors accomplished with Eichmann, it seeks to make you complicit in the killing of others, thus supporting the ethics of kyriarchy. Or, as we saw with the tactics of torture in chapter 2, it seeks to get you complicit in your own self-destruction. If neither works, it kills you outright. You become an accomplice in the destruction of the good order of creation and the solidification of the oppressive rule of certain creatures over all others, or you cease to exist at all.[29]

In relation to Jesus, evil accomplishes neither, and so its power is broken. Evil does not get Jesus to join in its ways, either as violent protagonist or a person of self-destructive despair. And despite its best efforts at Golgotha, it also does not get rid of him.

As the One sent by God the Mother/Father to act as the *go'el* for God's beloved but imprisoned creatures, like Moses before Pharoah, Jesus opposes the demonic forces. He counteracts and heals all the relations that idolatry distorts: social bonds, spiritual relations with God, psychological relations with the self, interdependent relations with nature. For healing to be effective, he acts to counter all of these compromised relations at once; if he simply worked upon one relation, the demonic

---

29. These two tactics were employed by the Joker in the movie *Dark Knight*. He successfully employed the first strategy against district attorney Harvey Dent, but both failed with Batman.

elements within the others would counterattack and overwhelm his efforts. The disease of sin, being systemic (indeed, multisystemic), must be addressed holistically.

His powerful actions include, yet go beyond, the kinds of liberators with which we are familiar: psychologists, exorcists, physicians, political activists, and warriors. His liberating acts go beyond those of all of the above, because he alone has the power of life over death. Jesus is the Jewish Messiah, bringing the expected "Day of the Lord," the day Yahweh would come directly to judge evil, ending its reign and establishing God's direct rule and its attendant justice and peace.

As the Jewish Messiah, Jesus acts in three ways to defeat evil. First, *Jesus pushes evil back through nonviolent resistance.* Jesus enacts grace as a power in the form of "reconciliatory emancipation," defending the poor and suffering the consequences with the goal of revealing a deeper, unifying grace which allows all creatures to flourish.[30] His nonviolent adversarial politics counter the forces of death in the multiple systems in which they reside. To heal bodies and psyches, he heals physical impairments and diseases which harm the body, sap the spirit, and can lead to social ostracism. To heal broken hearts alienated from God, he proclaims over and over again the everlasting mercy of God. To counter kyriarchal social relations, Jesus establishes a table fellowship based upon equality, reciprocity and mutuality. He breaks the Jewish purity system by which certain groups were deemed impure or outcast. He denounces spiritual and economic exploitation, such as in his act of cleansing the Jerusalem temple.

This portrayal of Jesus as performing acts of reconciliatory emancipation coheres with Jesus's liberative actions in the generative and enlightenment models. As in the generative model, his uprising to claim his and the poor's right to life entails resistance to those kyriarchal forces which repress such uprising. As in the enlightenment model, Jesus perceives the true nature of power, and acts as a teacher of alternative wisdom and a social prophet who challenges the purity and domination systems of his day.

What differentiates Jesus in the emancipation model is that Jesus not only resists like you or I or Martin Luther King Jr. might resist kyri-

---

30. On this unity-making liberation, see Taylor, "Christ of Reconciliatory Emancipation," in *Remembering Esperanza*, 175–89; and Taylor, "American Torture," 272–76. On "adversarial politics," see Taylor, *Executed God*.

archal forces. He does so with powers and authority only the triune God holds: The power of life over death, authority over chaotic forces in nature, and the authority to forgive sins. In the emancipation model, Jesus raises the dead back to life, as he did with the widow's son at Nain (Luke 7:11–17), with Jairus's daughter (Mark 5:21–24, 35–43), and with Lazarus (John 11:1–44). He not only casts out demons, as he did with the Gerasene demoniac (Luke 8:26–39), but he displays his further authority over chaos by calming the wind and sea (Luke 8:22–25; Mark 4:35–41; Matt 8:18, 23–27; cf. especially the last verses of each pericope). And Jesus does what no Jewish prophet or rabbi dared to do: he forgives sins, releasing people from the consequences and power of sin and guilt.[31] In each of these cases, Jesus acts to counter the "evolutionary progress" which is rooted in violence and is always willing to sacrifice the weak for the advance of group goals—whether such violent behavior and a callous ethic are active in nature, in social systems, or in a human heart. He seeks a different order, a nonviolent one in which the "losers" are not degraded, sacrificed, and forgotten.[32] While on earth, the Son of God counters demonic forces definitively.

Jesus not only counters the demonic present in the kyriarchal systems and human hearts. He also defeats evil nonviolently by refusing to allow it into his person and relations. *He resists temptation.* In this act, the Jesus of the emancipation model differs a second way from the figure in the generative and enlightenment models. In the latter, Jesus's resistance to evil is partial and episodic. In the emancipation model, Jesus's resistance to the demonic is total and continuous. This marks off Jesus as a human being unique in history, with a capacity to resist evil which no other human possesses. He alone is sinless (Heb 4:15). His sinlessness is essential to his liberating capacity to disentangle the demonic from the good creation.

While many in the gospels see Jesus as a madman, including his family (see Mark 3:20–35; John 7:1–5), in fact Jesus sees things as they are, and he is able to discern truth from falsehood and good from evil. He lives out of a community with God the Mother/Father and with the

31. For example, see the healing and forgiveness of the paralytic in Luke 5:17–26; Mark 2:1–12; Matt 9:1–8.

32. On this creative—and, frankly, surprising—idea of Jesus's acting against evolutionary forces of "progress," see Moltmann, *Way of Jesus Christ*, chap. 6: "The Cosmic Christ," esp. 287–305.

Holy Spirit, as well as one with his disciples, in which power is shared. In those communities, a "free space" exists between each person, allowing each to live from and toward one another in spontaneity, mutual responsibility, and delight.

From this free space, Jesus resists the move that leads all other human beings into idolatry, the unleashing of the demonic, and captivity. Instead of mistrusting God when he is anxious, he trusts God absolutely, and his creaturely neighbors and his own integrity relatively but surely. He refuses to submit to the lie that something other than God can secure his existence. He has faith, and in it, he prevents the idolatry that brings the demonic.

He also has love. He knows that the only eternal reality is found in communities of free and mutual subjects. Thus, Jesus refuses to objectify anyone—God, his neighbors, or himself. He continuously treats everyone he encounters as a fellow subject, as a mystery to be respected. As some in the gospels notice with contempt, not the least "the devil," Jesus refuses to use power demonically in order to gain mastery over others' freedom, even for good ends like their own happiness. He approaches all beings as the novelist Dostoyevsky did when released from ten years in prison:

> Love every leaf, every ray of light.
> Love the animals, love the plants, love each separate thing.
> Loving all, you will perceive the mystery of God in all.[33]

Jesus's resistance to evil is seen in his wilderness engagement with the Devil. In each case, the Devil tempts Jesus to use coercive power to gain his objectives, objectives which in themselves are not evil. When the Devil suggests that Jesus command stones to become loaves of bread, he is suggesting that Jesus use his unique relationship with God the Mother/Father to overcome the limitations of a finite, physical existence. Jesus refuses to renounce his trust of God by grasping for a power not given to human beings.

When the Devil suggests that Jesus throw himself from the pinnacle of the Jerusalem temple so that crowds below may see the hosts of angels save him, he resists both a guarantee of his own protection against suffering, and the use of a divine "sign" so obvious, all observers would

---

33. Quoted in Yancey, *Soul Survivor*, 137.

bow down to his status as Messiah. He did not want to compel belief nor turn them to God for ulterior motives—their own security.

When the Devil shows Jesus all the splendor of all the kingdoms of the world, and offers them to him if only Jesus will fall down and worship him, Satan is tempting Jesus to reach his rightful goal and status through the use of coercive force. Jesus, however, wanted truth and love to elicit a willing obedience.

Jesus must have faced such temptations all along the way, but there are two more key moments: in the garden of Gethsemane, and the period from his garden arrest to his last breath at Golgotha. In the garden, he forbids the use of coercive force to protect himself, and repairs the severed ear of one of the soldiers. Further, during his tortured prayer, when he perceives the horror approaching him, and on the cross, Jesus refuses to let go of the God whom he has known and always proclaimed as nonambivalent and nonviolent. God is for him, and Jesus refuses to deny the fact.

There is a third way Jesus acts to defeat evil. Here he defeats it not by moving against evil, but by growing its alternative. *Jesus grows a form of humanity free from idolatry and a form of community not based upon domination.*

In the emancipation model, Jesus—and Jesus alone—constitutes a new creation in his person and work by successfully resisting evil and opening its alternative. He becomes, as Paul says, "the second Adam," the seed of a new humanity (1 Cor 15:20–23, 45–49; Rom 5:12–21). The source of life is in Jesus himself, and he invites us to participate in that new human existence in and through him.[34]

The triune God begins growing this new humanity at the moment of Jesus's conception, and nurtures it throughout his life and ministry. The incarnation and Jesus's life itself are thus essential to God's victory over evil. The resurrection and Pentecost are essential to ensure that the seed of a new humanity spreads rather than becoming sterile. Like wheat growing amidst tares, like the tiny mustard seed sprouting and being nurtured by God unnoticed, like yeast hidden in the dough, God defeats evil by setting "the New Being" in the midst the old broken world and making it grow.[35]

---

34. Jesus tells Thomas that he himself is the life (John 14:6), and tells the Pharisees that he brings life in abundance (John 10:10).

35. On the triune God as a gardener and baker, see Matt 13:1–33. Paul Tillich cen-

For the Russian novelists Dostoyevsky and Tolstoy, the most star-tling moment in the gospel narratives is when Jesus thrice resists the temptation to evil in the desert. It was the miracle of restraint. George MacDonald summed up Christ's way of responding to evil:

> Instead of crushing the power of evil by divine force; instead of compelling justice and destroying the wicked . . . ; instead of gathering the children of Jerusalem under His wings whether they would or not . . . —He let evil work its will while it lived; He contented Himself with the slow unencouraging ways of help essential; making men good; casting out, not merely controlling Satan . . . To love righteousness is to make it grow, not to avenge it . . . Throughout His life on earth, He resisted every impulse to work more rapidly for a lower good—strong, perhaps, when He saw old age and innocence and righteousness trodden under foot.[36]

But how did he do it? If he was like us in all ways, how did he ac-complish what no other human being accomplished—the maintenance of his integrity and created goodness? Many point to the fact that Jesus is the Son of God, and thus must have supernatural powers which enable him, like Superman, to easily deflect threats we find overwhelming. But though Jesus is indeed the Son of God incarnate, the *kenotic* union of his divinity with fallen flesh means he does not have superhuman powers. He has human powers, like us. The victory he achieved over Satan was a human victory, not primarily a divine one.[37] How, then, did he resist when we cannot?

Jesus gains his power to resist evil by staying open, fully and at all times, to the presence of the One he calls "Abba." His knowledge that God the Mother/Father is unambiguously for him enables him to resist the temptation to mistrust God.

But how is he able to do that, when none of us remains fully open to God? The answer is found in a fourth figure present in the wilderness ac-count, beyond Jesus, Satan, and God the Mother/Father. "Then Jesus was led up by the Spirit into the wilderness to be tempted by the devil" (Matt

---

ters his soteriology on the idea of Christ being the new creation or "the New Being" in the midst of the old; see Tillich, *Systematic Theology*, Vol. 2, *Existence and the Christ*.

36. MacDonald, *Life Essential*, 24.

37. On the theme of a kenotic union of divinity and humanity, and of Jesus's not having superhuman powers, see Migliore, *Faith Seeking Understanding*, 174–82; see also Phil 2:1–11. On Christ as like us in all ways save sin, see Heb 4:15.

4:1). God the Holy Spirit, who descended upon him at his baptism in the Jordan, goes with Jesus as his constant companion, comforter and guide. Unlike any other human being, Jesus as Messiah is filled completely and continuously with the Spirit. When tempted, the Spirit convinces Jesus to continue to trust his Abba, enabling the human Jesus to resist sin.[38]

Is the cross necessary for Jesus's salvific act? No, in that Jesus has been successfully resisting evil throughout his journey. The resistance, not the cross, is the triune God's intentional will. Yet given the realities of a deeply fallen world, the cross is God's will in these circumstances. The movement of the demonic forces to execute Jesus is the logical consequence toward one who resists evil so effectively; Jesus is a threat to such forces. And God wanted Jesus to resist. By resisting evil even when his life is threatened, he brings his overcoming of evil to a climax—even the threat of death cannot sway him. To the bitter end, he refuses to use power demonically, and also refuses to let the demonic alter his interpretation of truth. He knows who he is, and what is real. Without this threat of death, it would always remain an open question whether he would renounce his trust in God, love of neighbor, and belief in his own integrity if his own survival was at stake.

In a momentous sense, the cross represents the fulfillment of Jesus's victory over evil, a struggle encompassing his public ministry. "It is finished," John records Jesus saying as his last word (John 19:30). By refusing to join evil in killing, or to become complicit in his own destruction, he has defeated the demonic forces. Thus in Revelation, John reveals that the One seated on the throne with authority to open the secrets of God's future is the Lamb who was slain (Revelation 5).

If the story stops at Golgotha, however, Jesus's resistance of evil is insufficient to save us from the demonic. If Eichmann had not acquiesced to the government's plans for the Final Solution, they would have gotten rid of him. Execution is the Devil's trump card, and it is effective. The executing forces also sufficiently humiliated Jesus; he would not likely have become a martyr. While he was a true threat as a human being who had successfully resisted evil, he could be erased.

The triune God's victory over evil depends upon Jesus's resurrection from the grave. The resurrection is the capstone of God's response to evil. God does not resist evil with evil, but with goodness. And then

---

38. See Matt 3:13—4:1; Luke 3:21–22; 4:1–2, 14, 18; Mark 1:9–13. On the Holy Spirit as Advocate and Helper who teaches, reminds, and guides, see John 14:26.

God ensures that God's goodness outlasts every effort of evil to destroy it. The risen Jesus returns, still holding the true power that generates life, and returns in a form of existence that cannot be killed. The demonic form of death, with its ability to seal evil into structures and time—"the last enemy"—is defeated.[39]

THE HOLY SPIRIT'S ROLE IN SALVATION

Jesus, the second person of the Trinity enfleshed, born of Mary and raised as a carpenter's son, disarms the principalities and powers (Col 2:15). Through his incarnation, life and ministry, death and resurrection, he constitutes for humanity new powers over sin, suffering, the demonic, and death. Through these unique acts, he saves.

Seen from another angle, salvation is the work of the Holy Spirit, for the Spirit's three works are essential. First, as we have seen, it is the Spirit who enables Jesus to remain connected to God the Mother/Father, to remain rooted in reality and resist temptations to secure the good through demonic means and to submit to lies.

Second, Jesus does not merely point to saving possibilities that humans then must take up and actualize. Jesus accomplishes salvation. Salvation is a past fact. In engaging us, the Holy Spirit does not get us to actualize salvation, for that is already done. But She enables us to participate in that new reality, and thus expand its scope. The Holy Spirit makes possible a transfer of power over evil from Jesus to us, but a transfer rooted in continuous covenantal connection. The Spirit connects us to Christ, and thus to Christ's powers, by creating a relation of mutual

39. This insistence upon the sinlessness and resurrection of Jesus as essential to the definitive way in which Jesus nonviolently resists evil is what differentiates liberation theologians like Gustavo Gutiérrez, James Cone, and Allan Boesak, feminist theologians like Elizabeth Johnson and Cynthia Crysdale, and womanist theologians like Jacqueline Grant, JoAnne Marie Terrell, and Kelly Brown Douglas from liberation, feminist, and womanist theologians who employ the generative model. Further, in contrast to the latter, the former use such traditional concepts as the incarnation of the Word or Sophia in Jesus, a Trinitarian form of theism or panentheism, and the cross as playing a role in Jesus's defeat of the demonic. The two groups hold significantly different theological conceptions of who Jesus is, and the way and extent to which he defeats evil. See, for example, Gutiérrez, *Theology of Liberation*, and *God of Life*; Cone, *God of the Oppressed*, esp. chaps. 6 and 8; Boesak, *Farewell to Innocence*; Johnson, *She Who Is*, esp. chaps. 8 and 12; Johnson, *Consider Jesus*, esp. chaps. 2 and 8, and 59–61, 90, 92, 110–11, 142–43; Crysdale, *Embracing Travail*; and Grant, *White Women's Christ and Black Women's Jesus*.

incorporation. Through the Spirit as go-between and by the faith She opens within us, Christ comes to dwell within us, and we dwell within Christ. His human capacity to resist evil and cling to God thus becomes available to us.

The Spirit's third saving role involves the broad work of the Spirit. As the Spirit did with Jesus, so with us the Spirit indwells and journeys with us to protect our freedom. As the Spirit of life and of the resurrection, She gives new energies for living within the New Being. Further, the Spirit of life works broadly, throughout history and different cultures, to enable individuals and groups to resist the forces of death and to create new communities not based upon domination. As Gutierrez and Cone recognized, She is present in historical movements of liberation.[40] The Holy Spirit and the risen Christ are active in Joseph Cinque's determined efforts to gain freedom; in Roger Baldwin's and former president John Quincy Adams's legal strategies; in Theodore Joadson's and Lewis Tappan's financial and moral support for the Mendians; in Olaudah Equiano's autobiography and Granville Sharpe and Thomas Clarkson's decades of efforts to end the British slave trade; in John Newton's conversion and repentance for his participation in transporting 20,000 free Africans across the Atlantic to their inhuman bondage; in William Wilberforce's dreams of shackled slaves, and dogged determination, placing bill after bill before Parliament for eighteen years; and in Barbara Spooner's question to William at a key juncture, when he was ready to give up in spring of 1797: "Is that the end of your story?"

OUR ROLE IN SALVATION

When the initial trial's jury looked bent to free Cinque and the other *Amistad* insurrectionists, President Martin Van Buren, worried for loss of Southern support for his upcoming reelection, pressured a transfer of the case to District Court. He wanted a trial without a jury, and with a young judge whose career was ahead of him.

U.S. district judge Andrew Judson was a Catholic, with a history of judgments against Negroes. After hearing the case, he went one night to pray in a church beneath a crucified Jesus. Like Christ in the wilderness, Judson was spiritually wrestling with a choice that could affect his

---

40. See, for example, Gutiérrez, *Theology of Liberation*, esp. parts 4 and 5; Cone, *God of the Oppressed*, esp. 152–62.

career, his family's livelihood, a President's election . . . and the freedom of thirty-eight human beings.

On January 13, 1840, he rendered his verdict: The thirty-eight captives had been born in Africa. They had been illegally kidnapped and sold into slavery. Ruiz and Montez were to be held for slave trading. And the United States Government was to take the freed Africans back home.

∽

"You told me that you live in the company of twenty thousand ghosts, the ghosts of slaves."

William Wilberforce had come to see his old pastor. John Newton looked up from the wet stones he was mopping and glared back. "I was explaining to a child why a grown man cowers in a dark corner." He walks away with his bucket.

"I need you to tell me about them."

"I'm not strong enough to hear my own confession."

"I thought time might have changed you."

"It has—I'm older."

Wilberforce continued. "Pitt has asked me to take them on. The slavers." Newton came close and looked William in the eye.

"I'm the last person you should come to for advice. I can't even say the name of any of my ships without being back on board them in my head. All I know is, twenty thousand slaves live with me in this little church. There's still blood on my hands . . . I can't help you. But do it, Wilber. Do it. Take them on. Blow their dirty, filthy ships out of the water. The planters, sugar barons, Alderman Sugarcane, the Lord Mayor of London, Liverpool, Boston, Bristol, New York—all their streets with blood, dysentery, puke! You won't come away from those streets clean, Wilber. You'll get filthy from it, you'll dream it, see it in broad daylight— but do it . . . for God's sake."

∽

Two common complaints against the classic model upon which the emancipation model is based are that the cosmic battle "happens over our heads," and in the model, salvation can be gained without spiritual or behavioral transformation. It is true that in the emancipation model, the triune God alone constitutes the New Being. It comes to guilty, broken, lost sinners—like John Newton and William Wilberforce and Andrew Judson—as a gift, as grace.

Nevertheless, there is a human role in salvation, and it is quite optimistic and demanding. As was true for Judson, Newton, and Wilberforce, God calls us to participate in spreading the scope of the new creation actualized in Christ—spreading it both deep within our own hearts, and out into social structures in the world. While it is true that Christ says, "take courage; I have conquered the world" (John 16:33b), it is also true that "the victory that conquers the world" is "our faith" (1 John 5:4). While the salvation of the world does not depend upon our actions, the route upon which salvation spreads, and the easing or deepening of sufferings upon humans, fellow creatures and even upon God, may well depend upon the choices we make.

How is it possible that Christ and the Spirit alone defeat evil, yet we also are involved in the battle, and our choices matter? As Dostoyevsky concluded about human nature after ten years in Siberia, all of our resources for perfectibility are tainted. "In every man, of course, a demon lies hidden."[41] As in *Aikido*, power is gained over evil not through accessing "pushing force" within the self, but through becoming attentive to the presence of divine power and allowing it to flow into and through you, for good.

Two sets of Christian symbols convey this relation between divine and human power over evil. The first set entails Jesus's *ascension* and the *Pentecost* descent of the Holy Spirit upon human beings. While in the generative and enlightenment models we have direct access to the presence of divine power, in the emancipation model, that access is mediated by the triune persons. Through a spiritual union with the risen Christ who is now available in all times and locations (a union enabled by the Spirit and faith), and by the power of the Holy Spirit moving within us, we gain Christ's and the Spirit's powers to resist evil and claim life.

The second set involves *baptism* and *Eucharist*. In baptism we renounce our use of demonic power. We rise to a new life in which we allow the divine power—present within us through the indwelling persons of Christ and the Spirit—to activate our capacities and guide our

41. Ivan Karamazov's summary of the human condition, quoted in Yancey, *Soul Survivor*, 143.

freedom. In the eucharistic meal and fellowship, we gain the generative power found in the new creation, a community of equality, reciprocity, and mutual empowerment.

The gospel is not moralized, nor are personal and social transformation based upon imitating Christ. Rather, Christ and the Spirit continue to spread the scope of the New Being. Our job is to let them move through us: To fill, vivify, and guide us. "In all things we are more than conquerors," Paul writes, but "through him who loved us," Jesus of Nazareth, who indwells us and gives us succor and courage (Rom 8:37).

While baptism is episodic, the messianic meal signifies that the Christian role involves a journey. Like Judge Andrew Judson, pressured by the president and his own inner demons to enslave thirty-eight innocent men, we must resist temptations. We must learn how to live in the new reality, learn how to "love every leaf . . . love each separate thing." And as in the generative and enlightenment models, so here, the Christian and the Church are called by God to rise up, to enter into the struggle for the continuing actualization of a very different possibility—the New Being—and against the first possibility, a world ruled by the demonic: by individual and corporate addictions; by the idolatrous worship of ego, possessions, and coercive power; and by kyriarchal unities based upon structures of domination and submission. In announcing God's reign, we are called to denounce the unjust orders. Like Wilberforce, we won't come away clean.

THE DEFEAT OF EVIL

If Christ effects a definitive defeat over evil, how come it does not look like it? This question points to the greatest weakness in this model. If wheat is growing, there are still numerous tares. When Joseph Cinque reached his home in Africa, he found his village destroyed by a civil war and his wife and children gone, likely enslaved. The American Civil War, the failure of Reconstruction, and the legacy of Jim Crow laws followed the successes of people like Baldwin and Tappan.

Evil, though defeated, continues to resist with power capable of great destruction. Further, the new creation enters a culture, community, or individual only through a free yielding and opening to it, for neither Christ, nor the Holy Spirit, nor God the Mother/Father will force the kingdom of God upon us.

Despite the raging of demonic forces during the past two millennia, which admittedly weaken the force of this theory, there are signs of evil's demise. As René Girard and Thomas Cahill point out, prior to Christ, every culture heard and amplified only the voice of the victors, of military heroes and those who wield coercive power effectively. Except for the Jews intermittently, no culture ever recorded the perspectives of the victims of such engagements of sheer might. Such victims were not even seen or remembered. But since the time of Jesus—who had compassion for the victims of demonic forces, who resisted such forces and who died defending the "losers" of history—people saw the victims in a new light, as innocent human beings who had rightful claims to life and just treatment. Those who resisted evil with the power of nonviolent love and upheld communities of life based upon reciprocity and mercy became alternative figures for cultural hagiography—perhaps minority figures in a world still suffused with the demonic, but present nonetheless.[42]

42. There is, of course, Eichmann, who failed to resist evil; but there is also Bonhoeffer.

8

Jesus, the Hospitable One

Hospitality

THE SONS OF JACOB AT SHECHEM

WHEN HAMOR'S SON SHECHEM took Jacob's daughter Dinah against her will, he committed an outrage. Whether her beauty or her spirit enticed him, he fell for her. Shechem then told his father he wanted Dinah for his bride.

With the son at his side, Hamor explained to Jacob that Shechem and Dinah had already been as man and wife, and that surely the gods were smiling on this union. Hamor wanted them to marry, and indeed, invited all the children of each community to marry one another, the tribe of Jacob remaining with them and the land open to them as if it were their own. They would all prosper together.

But the sons of Jacob, who were indignant that Shechem had committed an outrage against the entire tribe by forcibly lying with Jacob's daughter, answered Hamor and Shechem with deceit. Their condition for the marriage, they said, was the circumcision of every male of the city. "Then we will give our daughters to you, and we will take your daughters for ourselves, and we will live among you and become one people." Pleased by this response, Hamor and Shechem told their kinsmen, "These people are friendly with us," and all the men were circumcised.[1]

On the third day, with the men still in pain and unaware, two of Jacob's sons, Simeon and Levi, came upon the men with swords and

---

1. Genesis 34, verses 16 and 21. The above is a retelling of Gen 33:18—34:31, and also draws upon Frederick Buechner's own fictional retelling in *Son of Laughter*, chap. 16.

killed them all. Jacob's other sons plundered the dead. They took every-thing: their herds, all their wealth, all their little ones and their wives.[2]

When he became aware of what had happened, Jacob spoke to Simeon and Levi: "You have put us all in great danger by this thing that you have done. You have made us an abomination to all who live in this land. If ever they gather together against us, not one of us will be spared ... [T]his thing you have done is a stench before the heavens."

Simeon responded, "Was it right for him to use our sister like a harlot?"

And Jacob said, "God chose us to be a blessing to this world, and you have made of us a curse."[3]

ATONEMENT

It was her first crush. Briony Tallis was maybe ten. It was the early 1930s at their country estate, and Briony had fallen for the son of one of the staff, Robbie Turner, then seventeen. Robbie, however, was interested in Briony's older sister, Cecilia.

One afternoon, Briony looked out her window and saw Robbie and Cecilia make a chance encounter at the garden fountain. The two stood still, opposed. Robbie raised a hand up. Cecilia shed her clothes to her underwear, climbed into the fountain, and went under. Then her head emerged, she climbed out, reclothed "with difficulty pulling her blouse on over her wet skin. She turned abruptly and picked up from the deep shade of the fountain's wall a vase of flowers Briony had not noticed before, and set off with it toward the house. No words were exchanged with Robbie, not even a glance in his direction."

Briony wanted to run to Cecilia and demand an explanation for her behavior with Robbie, but she resisted.[4]

That afternoon, Robbie asked Briony to deliver a letter to Cecilia. While he thought he had given Briony the note that included a simple apology for knocking the expensive vase in the water, he had mistakenly brought the first note he had written, the one in which he graphically

---

2. Gen 34:28–29.

3. Dialogue from Buechner, *The Son of Laughter: A Novel*, 180. See Gen 34:30–31.

4. This key scene is from Ian McEwan's novel *Atonement*, 35–37; the quotation is from 37.

described his desire to make love to Cecilia.[5] Upon reading it prior to delivering it to her sister, Briony now felt disgust and anger at Robbie for spurning Briony's affections and crudely pursuing her sister.[6]

Robbie came for dinner. When Briony walked in on Robbie and Cecilia making love in the darkness of the library, it only confirmed for her that Robbie was a danger.[7]

After dinner, the family discovered that Briony's visiting twin cousins had gone missing, and everyone went looking for them. While searching, Briony came upon her older cousin Lola, seventeen, having sex with someone in the dark. The man left before Briony could see his face. Lola acted hurt and shocked, as if she had been raped, and later claimed she also could not see the man's face.

When the police came, Briony made a decision. She stepped forward and claimed that she had seen the man in the dark clearly. It was Robbie.

Robbie was arrested, tried, convicted, and sent to jail for five years. This destroyed the romantic relationship that was forming between Cecilia and Robbie, though Cecilia believed Robbie's assertions of innocence and remained faithful to him.[8]

Robbie got out of jail in 1941 to fight in France. By this time, Briony had left home and become a nurse, aiding wounded soldiers. She was estranged from her beloved sister, Cecilia.[9]

Slowly it became clear to Briony that, at ten, she had told the story to the police because she had wanted it to be so. She admitted to herself that she never saw the man's face.

When a wedding invitation came to her announcing cousin Lola's wedding to one of the house guests six years ago, Paul Marshall, she realized that Paul had been the man in the dark with Lola.

5. For Robbie writing, then mistakingly giving Briony the wrong version of the letter, see McEwan, *Atonement*, chap. 8, especially 73–74, 79–80, 84, and 88–89.

6. See ibid., 106–7, 130.

7. Robbie's encounter with Cecilia after she received his note occurs on ibid., 122–30; and Briony walking in on them, 130–31.

8. The search for the twins, Briony's encounter with Lola, her accusation of Robbie and Robbie's arrest occur on 133–35, 144–175.

9. *Part Two* (177–250) describes Robbie's experiences fighting in France, as well as Robbie's remembrance of Briony's crush on him and later disappointment (215–20).

Robbie, deemed a rapist, having lost six years and the promise of a life with Cecilia who loved him dearly, had been innocent.[10]

KIM BOK-DONG AND JAPANESE WARTIME USE OF "COMFORT WOMEN"

Kim Bok-dong was fifteen that spring day in 1941 when the Japanese man visited her home and told her she would have to go to work at a workshop producing army uniforms. Her mother resisted, but was forced to sign the agreement.

When Kim arrived in Guangdong, she still believed she was going to a workshop. But an army surgeon gave all the girls exams for vene-real diseases and assigned them to "comfort stations." Her first night, the army surgeon himself came to her and beat her badly. Each room had a number, and the girls were not allowed to go out. "During weekdays I received about fifteen soldiers a day, but it seemed more than fifty during weekends."[11]

Kim and the other women were moved to Hong Kong, then Sing-apore after three months. "There were so many soldiers rushing in that I could not even stretch my legs at night." After several more months, they went to Sumatra, Indonesia, Malaysia, and Java to receive soldiers.

Then, suddenly, the soldiers stopped coming. The war was over. But instead of freeing the women, the Japanese soldiers took the women to the 10th Army Hospital in Singapore and trained them in nursing in order to disguise them as nurses.

When Kim returned to Korea in 1946, her mother, hearing she had been a comfort woman, "died of sorrow." She married, but the marriage failed, since she could not have a child. She opened a small store to make a living.

In 1993 she testified to the World Human Rights Conference in Vienna "to demand acknowledgement and compensation from the Japanese government." "I wanted to tell of who ruined my life like this."

10. The first two-thirds of *Part Three* (251 through 300) describe Briony's hospital work in London, as well as Briony's realization, with the wedding invitation's arrival, that Robbie was innocent (268–69, 271–72).

11. Kim Bok-dong gave the first real-name record by a surviving former "comfort woman." Her testimony is from The Korean Council, Cyber Memorial, *Remember the Past: Testimonies* (Testimony No. 6). She made her report on January 17, 1992.

The Japanese government responded first by claiming there was no coercion involved; the women did it of their own free will to make money. Then, in 1995, the government said it would not provide compensation, but it would give money to an "Asia Peace Fund for Women." Kim opposed acceptance of the civil fund because she demanded that the Japanese government accept legal responsibilities for what happened. "My body is still covered all over with wounds. I cannot even properly digest a spoonful of rice, so that I have to depend on digestive medicines to eat. I feel sore all over my body as if I am pricked with pins. While other seniors have happy lives full of love from their children and grandchildren, I have had such a lonely life without children. Who made my life such a miserable one?"

WASTELAND

The movie *WALL-E* begins with nothing but a wasteland. All the humans are gone, having left the earth when their garbage became so voluminous, it crushed and suffocated and distorted the environment to such an extent no living thing would grow. For the first thirty minutes, the audience watches a small robot, WALL-E, move back and forth across the wasteland, attempting to compact the trash into little cubes, stacking them into skyscraper-sized towers, trying to clear space. No one has lived on earth for hundreds of years, but solar-powered WALL-E keeps at his task.

The humans had created a situation that took on a life of its own, that left destruction far beyond what was anticipated, that continued to reverberate, and that could not be fixed. Efforts at repair seemed futile, like WALL-E creating his little cubes of trash in a wasteland of garbage.

Similarly, each of the three stories above describes the creation of a wasteland. The sons of Jacob in their deceit and murder of the citizens of Shechem; Briony in her childish concoction of a story meant to wound Robbie over a momentary disappointment; the wartime government officers, doctors and soldiers of Japan who deceived, enslaved and brutalized Korean women in forced brothels: all committed crimes that polluted the perpetrators and all the interpersonal or intercommunal relationships. The damage, once done, could not be undone.

In ancient Israel as in most religions, the problem of pollution was dealt with by the making of a sacrifice to God. At first glance, however, a sacrificial view of atonement carries the same problems as the penal substitutionary theory. God appears bloodthirsty, unwilling to forgive guilty humans and reforge a relationship until blood has been shed. Humans propitiate God by offering up something of great value. As we discussed in chapter 2, such a saving scenario portrays God as ambivalent and violent toward humans, puts doubt about God's trustworthiness into human psyches, and fuels the sacrificial mentality that is the root of all violence. It simply reinforces the myth of redemptive suffering that keeps victims of violence from seeking their own healing.

Despite these seeming problems, the model of sacrifice is essential to the Christian view of salvation. Despite its archaic origins, the image has power because it connects to two elements of Christian experience: that of defilement and concomitant inability to restore wholeness, and of Jesus as one who gave his life to protect and restore the life of others.

The strengths of the sacrificial model can be separated from the weaknesses through two moves. The first move is to return to the Biblical understanding of sacrifice, which differs from the view that developed later in Christian practice. The second move is to retain the metaphor of sacrifice, but place it within a larger dominant model that includes yet goes beyond it: the model of hospitality. Jesus saves us by being hospitable, continuously open to God, his neighbors, and God's inbreaking reign of peace and justice. Thus, this theory I call *the hospitality model of salvation.*

THE PROBLEM WITHIN THE HUMAN CONDITION

In the emancipation model of salvation, the problem for humanity is the suffering caused by the "third factor" beyond God and creatures, the "demonic" forces that seek to destroy creation. In the hospitality model, the problem is the human act of betrayal that damages and defiles all parties involved: the perpetrator, the victim, and the network of trust between them.

As Martin Buber pointed out, human beings are fundamentally social. They live within covenant networks, and covenants are rooted in open and honest exchanges in which each party is treated as a "thou," a full subject. But humans not only make promises and keep promises; they also break promises in acts of disloyalty. Such violating acts create distrust in the other party. Such violations and the resulting distrust and estrangement can be seen in the three stories above. The sons of Jacob, Briony Tallis, and the Japanese government and soldiers all violate others through acts of betrayal. The Canaanites surrounding the city of Shechem now no longer see Jacob's clan as friendly. Robbie and Cecilia do not believe anything Briony says to them. Kim Bok-dong, the other Korean comfort women, and indeed perhaps all Koreans do not trust that the current Japanese government will treat them with respect and with justice.

The disloyal acts have polluted the relational ground. As Jacob told his sons, "You have made us an abomination to all who live in this land," and the "stench" rises to God in heaven. Frequently, such betrayals lead to cycles of violence filled with further betrayals and deeper mistrust, and to the downward spiral formed by the logic of mimetic exchange. Further, the damage cannot be undone by either retributive or compensatory justice. Can Jacob or his sons bring back the dead men of Shechem to their bereft parents, wives and children? Can Briony bring back Robbie's five years of life lost in a prison, or his budding relationship with Cecilia cut short? Can the Japanese government restore the life Kim Bok-dong then had stolen from her, or her dead mother, or her own life without children? The losses are both grave and permanent.

Toward the one who betrays, the logical question others will ask is this: "Why should we trust you?" The perpetrator's vandalism of God's peaceable kingdom leads to bloodshed, and the cries of the innocent rise up to heaven. The act brings estrangement from God, for as Jacob knew, it simultaneously violates other creatures and breaks a covenant promise with God. As the early stories of Genesis 3–11 tell, the human act of violation becomes God's problem. How can God trust the betrayer again? The humans break promises. They do not act with integrity. They do not do justice, love mercy, and walk humbly with their God.[12] Further, how can God get us betrayers to turn from our sin and freely fulfill our promises to God?

Not only in the divine-human relation, but also in interpersonal and intercommunal relationships, trust is broken. Why should the Canaanites trust the sons of Jacob?

The treacherous acts not only damage other lives and pollute relational ties; they also besmirch the life of the betrayer. Briony dirtied herself with her lie that reverberated far beyond her expectations. The defilement deepened when she failed to come forward upon witnessing the harmful consequences upon others. Since we were made to make

12. See Mic 6:8.

and keep our promises, the breaking of promises brings a degradation of human character. In interviews for her study of the Rape of Nanking and subsequent creation of forced military prostitution, Japanese veterans detailed to Iris Chang such devolution. Now a doctor in Japan, Hakudo Nagatomi spoke candidly: "I beheaded people, starved them to death, burned them and buried them alive, over 200 in all. It is terrible that I could turn into an animal and do these things. There are really no words to explain what I was doing. I was truly a devil."[13] After one acts in ways that betray one's own human nature, how is one to trust one's own self?

The victims rightly do not trust those who betrayed them. Yet the spoiling also affects their relationship with God. Where was God, when they were being violated? Why didn't God step in to stop it? The victim's experience of the absence of God may lead them to feel that God has also betrayed them, that perhaps God is also a promise-breaker, indifferent or malevolent or perhaps simply no longer present. Why should the victims or their loved ones trust God?

Sin as betrayal and violation and its corresponding response of distrust and retaliation brings forth a downward spiral in human relations, the divine-human relation, and even the stability of persons' inner lives. There is degradation, entropy. Distance grows, and soon the chasms seem unbridgeable. The past devours the present, and convinces all involved that a future different from the past is impossible. Each party, sequestered in its hate, becomes colder, harder, and awaits the unleashing of the dogs of violence.

THE MEANING OF SALVATION

They met in a white-walled, spare room in Rome's Rebibbia prison. There was a radiator, bars on the windows above, a low bed with a pillow and blanket. Nineteen months earlier, Mehmet Ali Agca had shot Pope John Paul II four times in St. Peter's Square. Now, they sat in simple plastic chairs, each leaning toward one another, heads bowed. The pope held the hand that had held the gun that had tried to kill him. They talked for 21 minutes. Once or twice, Agca laughed. Mostly, Agca's face reflected confusion and uncertainty.

The pope forgave him for the shooting.

---

13. Chang, *Rape of Nanking*, 59.

At the end of the meeting, Agca either kissed the Pope's ring, or pressed the pope's hand to his forehead in a Muslim gesture of respect.

"What we talked about will have to remain a secret between him and me," the pope said as he left the cell. "I spoke to him as a brother whom I have pardoned, and who has my complete trust."

In 2000, at the pope's urging, the Italian president pardoned Agca.

In 2005, recovering in a hospital from the flu, the pope received a handwritten letter in Italian from Agca, wishing him "a speedy recovery."[14]

If the cycle of betrayal and mistrust brings forth a world on a descending trajectory, salvation is the opening up within history of a future different than the past, one hopeful and life-giving. It is the beginning of an upward spiral, a movement toward light instead of darkness, good instead of evil.

For the perpetrators, those who have defiled themselves through treachery and violence, those covered in blood and guilt and shame, salvation is cleansing, purification, the restoration of one's status and good name within a community and integrity within oneself. It is like coming up out of the waters of baptism, clean.

Salvation interrupts the increasing cycles of betrayals and mistrust with a word and a human movement different from the law of mimetic exchange. For both perpetrators and victims, salvation brings reconciliation through a renewal of trust and an upward spiral of trust and fidelity. Salvation is imaged by the Pope holding Agca's hand, and Agca pressing that hand to his forehead. It is seen in the long, quiet pause of the prodigal father holding his kneeling son in Rembrandt's painting. When salvation comes, all three parties are brought together again and reconciled: the promise-breaker, the victim, and God. As Jürgen Moltmann writes:

> Victims have a long memory, for the traces of suffering are deeply etched into their souls and often into their bodies too. People who have committed the injury always have short memories. They do not know what they have done because they do not want to know. They are dependent on the memory of the victims if they want to see who they are and be reconciled. They must learn to see themselves with the eyes of their victims. Reconciliation is not

14. Lance Morrow, "I Spoke . . . as a Brother." Agca shot John Paul II on May 13, 1981; John Paul's visit with Agca at Rebibbia prison was December 2, 1983.

an individualistic act between "me and my God" but a communal
act between God, the perpetrators, and the victims.[15]

The descendants of Jacob and the children of Hamar prosper together. Briony reclaims the intimate relationship she once had with her
sister. Koreans and Japanese move toward a shared future.

The victims not only gain reconciliation with their enemies. Their
life is restored, opening for them a future different from the painful
past. Further, their future is opened because they experience something absent during their sufferings—a certain knowledge of God's
love and advocacy for them. Like the prodigal father to his sons, God
is not indifferent toward any of God's beloved creatures, but is unambiguously for them.

THE COMING OF SALVATION

She stepped out from under the bridge, heading towards the church.[16]
She needed backbone. She thought of the rejection letter from the pub-
lisher in her pocket. In her novella, she had concocted a fiction that satisfied her vanity but evaded all the key elements of what had happened
that morning by the fountain.

As she sat watching cousin Lola marry Paul Marshall, she knew that
she and the two of them "had conspired with silence and falsehoods to
send an innocent man to jail."[17]

Afterward, she wavered, looked for a café, had tea, but found her
courage and walked to Cecilia's flat.

"Oh my God," Cecilia said, and sat down on the steps.[18] They looked
at one another. Scanning her sister's face for the first time in five years,
Briony scarcely knew her. The conversation was awkward and abrupt.
Cecilia was cold, then derisive, then sarcastic toward her sister. They
went inside.

Cecilia mentioned Briony's letter, in which Briony said she wanted
to tell their parents the truth of what had happened. "If you were lying

---

15. Jürgen Moltmann and Elisabeth Moltmann-Wendel, *Passion for God*, 77.

16. The following retells the climactic scene in McEwan's *Atonement* from the last
third of *Part Three* (300–330). (Direct quotes are in quotation marks.)

17. Ibid., 306.

18. Ibid., 312.

then, why should a court believe you now?"[19] Cecilia's confirmation of her crime stung, because "the perspective was unfamiliar. Weak, stupid, confused, cowardly, evasive—she had hated herself for everything she had been, but she had never thought of herself as a liar."[20]

"What I did was terrible. I don't expect you to forgive me."

"'Don't worry about that,' [Cecilia] said soothingly, and in the second or two during which she drew deeply on her cigarette, Briony flinched as her hopes lifted unreally. 'Don't worry,' her sister resumed. 'I won't ever forgive you.'"[21]

Robbie came in the room; he had been sleeping, and when he saw Briony, he just looked at her. Though intimidated, she did not glance away. He grew furious. "I don't know why you let her in," he said to Cecilia. Then to Briony, "I'll be quite honest with you. I'm torn between breaking your stupid neck here and taking you outside and throwing you down the stairs." She took in his words, her due. His voice had contempt when he explained what life in prison was like.

"Do you think I assaulted your cousin?"

"No."

"Did you think it then?"

Briony fumbled her words. "Yes, yes and no. I wasn't certain."

"And what's made you so certain now?"

"Growing up."[22]

Briony heard her sister's voice. "There isn't much time. . . . So sit down. There are some things you're going to do for us."

Robbie turned to her. "You're to go to your parents as soon as you can and tell them everything they need to know to be convinced that your evidence was false . . . [T]omorrow . . . [y]ou'll go to a solicitor, a commissioner for oaths, and make a statement which will be signed and witnessed. In it you'll say what you did wrong, and how you're retracting your evidence. You'll send copies to both of us. Is that clear?"

19. Ibid., 317.

20. Ibid., 318.

21. Ibid., for these last two paragraphs.

22. This dialog between Briony and Robbie comes from ibid., 322–23.

"Yes."[23]

Then they walked her to the London Underground. She wanted to ask her sister about her new address, or where Robbie was going, but she couldn't. They had only one subject together, "and it was fixed in the unchangeable past." Outside the station, they bid a cool farewell, but Briony had one last word she had yet to say.

"I'm very very sorry. I've caused you such terrible distress."

Robbie said softly, "Just do all the things we've asked."

"She paid her fare to Waterloo. When she reached the barrier, she looked back and they had gone."

"She had hardly expected to be forgiven. What she felt was more like homesickness, though there was no source for it, no home. But she was sad to leave her sister. It was her sister she missed . . . That tenderness in her voice . . . when Cecilia was sixteen and she was a child of six and things went impossibly wrong. Or in the night, when Cecilia came to rescue her from a nightmare and take her into her own bed. Those were the words she used. *Come back. It was only a bad dream. Briony, come back.* How easily this unthinking family love was forgotten . . ."

"[When she reached the stairs' bottom,] she considered what she had to do . . . She knew what was required of her. Not simply a letter, but a new draft, an atonement, and she was ready to begin."[24]

～

Briony Tallis's act is atoning, and it involves a twofold sacrifice—but not the kind of sacrifice we expect. As we have seen, often the context in which religious sacrifice is imagined is one in which God is enraged by human infidelity—as God was when Moses returned from the mountaintop and saw the Israelites dancing around the golden calf. Somebody has to die. Within this context, sacrifice is perceived as a way for the wayward humans to placate God. The premise is that the suffering and selflessness of the innocent is redemptive.

Is it possible to understand Briony's act as an act of sacrifice that atones, without supporting the myth of redemptive suffering? It is, if

23. This dialog comes from ibid., 325–26.

24. This last scene, where Robbie and Cecilia walk Briony to the London subway, is from ibid., 328–30.

two moves are made. First, we must return to the Biblical meaning of sacrifice, which has nothing to do with the distorted understanding of sacrifice immediately above. Second, the act of sacrifice cannot stand alone for a correct interpretation; it must be placed within the larger act of hospitality.

In the Bible, there are three types of sacrifices: gift-offerings, communion-offerings, and sin-offerings. In a *gift-offering*, something of value to the community was given to God as an act of gratitude in response to God's gracious acts. An animal or inanimate substitute such as flour, oil, incense, or wine was completely burned up and sent via the smoke to God.[25] All such offerings were not bribes, but rather, responses to the central gracious act in Israel's history, the freeing of the Jews from slavery in Egypt. They knew that everything about their lives depended upon that act of God, and was a gift. The spring Passover Festival, in which a lamb was sacrificed, reflects this meaning of gratitude and sharing of the gifts God has given back to God.[26]

Very early in the Old Testament, however, the idea of "sacrifice" became a metaphor for the giving of one's whole life to God in covenant fidelity, rather than just a representative portion. One offers up to God one's well-being in gratitude, and like a circumcision of the heart, one lives as if the law is written naturally upon her or his heart.[27] In the New Testament, Jesus tells his followers to "be perfect, as your heavenly Father is perfect," while Paul tells new followers of Christ, "present your bodies as a living sacrifice, holy and acceptable to God, which is your spiritual worship." They offer God a gift of praise by refusing to be conformed to the old aeon and instead following God's will.[28]

In the *communion-offering*, such as occurred when the people entered into covenant partnership with God, only the blood and fat were burned up. The lean meat was eaten by the people as they joined together

---

25. See, for example, Exod 29:38–42; Lev 23:9–21; Num 15:1–21; Deut 26:5–10; 2 Sam 6:18.

26. On all sacrifices having their root and center in God's gracious liberative act in the exodus, see Rogerson, "Sacrifice in the Old Testament," 57.

27. See Lev 7:11ff.; Jer 31:31–34; Ps 40:6–8; Heb 10:5–9; and also Amos 5:21–24; Hos 6:6; Mic 6:6–8; Matt 9:13; 12:7; Mark 12:33.

28. Matt 5:48; Rom 12:1–2; and also Heb 13:15–16; Phil 4:18. For sacrifices of thanksgiving, see for example Pss 24:3–6; 27:6; 50:14; 107:22.

with God in a feast.[29] The New Testament Eucharist reflects such a peace offering and event of hospitality.

Gift- and communion-offerings, however, apply in situations in which the divine-human relation and social order are peaceful, not for situations in which the divine-human relation has been damaged by the violating acts of humans against one another. For the ancient Jews, such a break in harmonious relations is seen as a stain that mars social life, or as a contagious infection. As Jacob knew after his sons committed murder, the "abominating," "stinking" act brings a cursed likelihood of further destruction descending upon the person or community, either as a social consequence of such behavior (human retaliation), or a divine act of punishment. Thus, the "stink" or "stain" or "contagion" needs to be removed in order to protect the life of the person and community. Further, the Jews presupposed that access to a holy God was impossible unless the sin was removed and righteousness restored.

Sin-offerings were the means by which the degenerating impact of sin was removed. The atoning sacrifice, however, was not something humans initiated to placate God, but something God did to sever the link between sin and its otherwise inevitable consequence of destruction. Before the pure, whole, unblemished animal is slain, the sinner lays his hands upon the animal to symbolize an identification between the two. Somehow, the slaying of the animal and placing of its blood upon the sinner and community "cleanses away" the contagion like a disinfectant, or "covers over" the marring stain. The blood neutralizes the abomination's power to harm the body of the sinner or the community.

The Old Testament never explains how the pure animal's blood brings about this effect. Leviticus 17:11 comes closest to describing a mechanism: "For the life of the flesh is in the blood, and I have given it to you for making atonement for your lives on the altar; for, as life, it is the blood that makes atonement."

It is as if God uses the purity of the animal's blood to wash over, overcome, and renew the tainted life of the sinner, much as how clean, flowing water can refresh a stagnant pool.[30] The sacrifice was costly for all involved: for the animal; for the sinner, who chose the best animal to

29. See Exod 24:1–18, and also Genesis 15.

30. In Jewish and Gentile traditions, the death of martyrs seemed to have similar cleansing power. Their spiritual sacrifice was great enough to cover more sins than their own. See Fiddes, *Past Event and Present Salvation*, 67.

use; and even for God, who used an innocent animal's life, beloved of God, to purify sinners' lives. What is clear is that the life-bearing blood brings the change, not the death. And neither the blood nor the death are aimed at God as propitiation, but at the stain of sin, and employed by God to heal.[31]

The blood by itself, however, could not effect the cleansing change. The repentance of the sinner was also necessary for the sins to be wiped away, as well as a change of behavior toward justice and compassion.[32] As the psalmist says:

> O Lord, open my lips,
>   and my mouth will declare your praise.
> For you have no delight in sacrifice;
>   if I were to give a burnt offering, you would not be pleased.
> The sacrifice acceptable to God is a broken spirit;
>   a broken and contrite heart,
> O God, you will not despise.[33]

Many of the New Testament authors' presentations of Jesus's blood on the cross as having saving power reflect this Jewish understanding of the life-bearing blood of a pure creature having the ability to cleanse sin. It is Jesus's giving of his powerful life-bearing blood that renews life, not his death. Nor is his death that of a vicarious substitute for divine punishment. In other passages—such as when John the Baptist points to Jesus as "the Lamb of God who takes away the sin of the world"—a merging of the sin-offering and gift-offering, of the Day of Atonement and Passover sacrifices, occurs.[34]

The fact that the three forms of sacrifices were so commonplace in first-century Judea explains why the authors of the New Testament employed "sacrifice" so readily to explain how Jesus's death cleanses humans

---

31. The fact that a cup of grain could be substituted if one were too poor to sacrifice an animal shows clearly that the animal was not a vicarious substitute that was punished. One cannot punish a cup of barley. There was no transfer of sin from the sinner to the animal slain (or grain burned). Only with the scapegoat on the Day of Atonement (Leviticus 16) was there a transfer of sin from the community to the goat. But the goat was not offered to God as a substitute for punishment. Rather, it was driven out of the community, again revealing that the goal of such rituals was to remove the stain of sin from the community. Death was not involved in that removal.

32. Animal sacrifice contained no automatic mechanism.

33. Ps 51:15–17; see also Mic 6:6–8 concerning the change of behavior required.

34. John 1:29; see also 1 Cor. 5:7; Luke 22:7; Mark 14:12; Exod 12:3–8.

from sin and restores the divine-human fellowship. The ritual, however, is problematic for modern people. It was already somewhat problematic in the first century. Though he uses the sacrifice as his primary metaphor, the author of Hebrews states "it is impossible for the blood of bulls and goats to take away sins."[35] For modern people, sin, as offense against God and neighbor, is not literally a disease or a piece of dirt from which the personal or communal body can be cleansed. Nor is life a kind of "stuff" identified with blood, so that its shedding and application can transfuse new life into sin-corrupted bodies. For moderns, the usefulness of the sacrificial metaphor falters upon its magical thinking. Further, the premise that the blood of martyrs or of the innocent has revivifying power functions to support the myth of redemptive suffering that legitimates violence and the acquiescence of victims to abuse. The renewal of life is seen as the result of sacrificial death.

Despite the problems of magical thinking and of valorizing suffering, the biblical meanings of sacrifice provide a powerful way to understand how cleansing and reconciliation are possible, for five reasons:

- In none of the three forms of Israelite sacrifice is propitiation a goal, so the framework of an angry God ready to kill wayward humans is excluded from the metaphor.

- All three forms come at God's suggestion, as ways to either maintain or restore the divine-human relation.

- In all three, the human posture of the worshipper is one of hospitality. In the gift-offering, one gives a portion of one's life to symbolize one's gratitude for God's generous gifts, and an opening of one's life fully back toward God. In communion-offerings, it is as if the meal is being shared with God. And in the sin-offering, the spiritual posture of openness is present in the corresponding spiritual act of repentance and promise to change behavior.

- All three forms of sacrifice have their setting within the broad theme of Exodus and Sinai. In other words, they are meant to facilitate the movement of God's people from bondage to freedom. That freedom is envisioned as a new form of community

35. Heb 10:4.

not based on domination, one in which ultimately God dwells fully with humans in a just and peaceable kingdom.

- While the elements of magical thinking and the glorification of suffering are not helpful, the biblical understanding of a sin-offering nevertheless reveals how a sacrifice may cleanse personal and social defilement, making new life and reconciliation possible. The basic principle found within the sin-offering is that a "good" life "covers" or "removes" a defiled life. Or, a life of truth and fidelity may "cover over" a life lived in deceit and infidelity. The magical thinking is no longer present in the metaphor: The acts of violation cannot be "removed," any more than the dead of Shechem can be revived, or Robbie's five years of lost freedom returned to him, or Kim Bok-dong's teenage dreams of a happy life recovered. But the metaphor of a sin-sacrifice retains the idea that it is possible to move beyond the personal and social defilements without denying their damaging realities. The "good" life that may cleanse the pollution occurs when the betrayer *acknowledges her or his act of violation* and its damaging consequences, and when she or he *states that she or he wants a different form of relationship in the future*, and makes concrete acts toward that new way of relating.

This twofold sacrifice that may cleanse the perpetrator of sin and guilt while effecting atonement between perpetrator and victim is illustrated in the narratives, agonizing debates, and torturous confessions that occurred in South Africa during the Truth and Reconciliation Commission's work. The goal of the commission was to get to the truth about the past, and also foster national reconciliation. In *Reconciliation: Restoring Justice*, theologian John de Gruchy describes the Commission's process that closely reflects the twofold sacrifice that atones.

The Commission created a space in which perpetrators, beneficiaries, and victims could encounter one another around the truth. The space involved an actual triangle: between perpetrator and victim was a space that held images of the crime committed. In the conversation across the middle space, the 'other' was initially experienced as a barrier, as someone who stood in the way of achieving self-interested goals. Yet the very conversation entailed a decision for each party: Will I continue to perceive the "other" as fundamentally different than myself, as polluted and ethnically unacceptable? Or will I regard the "other" as a fellow human being struggling with me to find a way beyond the impasse of endlessly opposing claims? In itself, the latter involves a reversal of the act of objectification against the "other." Further, I become vulnerable to the 'other,' and allow the conversation and relationship to develop its own momentum and direction.

This choice to converse with my adversary on equal terms, as subject to subject, opens up possibilities. Like Briony, who stood still as Robbie angrily told her what it was like for him in prison, the perpetrator will listen to what de Gruchy calls "the sound of fury,"[36] the rage of victims angered by the injustice of the perpetrator's acts and their horrific consequences. To listen to this rage is to recognize that they are not simply passive objects of oppression.

The possibility opens for the perpetrator to make the twofold sacrifice that atones. *She may tell the truth about what happened.* Like Briony, who comes to Cecilia and Robbie, and the next day heads to her parents and a notary, she may accept responsibility for her hideous crimes and apologize. She may feel remorse, an act in which the perpetrator identifies with the victim, an act that re-humanizes both perpetrator and victim. Remorse acknowledges the victim as a person like oneself. By acknowledging that one has committed not merely a mistake, but a sin, it uncovers for the perpetrator her or his agency in relation to the evil unleashed, and thus a resource for turning oneself around, for being a different person. Truth-telling involves a self-sacrifice, not in the sense of self-negation, but in the sense that the perpetrator puts aside the various self-defensive strategies by which she or he evades the truth—lying, denial, repression, self-justification, blaming others. It involves a risk, for one is putting one's real self forward.

The atoning sacrifice involves for the perpetrator a second risk-taking venture in relation to the victim. *The perpetrator commits to a different kind of relationship with the victim in the future, and also makes concrete steps to begin living in that new way.* The steps likely include corrective justice (the restoration of land and resources, for example) and compensatory justice (reparations). Reparations are always inadequate, and often mostly symbolic, since it is impossible to redress all the wrongs. Dead loved ones cannot be brought back to life; land cannot be returned to First Nations in total. But in giving reparations, the perpetrator signals

36. De Gruchy, *Reconciliation*, 164–70.

something to the victim: The perpetrator committed a crime that never should have happened, and seeks to undo its effects.

The twofold sacrifice of truth-telling and movement toward an alternative way of relating is atoning; yet the sacrifice does not necessarily lead to reconciliation. This is because the victim has a right to vengeance and a full recompense.[37] The victim is not required to forgive; or, if she forgives the past acts, may still say, "I want nothing more to do with you in the future." If she forgives, it is a gift, an act of grace by which she freely chooses to forego her right to retribution, since of course everything lost cannot be restored. At its most basic level, forgiveness is the act by which the victim takes her hands off the perpetrator's throat, and gives him back to God that God may try to redeem him.

The atoning act of twofold sacrifice is a creative act by the perpetrator within a context of endless patterns of betrayal and mistrust. Forgiveness is also a creative act introduced by the victim into the pattern, one that opens up the possibility of cleansing for the perpetrator, and a future for both parties different than the past. Through these intentional acts of entrustment, new relationships can be forged in which power relations are restructured in a just fashion, and both parties find a way to forge a common future. The status of each is changed. The victim is now the survivor, the living one whose subjectivity has been restored and acknowledged. The perpetrator is also human again, this time as a forgiven sinner.

One question remains concerning this twofold act of atonement that brings cleansing and reconciliation. Is the forgiveness prevenient or consequential to the criminal's atoning sacrifice? Like Jesus who forgave his executioners before they ever made any sacrificial moves, or like the prodigal father who was embracing his son and calling for the fatted calf before the son could blurt out his apology, the victim's offer of forgiveness may precede the perpetrator's confession. Forgiveness of course is a gift; it is not earned by perpetrators, and the prevenience shows this. Further, forgiveness may enable the perpetrator's remorse and confession and change in behavior. Yet forgiveness's effectiveness in leading toward reconciled relations and a new future depends upon that twofold sacrificial act by the sinner. The order of atoning sacrifice and forgiveness may be contingent, but both are necessary. And truth-telling and compensatory acts increase the likelihood that the victim will offer

37. See the *lex talionis* in Lev 24:19–20.

forgiveness. When offered, even after the twofold sacrifice, the forgiveness is still a gift, since one is still foregoing one's right to retribution and full compensation.

GOD'S ROLE IN SALVATION

God is the one who cleanses and restores us, as God reveals in Ezekiel: "I will sprinkle clean water upon you, and you shall be clean from all your uncleanness, and from all your idols I will cleanse you. A new heart I will give you, and a new spirit I will put within you; and I will remove from your body the heart of stone and give you a heart of flesh."[38]

The way that God does this is not by relying on the humans to cleanse themselves, to bring the sin-offering. It is true that in the Bible, God makes the cleansing of defiled sinners and the restoration of divine-human fellowship possible by creating the sacrificial rituals. But the problem for sinners who have corrupted themselves through betrayal, violence, and delusional rationalizations is that they no longer have the capacity to return to God with an appropriate response of honesty, remorse, and new commitment to changed attitudes and behavior. Thus, the triune God brings about cleansing and reconciliation by sending the Son to take on a representative piece of human life—life in the "flesh," fallen—and cleanse that life and restore it to God on humankind's behalf. The Son is sent to constitute salvation by giving an appropriate human response to God, given human corporate and individual acts of betrayal, self-defilement and denial. As in the emancipation model, so here, Jesus becomes the Second Adam, the seed of a new humanity.

Startlingly, God the Mother/Father also sends the Son so that, on behalf of God, Jesus may perform a similar twofold sacrifice toward humanity, one that enables the victims of human atrocities to move from mistrust to trust in God.

JESUS'S ROLE IN SALVATION

In the betrayal of our promises, we violate others and engender escalating patterns of distrust and betrayal. Cut off from God, from our neighbors, even from our own self, we look to the future and believe it will always be like the past: without hope.

---

38. Ezek 36:25–26.

Jesus, in contrast, is the person who is open, and thus the one who opens up a future different than the past. He saves humanity by effecting three accomplishments unique in history, accomplishments that change the human situation.

First, in the midst of a polluted human world, *Jesus becomes the seed of a new humanity*. Though the Son has taken on fallen flesh, he reverses Adam's steps, leading that human flesh in an ascending rather than descending course. In Rublev's painting of the Trinity, three persons are seated around a table, open to the viewer and filled with life-giving food. The three persons live every moment of their existence from and toward the open generosity of others. Like those persons, Jesus is the hospitable one, living every moment of his existence from and toward God, gaining his power from the continuous flow of grace and gratitude.

At every moment of his existence, Jesus is open to God the Mother/Father, the one he calls "Abba." Having taken on a random but representative sample of the infected whole of humanity, Jesus offers to God a life of openness, a life in which the law is written upon his heart and he follows God's ways with joy.[39] Jesus clings to the Abba he understands as being unconditionally for him and nonviolent, and he resists the Devil's suggestions that God might be otherwise. In this rejection of demonic deceptions and this clinging to God, Jesus reverses the fall of Adam and Eve. He fulfills the divine-human covenant based upon trust and fidelity, the open relation of giving and receiving that is the inner meaning of the gift- and communion-offerings.

Jesus is continuously open to himself. As Drewermann rightly perceived, trust in self is directly proportionate to trust in God. He is able to trust his knowledge of God's generosity and thus resist Satan's lies. He is able to trust his understanding of the true nature of power, and distinguish it from false forms. He lives with integrity, never burying who he truly is.

Jesus is continuously open to his neighbors. As we saw in the emancipation model, Jesus acts as a *go'el*, denouncing injustice and refusing to compromise with kyriarchal powers. Yet while never passive in relation to evil, he is also not aggressive or defensive of his ego. Toward violent betrayers, he refuses to use power demonically or cut relations. Again reversing the fall, Jesus refuses to treat anyone as an object—God, himself, or his neighbors, even those who haul him into trumped-up trials and

---

39. See Jer 31:31–34.

hang him to a tree. In healing the severed ear of the high priest's slave in the garden of Gethsemane, in asking God to forgive his torturers and executioners "for they do not know what they are doing," Jesus refuses to place anyone in the category of an "evil-doer" who is beyond hope of redemption. He returns good for evil, precisely because he refuses to imagine his future, or God's future, without such persons. In this, he differs from us.

Through this gift-offering and communion-offering of a life lived in complete hospitality, a life that fulfills God's goal for humankind, Jesus is himself already the seed of a new humanity. This is seen in the power of life he is able to offer others. In his incarnation, life, and ministry, Jesus already opens up the possibilities for change. As Leonardo Boff writes, "Christ would have been a sacrifice even had he never been immolated, had never shed his blood."[40]

Yet the cross is not insignificant in Jesus's creation of this new form of humanity. The sacrifice model borrows here from the emancipation model, in which Jesus resists temptations in the wilderness, at Gethsemane, and on the cross. Jesus holds onto God's new form of "kinship group" based not in ethnicity, class, gender, or other forms of power, but in mutual regard, forgiveness of faults, and the glad receiving and giving of aid. Further, in Gethsemane and at Golgotha, Jesus refused to base his religion in fear, refused to reject his belief that God was unambiguously for him and all others, or that God's future reign of *shalom* would win out over the demonic. He trusted the truth of his own existence, rooted in such hospitality.[41]

Beyond fulfilling the existential intent of the gift- and communion-offerings, *Jesus also fulfills the existential and relational intent of the sin-offering, cleansing polluted humanity and bringing about divine-human reconciliation.* He fulfills the twofold sacrifice to God.

The Son of God takes on a random but representative sample of the infected human community, and acts as our representative in performing the sin-offering to God the Mother/Father. Though himself without sin, he does not dissociate himself from humans as violators. He stands with us, as a member of our broken, polluted lot. As the hospitable one,

40. From Boff, *Passion of Christ, Passion of the World*, quoted in Brock and Parker, *Proverbs of Ashes*, 42.

41. On his refusal to mistrust God or his own existence, switching to a religion based in fear, see Beier, *A Violent God-Image*, 219–26, 235.

Jesus opens himself to the triangular space of betrayers, victims, and the images of the crimes committed. He sees all parties as subjects—the victims, the perpetrators, God. He hears without ego-defense "the sound of fury," the rage of the human victims, and also the anger of God for the violation of God's beloved creatures and the betrayal of the divine-human covenant. He takes in the divine disappointment, broken heartedness and fury, divine sentiments expressed to humanity (represented in the people of Israel) in Jeremiah:

> Thus says the Lord:
>
> What wrong did your ancestors find in me
>   that they went far from me,
> and went after worthless things,
>   and became worthless themselves?
>
> ....
>
> I brought you into a plentiful land
>   to eat its fruits and its good things.
> But when you entered you defiled my land,
>   and made my heritage an abomination.[42]

As one of us and representing all humans, Jesus then effects the two-fold sacrifice that atones. First, Jesus agrees with the divine indictment, thereby creating a oneness of mind between God the Mother/Father and a human being. He says "Amen" to it, taking in fully the horror of what we have done to God, to our neighbors, and to ourselves. In this confession, Jesus overcomes the lying, denial, repression, self-justification, and blaming of others by which humans evade the truth. Further, identifying with the divine and human victims, he feels a complete remorse, a full sorrow for the sins of the human community across time and place of which he counts himself a member.

Then on our behalf, he makes the second atoning sacrifice. He commits to a different kind of relationship with all the victims in the future—God and his neighbors. As we have seen, he lives a life of integrity and hospitality, actualizing a form of human being that not only makes promises, but keeps them. As the New Being, Jesus lives out of the power of humanity's future existence, not out of the demonically-binding power of its past.

Does God the Mother/Father need such a vicarious sacrifice in order to be reconciled to humanity? Advocates of the generative and

---

42. Jer 2:5, 7.

enlightenment models found in Part II deny this need for Jesus to give a sacrifice on our behalf, since sin does not cause God to be estranged from sinners. God's unconditional acceptance, love, and forgiveness are based in God's own decision to embrace us. They are thus continuously available; we just need to recognize that fact.

In contrast, the hospitality model imagines God and humankind within a covenant partnership in which acts of deception, betrayal, and violence create estrangement not only of humans from God, but of God from humans. The acceptance, love and forgiveness of God are indeed unconditional, rooted solely in God's decision to be God with and for us. But the effectiveness of God's gracious act of forgiveness depends upon the responsive, twofold self-giving of human beings back toward God in the forms of truth-telling and commitment and concrete action toward a new relationship based on fidelity and trust. Jesus fulfills this condition on our behalf, acting like a mountain guide who knows the terrain and who goes before us to obtain "the freedom of the glory of the children of God."[43]

In a third way—one counterintuitive for a metaphor like sacrifice, which makes us think of humans sacrificing to God—Jesus overcomes divine-human estrangement. Here, the problem is not that of human betrayal and self-defilement, but of human suffering and the experience of the absence of God. Where was God when the sons of Jacob fell upon the men of Shechem? Where was God when Kim Bok-dong was taken from her mother at fifteen through Japanese deception and coercion? Might not victims of human violation feel that God has betrayed them as well? Why should they trust God? And even the perpetrators—those who dirty themselves and who perhaps experience just but painful consequences of their sins—is it not possible that they, too, may feel God has abandoned them to their sin? Though the people of Judah knew their sins, they still cried out to God: "O hope of Israel, its savior in time of trouble, why should you be like a stranger in the land, like a traveler turning aside for the night?"[44]

In the midst of a polluted relational world, Jesus not only represents humans to God, but also God to humans. *In his divine nature, Jesus offers*

43. Rom 8:21. Jesus is the "pioneer and perfecter of our faith" (Heb 12:2). Jesus's twofold sacrifice is teleological in character, not done to placate God or fulfill retributive justice.

44. Jer 14:8. See verses 1–9.

a twofold self-offering to humanity. Like the prodigal father who looks for his lost son, God comes and tells again the truth of God's unconditional love for humanity through Christ's own lips and actions. God also moves toward a new form of relationship with humanity, one more costly and committed. In Christ, without ceasing to be God, God becomes one of the creatures, identifying the future fulfillment of God's own life with the creature's life. This act by God to literally take the creature's side, an act of concrete steps that correspond to God's renewed declaration of fathomless love, may move human beings from mistrust to trust in God.

Creating a form of humanity that does not betray others and close itself off from others; taking in the whole truth of our human acts of violation and the horrors that trail them; as God, becoming a human being in order to convey the unconditional love and mercy of God, and move mistrustful humans back toward trust in God: These are things we cannot do, or do not do. Christ does them for us, and for God.

Yet these three cleansing and reconciling accomplishments would be nullified without the resurrection. What good is it to know that God is here with us and for us, if God is defeated by acts of betrayal and violence, and is buried in a tomb? What good is a new form of humanity and a reconciled relation with God if the one person who accomplishes it is in the grave? Such an end simply confirms that entropy is the ultimate principle, not levity. There is no "different future," no matter how lofty Jesus's existence was for thirty-three years.

But the resurrection confirms that the God who takes our side is also the God of the future who will fulfill God's purpose of a new creation. The resurrection secures the everlasting existence of the New Being, and of the reconciled relation between human beings and the forgiving, cleansing God who brings us up out of the water, shining like suns.

THE HOLY SPIRIT'S ROLE IN SALVATION

In Jesus of Nazareth, the triune God actualizes the New Being, a form of humanity that gives the appropriate response to God's gracious invitation to fellowship. In him, faith, love, and hope come to fruition. Through his three accomplishments, he cleanses and reconciles defiled sinners to God. The status of all human beings is changed. Victims of violation are now, like Jesus, raised into new life, survivors; perpetrators and bystanders of violations are now forgiven sinners. All are adopted children of God the Mother/Father, and Christ's sisters and brothers.

Yet all of this is true "in him," in Jesus our forerunner and the first fruit of the new creation. It is real, and thus the Christian community need not replicate his three accomplishments. Which is good news, since it can't. "Here is the Lamb of God who takes away the sin of the world," John the Baptist declared upon seeing Jesus, and that is the gospel.[45] Yet the scope of the new creation must be spread, and thus the broad work of the living, risen Jesus and of the Holy Spirit is essential if we are to understand how communities and individuals come to participate in the new future opened by Christ.

The role of the Spirit in salvation is the same here as in the emancipation model. During his ministry, particularly at Gethsemane and Golgotha, Jesus is tempted to abandon his hospitality—to God the Mother/Father; to himself and his integrity; to the poor who are violated; and to the violators themselves. He is not able to retain his openness by his inner strength alone. He depends upon his constant companion, God the Holy Spirit, who guides and strengthens him.

The risen Jesus and the Spirit then act together to transfer the power to become gracious and thankful from Jesus to us. The transfer occurs through our participation in the new reality in Christ, rather than through imitation of his way of life. The Spirit connects the Christian community with its Lord and head, Jesus, and as branches connected to a vine, this connection enables the Church to participate in the new form of human being and human community.

Finally, the risen Christ and the Holy Spirit work broadly, throughout different historical periods and cultures, to enable groups and individuals to begin living in the new reality shaped by grace and gratitude, rather than the old aeon subjected to endless cycles of betrayals and mistrust.

The Spirit of truth is simultaneously the Spirit of love who moves estranged parties toward reconciliation. For perpetrators and beneficiaries of violence, the Spirit enables them to listen to the sound of fury and participate in Christ's twofold sacrifice. Under the Spirit's teachings, they tell the truth, and commit to a different way to live. The Spirit encourages victims to rise up, give voice to their own fury and claim their right to life. She also teaches the meaning of forgiveness, and opens the way for

45. John 1:29.

it. For both perpetrators and victims—and to the extent that we share elements of both—the Spirit teaches us to love our enemies, a fruit of the Spirit essential for the openness and hospitality found in the new community.[46] In the new form of community not based upon domination, the categories of "us" and "polluted, tainted, inferior other" are ended. Each person is both a survivor of horrors and a forgiven sinner. Each is now a brother or sister of Christ's, and part of a new form of kinship rooted not in ethnic, clan or class differences, but in mutual mercy and forgiveness.

OUR ROLE IN SALVATION

Under this same section in chapter 7, I described an encounter between William Wilberforce and John Newton from *Amazing Grace*. Wilberforce sought out the advice and aid of his former pastor before he began to oppose the slave trade in the mid-1780s. Newton resisted. Dressed like a penitent and mopping the church floor, Newton refused to tell Wilberforce about the 20,000 ghosts of dead slaves with whom he kept spiritual company.

In 1797, Wilberforce visits Newton again. Newton, now completely blind, sits dictating his account of his acts as a slave trader to a secretary. "This is my confession," he tells Wilberforce, picking up the written pages. "You must use it." Then, with emotion, he says these words: "I wish I could remember all their names. My twenty thousand ghosts. They all had names. Beautiful African names. We called them with just grunts. Noises. We were apes. They were human."

Newton lived to see the British Parliament abolish the slave trade.

What is the relation between our faith, repentance, and attempts to restore justice to those whom we have violated, and our own cleansing from defilement and reconciliation with God? One of the criticisms of the penal substitutionary theory of atonement is that it imagines a form of salvation that does not necessarily entail personal or social transformation. A similar charge is often given to the popularized version of the sacrifice model of atonement. Because of Christ's sacrifice, one can be cleansed and reconciled to God while never changing one's heart or behavior in relation to kyriarchal structures. One wonders if this is not

---

46. See Gal 5:22; Matt 5:43–48; Rom 12:17–21; Rom 8:26.

true of Newton who initially hides from the world's social problems and, when asked whether he has changed, says simply that he is older.

But the criticism is not true for the hospitality model. The triune God sends the Son into the world in order to transform it through inaugurating the New Being, the fulfillment of God's just world. Further, while the Son gives a vicarious sacrifice, his act is not a substitute for our own, but rather the basis and ground upon which we then can and must act. He acts as our representative, and because of that role, he pulls us into covenant obligations for our own acts of truth-telling and movement toward a different form of relationship with the 'other.'

With the risen Jesus—and his hospitable humanity—living inside us, and the reconciling Spirit also indwelling us, we are called by this duo to offer ourselves in self-giving. Moving from their power, we repair the relations of trust that we have broken. As betrayers, we tell God the truth, and take concrete steps to live out Christ's new way of hospitality. In these faith acts, we participate in Christ's twofold sacrifice to God. Further, we put aside our false selves, lies, self-justifications and the blaming of others, and commit ourselves to living with integrity. To those we have betrayed, we risk entering the triangular space between us, the space filled with our crimes and their effects. We risk telling the truth about what we have done, expressing our sorrow, committing ourselves to a different kind of relationship, and taking concrete steps to actualize it.

This is what John Newton does when he finally faces the truth of his acts, not simply with emotions, but with names and dates and acts described in narrative form. He tells the truth: all the Africans he hauled to the New World, all those who died on the Middle Passage, "They all had names. Beautiful African names." His contrition is exemplified in his wish that he could remember them all. He tells the truth: "We were apes. They were human." But he not only tells the truth; he also takes concrete steps to live a different kind of relationship to the ones he enslaved, to his former fellow slavers, to the beneficiaries of slavery. He writes down the facts of the slave trade and gives it to Wilberforce to use in overturning the system of slavery.

Briony Tallis also makes the atoning twofold sacrifice. That the act is risky is seen in her numerous thoughts of turning back as she walked to Cecilia's flat. But when she sees Robbie and Cecilia, she tells the truth, expresses her sorrow, and then takes concrete steps to try and undo the damage she has done. With Cecilia at least, she longs for a different relationship, missing their sisterly love and intimacy.

Victims of violation participate in Christ's twofold sacrifice by rising up and speaking the truth about what happened to them, as Kim Bok-dong did as the first Korean "comfort woman" to allow her name to be used publicly. Victims express "the sound of fury," and refuse to either treat the perpetrator as a victim, or objectify them as not human. They participate in Christ's sacrifice by demanding justice. Such justice may include retributive justice, but the larger framework is that of reconciliatory justice. They participate by entering the triangular space, engaging in confrontation and dialogue, and allowing Christ to open them to the possibility of giving the gift of forgiveness.

This gift of forgiveness and possible embrace of former victims and perpetrators is essential to God's cleansing and restorative act. For while God can forgive us for our betrayal of God, only our neighbor can forgive us for having broken trust with her or him.[47]

Perpetrators' unwillingness to tell the truth makes forgiveness by the victims and a new future impossible. At war's end and to the present day, for example, the Japanese government has denied the creation of institutionalized brothels with enslaved women. Can Kim Bok-dong trust the Japanese government, based upon this behavior?

Even when confession and contrition are offered, the second sacrificial act of commitment to new power structures is often insufficient to convince victims to trust victimizers when no concrete steps are taken. This is why acts of compensatory justice are necessary, for the attempt to undo the damage of one's violent acts—particularly if it is costly to oneself—makes the "I'm sorry's" and commitment to a different form of relating much more believable. For example, in 1953, West Germany paid Israel 3.45 billion Deutsch Marks as reparations for the persecution, pillaging and murder of the Jews during the Holocaust. Can such money

---

47. Miroslav Volf writes: "[D]ivine forgiveness cannot substitute for a victim's giving and a perpetrator's receiving of forgiveness. If it could, it would make nonsense of Jesus' command that persons who remembered that their brother or sister had something against them go and be reconciled to them before offering their gifts at the altar (Matt 5:23–24). Reconciliation with one's estranged neighbors is part and parcel of reconciliation with God. The divine embrace of both the victim and perpetrator has, in a sense, not come to completion without their own embrace" (Volf, "Love Your Heavenly Enemy," 96.)

bring back the dead? No. But it signals to the Jewish people Germany's sincerity in its sorrow and commitment to be a transformed people.

A serious attempt to undo the damage of the past signals that the perpetrator wishes more than just co-existence; she or he wants a future together with the one betrayed.

SACRIFICE AS AN ACT AND A WAY OF LIFE

Jesus alone as savior creates the New Being. He alone cleanses and reconciles all things. The Christian participates in his twofold atoning act through the downward movement of renunciation and the upward movement of claiming the new form of humanity for oneself that occurs in baptism. Yet as John Newton reveals, baptismal participation in Christ's twofold act inaugurates a journey for the Christian in which one slowly and painfully learns how to live accepting and giving grace, feeling thankful, and remaining open. We do the hard work of finding the names we have forgotten, or never bothered to learn—whether they are names of our neighbors, or our own name.

FORGIVING GOD

There is one more way we participate in Jesus's sacrificial act. As we have seen, surprisingly, Jesus gives a twofold sacrifice on behalf of the triune God toward humans, communicating God's unconditional love to the victims of human violence who feel godforsaken. God binds God's fate with our fate, becoming a human being.

We participate in God's twofold atoning risk by forgiving God, and beginning again a relation of mutual trust.

9

Jesus, the Just One

Divine Justice

THE VINEYARD OF THE LORD OF HOSTS

And now I will tell you
 what I will do to my vineyard.
I will remove its hedge,
 and it shall be devoured;
I will break down its wall,
 and it shall be trampled down.
I will make it a waste;
 it shall not be pruned or hoed,
 and it shall be overgrown with briers and thorns . . .
For the vineyard of the LORD of hosts
 is the house of Israel,
and the people of Judah
 are his pleasant planting;
he expected justice,
 but saw bloodshed;
righteousness,
 but heard a cry!
Ah, you who join house to house,
 who add field to field,
until there is room for no one but you,
 and you are left to live alone in the midst of the land!
The Lord of hosts has sworn in my hearing:
Surely many houses shall be desolate,
 large and beautiful houses, without inhabitant.
For ten acres of vineyard shall yield but one bath,
 and a homer of seed shall yield a mere ephah.[1]

---

1. Isa 5:5–10.

THE PARABLE OF THE WICKED TENANTS
OF THE VINEYARD

[Jesus] began to tell the people this parable: "A man planted a vineyard, and leased it to tenants, and went to another country for a long time. When the season came, he sent a slave to the tenants in order that they might give him his share of the produce of the vineyard; but the tenants beat him and sent him away empty-handed. Next he sent another slave; that one also they beat and insulted and sent away empty-handed. And he sent still a third; this one also they wounded and threw out. Then the owner of the vineyard said, 'What shall I do? I will send my beloved son; perhaps they will respect him.' But when the tenants saw him, they discussed it among themselves and said, 'This is the heir; let us kill him so that the inheritance may be ours.' So they threw him out of the vineyard and killed him. What then will the owner of the vineyard do to them? He will come and destroy those tenants and give the vineyard to others." When [the chief priests, scribes and elders] heard this, they said, "Heaven forbid!" But he looked at them and said, "What then does this text mean:

> 'The stone that the builders rejected
> has become the cornerstone'?

Everyone who falls on that stone will be broken to pieces; and it will crush anyone on whom it falls." When the scribes and chief priests realized that he had told this parable against them, they wanted to lay hands on him at that very hour, but they feared the people.[2]

TALAAT PASHA AND THE ARMENIAN GENOCIDE

I asked no privileges for them, but simple justice
between man and man.[3]

The Armenian people are the oldest ethnic group in Anatolia, the region of East Turkey and Southern Russia. They were early converts to Christianity.

---

2. Luke 20:9–19.

3. Lord Salisbury confronting the Ottoman ambassador in 1896, quoted in Balakian, *Burning Tigris*, 53, 57.

In the nineteenth century, in contrast to Turkish households, the Ottoman Empire would "double-tax" the Armenian households. The government allowed the Kurds or Turks of the region to collect the taxes, and every year, two sets of collectors would come by. The Kurds—an ethnic group that functioned as mercenary soldiers of the Turks—would billet their troops in Armenian homes during the winter: raping the women, eating the food, taking what they wanted. Armenians were not allowed to become citizens in the Empire, though they predated its existence.

The first phase of the massacres began in the 1870s until the 1890s. Turks killed roughly two hundred thousand Armenians. The killings were in response to Armenian attempts to gain government approval of state protection for themselves from abuse—difficult to obtain, seeing that it was the government that was committing the persecution.

From 1915 to 1922, however, a "final solution" to the "Armenian question" was drafted and executed. Tens of thousands of Kurds and Turks took part in these killings. Many of Hitler's ideas for techniques on genocide came from the Ottoman killings.

During a secret party meeting in late 1914 or early 1915, the Turkish government drew up a blueprint for its Armenian extermination operation. One page was headed, "Documents Relating to Comite Union and Progress Organization in the Armenian Massacres," and subtitled, "The 10 Commandments."

1. [C]lose all Armenian Societies, and arrest all who worked against Government at any time among them and send them into the provinces such as Bagdad or Mosul, and wipe them out either on the road or there.

2. Collect arms.

3. Excite Moslem opinion by suitable and special means, in places as Van, Erzeroum, Adana, where as a point of fact the Armenians have already won the hatred of the Moslems, provoke organised massacres as the Russians did at Baku.

4. Leave all executive to the people in the provinces such as Erezeroum, Van, [etc.], and use Military disciplinary forces ostensibly to stop massacres, while on the contrary in places as Adana, Sivas, Broussa, Ismidt and Smyrna actively help the Moslems with military force.

5. Apply measures to exterminate all males under 50, priests and teachers, leave girls and children to be Islamized.

6. Carry away the families of all who succeed in escaping and apply measures to cut them off from all connection with their native place.

7. On the ground that Armenian officials may be spies, expel and drive them out absolutely from every Government department or post.

8. Kill off in an appropriate manner all Armenians in the Army—this to be left to the military to do.

9. All action to begin everywhere simultaneously, and thus leave no time for preparation of defensive measures.

10. Pay attention to the strictly confidential nature of these instructions, which may not go beyond two or three persons.[4]

The main motive of the murderous Turks and Kurds was envy. In every city, town, and village a significant part of the Armenian population was financially stable. They were disproportionately successful in small business and trade. They were artisans, craftsmen, teachers, clergy, physicians, and farmers. They were the academic elite throughout the Empire. Whether modest or affluent, Armenian homes were often furnished with art, carpets, and European furniture. When Armenian families were being forced from their homes, Turkish women and men would seek bargains, buying organs, sewing machines, furniture, and rugs for almost nothing. "The scene reminded me of vultures swooping down on their prey," wrote Leslie Davis, the American consul in Harput, who witnessed the pillaging. "It was a veritable Turkish holiday and all the Turks went out in their gala attire to feast and to make merry over the misfortunes of others."[5] When American consul Jesse Jackson in Aleppo sent his associate Auguste Bernau to surrounding villages, Bernau found concentration camps in which the Armenians were naked, starving, robbed of everything, and "penned up in the open like cattle." "I thought I was passing through a part of hell . . . everywhere it is the same Governmental

---

4. Ibid., 189–90.
5. Ibid., 234. See 233–36.

barbarism which aims at the systematic annihilation through starvation of the survivors of the Armenian nation in Turkey."[6]

By the end of 1922, between 1.2 and 1.3 million of the more than two million Armenians living on their historical homeland had been annihilated.[7]

Economically, it was a self-destructive act. No one was left to till the soil, leading to famine. Nearly all the merchants, bankers, doctors, dentists, lawyers, teachers, carpenters, tailors, and other artisans were Armenians. "By one stroke," Davis wrote, "the country was to be set back a century." It didn't matter. When Ambassador Henry Morgenthau argued with Talaat Pasha, the Minister of the Interior and chief director of the genocide, Talaat got angry.

"Yes, we may make mistakes, but we never regret. I have accomplished more toward solving the Armenian problem in three months than Abdul Hamid accomplished in thirty years!"[8]

DOWNWARD SPIRALS OF VIOLENCE

Each of the three vignettes above describes acts of escalating human violence. In each case, the violence of one faction upon another was fueled by a combination of envy, avarice, and hatred of the 'other.' In each case, the groups of perpetrators knew they were courting danger, overstepping boundaries of civility and justice, but they did not care enough to stop. Their acts had an apocalyptic element, as the destruction of the 'other' seemed to diminish their own possibilities for life.

If God is to save, God must restore justice. I term this model *the divine justice model of salvation.*

THE PROBLEM WITHIN THE HUMAN CONDITION

In the 1090s, St. Anselm developed a theory of the atonement that contrasted sharply with the "Christ the Victor" theory and its subset, the "Ransom" theory.[9] His theory, called the "satisfaction" theory of atone-

6. Ibid., 261–62.

7. Ibid., 195–96.

8. Ibid., 274–75. Abdul Hamid II was sultan over the Ottoman Empire from 1876 to 1908. Between 1894 and 1896, he was responsible for the massacre of 200,000 Armenians.

9. See Anselm, *St. Anselm, Cur Deus Homo* (*Why God Became Man*).

ment, has often been misconstrued. In this misinterpretation, sin as the breaking of a covenant promise is perceived as creating a problem for God primarily because it insults God's dignity as sovereign Lord. The problem is the besmirching of God's honor, for God takes the betrayal as a personal affront. God is angry about this, and this "God of justice" needs the humiliation or blood of the perpetrator before God will pardon the insult.

No doubt, there is an element of the dishonoring of God in the three stories above. The LORD of Hosts takes it personally that the houses of Israel and Judah commit bloodshed and oppress the poor. In Jesus's parable, certainly the vineyard owner's authority is mocked by the tenants who rough up or kill all persons the owner sends on his behalf. And God the creator of all human beings is surely mocked by the tens of thousands of Turks and Kurds who murdered the Armenians in the most brutal of fashions with impunity. In contrast to such brazen behavior, the Bible announces, "God is not mocked."[10]

While there is an element of disdain for God in the vignettes, for Anselm, the main problem created by human murder and betrayal is not the tainting of God's honor. It is the breaking of a covenant. As did the Old Testament authors, Anselm understood the divine-human relationship according to a covenantal framework. As we saw in the hospitality model of the previous chapter, the breaking of promises ruptures mutual relations of trust, setting those relations into a downward spiral of mistrust and further betrayal. The downward spiral of violence and betrayal does not threaten God's honor: God's being as holy and just cannot be altered. Rather, as the world discovered in the Balkans during the 1990s and Rwanda in 1994, the transgression of boundaries of civility threatens the order and beauty of the good creation. Like Yahweh confronting the bloodshed and thievery of Israel, what angers God is the threat to the world God loves.

God is the upholder of the universal order in creation—the order of justice, of human rights and obligations without which society would collapse. God cannot simply overlook breaches of the universal law of human rights, or the universe is shown to be an unjust, violent, and irrational place, and God to be "no God," a weak and inconsequential being.

---

10. Gal 6:7.

Further, the perpetrators of such serious breaches of the moral law are powerless to put such order right again. They are unable to return the world to its previous balance. Once the three slaves are brutalized and the beloved son is dead, what are the tenants to say when the owner comes? Once one half to two-thirds of the Armenians—a people with whom the Kurds and Turks have lived for over a thousand years—are dead and shoved in mass graves, what is to be done when the descendants of these Armenians, or the God who is their maker, return?

In *Collapse: How Societies Choose to Fail or Succeed*, Jared Diamond describes a similar crossing of a threshold. Social acts begun in freedom take on a life of their own, creating self-moving dynamics which overtake the agents and lead to their destruction. The Polynesian culture of Easter Island, for example, was thriving in its earliest stages. However, the various clans began to compete with one another in erecting huge stone statues to the gods. Such elaborate constructions displayed the potency of a clan, and so there were escalating attempts to "out-do" one another in the size of statues erected.

To transport and erect such large stones carved at the quarries, the Islanders dragged the statues across sometimes mile-long wooden ladders. The Islanders needed logs. In their acts of escalating bravado, the Islanders deforested their island. The consequences were catastrophic, for the loss of trees disrupted the ecosystem to such an extend that the Islanders lost first wild-caught foods, then the high yields of their own crops. As the generations progressed, the eventual consequences were starvation, a population crash, and a descent into cannibalism. The few who survived recorded their state in small statues depicting starving people with hollow cheeks and protruding ribs. When Captain Cook visited in 1774, he described the Islanders as "small, lean, timid, and miserable."[11]

Jared Diamond often asked himself, "What did the Easter Islander who cut down the last palm tree say while he was doing it?" They overexploited their natural resources, Diamond concluded, through failing to perceive what was occurring or to anticipate its impact. What Diamond calls "rational bad behavior" also contributed. Cutting the trees to erect a statue brings immediate benefit to that clan, while the loss is spread out over all the clans. Disastrous values sealed the downward spiral. The

---

11. Diamond, *Collapse*, 109. See 108–9, and chap. 2 on the case of Easter Island.

clans valued status achievement and competition over more cooperative or benign ways of defining one's group identity.[12]

God's primary problem is not that God is personally affronted by human transgression (though this is true). God's main problem is finding a way to objectively "right" the balance of the social order (along with its impact upon the natural world). God is unwilling to let the humans destroy themselves and the world.

THE MEANING OF SALVATION

Salvation is the restoration of order, and thus of beauty and fecundity. It is the establishment of *shalom*, of peace that entails moral righteousness and justice in human relations and the humane treatment of the other creatures. People of differing ethnic groups—in Rwanda, the Balkans, Anatolia—live together in peace as neighbors. Instead of the rapacious grabbing of real estate and personal property, resources are distributed in such a way that each has a sufficient amount to live and thrive. They plant their small vineyard, and enjoy its fruits.[13]

THE COMING OF SALVATION

For Anselm, the disintegrating social situation in the created order presents God with a choice. The framework of universal obligations has been broken. Justice demands the satisfaction of God's demands that the world order be set right. God can set the framework right either by punishing the sin of the transgressors,[14] or through satisfaction from some other source.[15] Anselm's entire point concerning the grace of God is that God chooses to "set right" the moral order of the universe by the latter route rather than by punishment. Since, as we have seen, the humans

---

12. See ibid., chap. 14: "Why Do Some Societies Make Disastrous Decisions?"

13. Jer 31:5.

14. A penalty—a placement of suffering upon the perpetrators—that compensates for the suffering caused, as we saw in the penal substitutionary theory in chapter 1.

15. Surprisingly, Stott gives one phrase in his argument for the penal substitutionary theory in which he acknowledges there may be another way for God to effect justice. "For Yahweh is 'a consuming fire'. The fire of his anger was 'quenched', and so 'subsided' or 'ceased', only when the judgment was complete, *or when a radical regeneration had taken place, issuing in social justice*" (Stott, *Cross of Christ*, 125–26, italics mine). He then cites Jer 4:4; 21:12. On the next page (127), Stott then talks about the divine forbearance, showing that God does not always respond to transgression with retributive justice, as if punishment were a necessity.

who started the downward spiral of violence and betrayal are unable to "set it right," God acts on their behalf to do so. God's act in Jesus Christ is "the other source of satisfaction."[16]

For Anselm, God does not act to "satisfy" the divine justice by punishing the offenders, or even by punishing Jesus as a substitute. Satisfaction here is interpreted teleologically. "Satisfaction" means to fulfill the intended end of a project, to bring it to fruition. Within a covenantal framework, humans were created to make and keep promises; thus satisfaction refers to God's call to "satisfy" the requirements of relationship within a covenant (rather than the penal demands of a law code).

The triune God fulfills the divine justice by acting as the Just One. In this teleological justice, God ends the downward spiral and restores the right relations which heal the social and natural communities. This form of justice is compensatory and reconciling rather than retributive.

GOD'S ROLE IN SALVATION

What allows for a righting of the moral order other than through punishment is a change of behavior. Indeed, something even deeper than a mere change in outward action: a change in one's very heart, in the "basic act" or choice of values which sit at the foundation of one's emotional and spiritual life, one's free will and choice of actions. One begins not only to make promises, but to keep them, and to execute justice for all, particularly the weak and marginalized.[17]

But such a change in behavior, indeed of heart, is precisely what human beings cannot do. So God the Mother/Father sends to earth the Son, and the Holy Spirit as a companion and encourager for the Son. On behalf of humankind, the incarnate Son offers to God the Mother/Father something to compensate for what human creation has failed to offer. The Son offers the end of the old way of living as a human, rooted in moral breach and traitorous violence, and the beginning of the new way of living as a human, as one who is faithful and just, re-establishing the moral order. Jesus of Nazareth objectively rights the balance of the world, re-creating its beauty.

16. On this key element of Anselm's theory, see Gunton, *Actuality of the Atonement*, 90–91.

17. On God desiring *metanoia* rather than punishment, see, for example, Jer 4:3–4; 21:12.

Instead of the expected use of sheer might, however, he does so from within the breached moral order, and in counter-intuitive ways.

JESUS'S ROLE IN SALVATION

A will cannot be free *to choose evil—*
for in the very act it forfeits its freedom,
and so becomes a corrupt Nature, self-enslaved.[18]

Like the emancipation and hospitality models, the justice model assumes Paul's anthropological and soteriological vision that all human beings find their identity "in Christ."[19] Initially, the justice model borrows from the emancipation and especially the hospitality models for its content. In breaching our moral obligations to our neighbors and to God, we have submitted to the temptations of the demonic, and become enslaved to them, and are thus unable to return to the good. As our representative, the incarnate Son satisfies the obligations of our covenant with God, setting the covenant right, by offering something to God the Mother/Father to compensate for our transgressions. Jesus offers the truth-telling and movement toward a new form of relating with God and with other humans and creatures.

While Anselm acknowledged the free obedience of Jesus to God during his life as a part of what he offers to God, he focused upon the value of a death given freely. Seeing the problems of this death-oriented model which seems to reinforce the myth of redemptive death and violence, I argue that the weight of the gift should be shifted to his fidelity during his lifetime, including his last moments. As David Bentley Hart suggests, perhaps Anselm agreed:

> [F]or Anselm it is not Christ's *suffering* as such that is redemptive (the suffering merely repeats sin's endlessly repeated and essential gesture), but rather his innocence; he recapitulates humanity by passing through all the violence of sin and death, rendering to God the obedience that is [God's] due, and so transforms the event of his death into an occasion of infinite blessings for those to whom death is condign. Christ's death does not even effect a change in God's attitude toward humanity; God's attitude never

18. Coleridge, quoted in Gunton, *Actuality of the Atonement*, 84.
19. See Parfit, *Reasons and Persons*, esp. part 3.

alters: [God] desires the salvation of [God's] creatures, and will not abandon them even to their own cruelties.[20]

God the Mother/Father graciously accepts Christ's gift of fidelity on behalf of the offender, humankind, thus restoring the covenant relations and the flow of rights and obligations.[21] Christ's participation in the movement of donation and redonation with God the Mother/Father reflects the movement of grace and gratitude found within the triune God's own inner life, thus restoring in humanity the beauty that reflects God's beauty.

We are included within Jesus's offer of an infinite sorrow and a new way of life. Yet the justice model also describes us as being included in a different and deeper direction which Jesus traverses. This view of Jesus's journey borrows from the apocalyptic and eschatological perceptions of the Bible. As we saw in the emancipation model, in his person and his public ministry, Jesus inaugurates the coming "Day of the Lord's Wrath." As the figure who brings this day, in Jesus two conflicting histories meet: the *apocalyptic history* of human betrayal, violence, and self-annihilation and the divine "No" against that self-destruction; and the *eschatological history* of the new divine act by which God graciously reconstitutes human life. In the long-awaited Messiah, these histories definitively meet: the judgment and end of the world; and the "standing up" of the One with integrity, the One filled with the Spirit of new life and righteousness. Throughout his entire narrative, Jesus exhibits both the end of the sinful "flesh" in apocalyptic sufferings, and the "breath of the resurrection."[22]

The apocalyptic and eschatological movements begin their histories with the incarnation, life and public ministry of Jesus. The breath of the resurrection is evident in his new way of being. He is filled with joy and the love of life, with fidelity and trust, and with integrity. From the beginning and comprehensively, he is the human being filled with the Spirit of life and new life.[23] Yet from the beginning, the presence of

---

20. Hart, *Beauty of the Infinite*, 371 (inclusive language changes are mine); see also ibid., 367.

21. On Jesus giving a representative offering and achieving a definitive reconciliation, see Rae, "A Remnant People"; and Hart, *Beauty of the Infinite*, 360–72.

22. This theme of the simultaneous occurrence of apocalyptic and eschatological histories in Jesus is found in the works of Reformed theologians Barth, Moltmann, Welker, and Hall, as well as New Testament scholar N. T. Wright.

23. "In retrospect the evangelists took care to show that the 'breath of the resurrection' (J. A. Bengel) filled and penetrated the life, words and acts of Jesus even before

the new life in him must struggle with the opposition, and consequent painfulness, of sinful humanity. He is misunderstood, mistrusted, and dismissed. He is called an agent of Satan, one filled with the demonic, or just plain crazy. He is tempted to abandon his way. As the Messiah, he opposes kyriarchal forces, and quickly earns their suspicion. Ultimately, what little success he has in drawing people to repent of their old ways of the flesh and to accept an alternate basis for life in the Spirit comes to naught in the last days of his life.

More than any of the other models in Part III, the cross takes the central place in the justice model of salvation. The confrontation of the old and new aeons—the self-destruction and divine judgment of human history, and the reconstitution of humanity on a new, divine basis—while present throughout Jesus's life reaches an intensity during his last week. For the perpetrators of violence—for Judah who uses bloodshed and thievery to steal from the poor; for the wicked tenants who abuse the owner's slaves and even his beloved son; for the Turks and Kurds, the executioners and beneficiaries of genocidal madness—Jesus's last week brings the trajectory of sinful human choices to their inevitable end: tragic and all-encompassing destruction. This fact appears only after Jesus returns, in light of the resurrection. On Good Friday and Holy Saturday, the beneficiaries of kyriarchy thought only that they had dodged a threat and safely eliminated a mere rabble-rouser who could cause trouble. Bystanders either agreed with this assessment, or acknowledged sadly and with cynicism the death of another prophetic Rabbi, or were indifferent altogether. But after the resurrection of Jesus from the dead, it becomes clear what has occurred in the last few days. Human beings who deceive themselves and others that in their betrayals and violence they only want to take a few things, and those theirs by right; that they only want to get rid of a few troublesome groups of people, again by right, find that the evil that runs in their individual and collective hearts runs much deeper than this. Like the tenants, they are ready to murder the only whole human being who has existed, God's beloved son, if that "new human being" gets in the way of their interests.

His resurrection, and that from the earliest beginnings the quickening and coming to life of the flesh were in full train. The resurrection of Jesus adds nothing new to what happened from the beginning. It only crowns this event as its disclosure and revelation" (Barth, *Church Dogmatics* III/2, 336–37).

They are ready as well to do a novum in history—to murder God, if God gets in their way.

In these quickly-fluctuating and oppositional encounters between Jesus and human beings during his final week, evil is taken to its logical end and made explicit and undeniable. We are humans ready to kill our neighbor, ready to kill God, in order to inherit that which does not belong to us, and that which it is not ontologically possible for us to possess. And in killing the new human being and God, who is the very ground and meaning of all created life, the human pretension that we are in fact building up life and bringing about glory for humanity is torn asunder. As with Talaat Pasha and the Easter Islanders, our cries of greatness are exposed for what they are—ejaculations of madness that can no longer hide the suicidal bass note in our entire enterprise of homicide and deicide. We are the ones cutting down the last palm tree and calling it a great and necessary moment. We are the ones who will soon be starving, diminished, timid, cannibalistic, and miserable.[24]

How does Jesus bring treacherous human history to its apocalyptic end? He does not use armies or violence. Significantly, he does not create a faction, a zealous and righteous faction that sees its role as exposing and destroying the unrighteous. He brings history to an end in an unexpected but definitive way. Paradoxically, as Emmanuel and as the new human being, *Jesus judges human sin precisely by refusing to judge*. In his silence during his interrogations and last moments, Jesus refuses to participate in the core human sin—the presumptuous move by humans to judge other groups, or judge the self, as "unworthy" and thus as candidates for being cast off permanently, like Talaat Pasha "finishing the job" of exterminating the Armenians.

In Jesus as the messianic bearer of the Spirit of righteousness, Jesus brings together justice, mercy, and the knowledge of God. He expects judicial equity; but he also expects the application of mercy in a socially established pattern, so that the weaker members of society are protected: strangers, the poor, those with neither influence nor power. Mercy—the act of going to meet those who are weaker, the suffering, and

24. The cross as the revelation of the cataclysmic end of our apocalyptic history of sin—as homicide, deicide and suicide—is a central argument of Barth's soteriology. See *Church Dogmatics,* IV/1, 231–35; 289–96. It is also found in René Girard's theory of scapegoating and mimetic violence. Further, it is found in African American theologians such as James Cone and Matthew Johnson. For the latter, see Johnson, "Lord of the Crucified," esp. 7–8.

the disadvantaged—is the mark of his justice, and of God's justice.[25] The law of mercy prevents the perversion of justice by humans who want to differentiate and discriminate against persons.

Jesus establishes the reign of God and its inbreaking fulfillment of justice. He creates a sphere of power in which humans can enter. Yet he does so while telling exorcised demons or those healed not to make him known, as one who will "not make his voice heard in the street."[26] He calls for and keeps silence to prevent his identity from being known too soon and defined in too narrow a fashion.[27] He embodies a superior power, one able to displace the demonic, because he is a person and a power who claims nothing for himself. He does not seek to be a hero, or a success story. He sets up no "faction," no power apparatus that can then be used by sinful humans in a process of institutionalization. His power, the power of the Spirit, thus cannot be controlled by sinful humans and can move into the most concrete of situations to heal and to empower resistance to the demonic.[28]

In similar fashion to his use of this method during his public ministry, during his last week, Jesus refuses to bring attention to himself, to make himself central, a heroic figure. He consciously claims for himself no recognizable forms of political power, rule, or success. If he were to speak up in defense of himself, or by taking sides with one or another human group in the fractious sociopolitical battles of first-century Palestine, he would have drawn to himself opposition from some groups. But others would have claimed him as supporting their cause, and used him in their battles of hatred against other factions. Instead, he stays silent. He refuses to join the Zealots, the Essenes, the Pharisees, or the Sadducees.

Through his silence, his unwillingness to join any group, he brings about a convergence of unanimity amongst the many factions. They all hate him. They all agree he is despicable in his weakness. They share a negative, aggressive, and scornful relationship to this one suffering man. He is not what any of them expected in a Messiah, a religious or political leader.

---

25. See Isa 42:1, 6–8; and Welker, *God the Spirit*, 108–24.

26. See Matt 12:16; Luke 4:41; Isaiah 42.

27. See Welker, *God the Spirit*, 203–11.

28. See ibid., 211–27.

Ironically, it is precisely his mercy that establishes the true justice of God and acts to judge those who judge him. He refuses to solidify his individual or his "group's" well-being through casting others out. He refuses to act as all fallen humans do—taking upon themselves the ability to decide the meanings of "justice" and "mercy," and using those self-adjudicated definitions to determine who is expendable and to justify attempts at self-protection and aggrandizement through violence. He recognizes only God as the one who can judge, who can determine the meanings in any given context of "justice" and "mercy."[29] Precisely as the one with whom all groups refuse to be associated, yet the one who turns out to be God, Jesus judges human ignorance and arrogance definitively. We do not want anything to do with God's justice or God's mercy.

For the godless, the cross brings human evil to its apocalyptic end. For the godforsaken, the victims, the final week brings God into the utmost solidarity. The second person of the Trinity becomes a "non-person" and dies the death of a cursed-one, descending into hell. Because of that act, something new occurs—the "godforsaken" now find God beside them, as their friend and advocate. For all those caught in the destructive machinations of human apocalyptic history, they now find that God has tied God's history with theirs. The Just One stands beside them as their brother and advocate, clarifying their status as truly human and as beloved ones of God.[30]

As we have found in the previous two models, so with the justice model, the resurrection of Jesus from the dead is essential for salvation, for Jesus's establishment of justice would be impossible without it. The resurrection of Jesus is essential, for in his return he acts to bring together all three parties in the moral covenant: the godless, the godforsaken, and God. No salvation is possible for one party without the others, and thus Jesus must effect the coming-together of all.

At the resurrection, the crucified yet living, risen Jesus returns with the victims to the perpetrators and together, Jesus and the victims confront the violators with their crimes. In light of God's vindication of him in the resurrection and his identity as God incarnate, Jesus's crucifixion

---

29. See ibid., 124–34.

30. This theme of divine solidarity with the victims of violence is one shared by theologians of the cross like Luther, Bonhoeffer, Moltmann, Hall, and Alan Lewis, as well as African American and womanist theologians like Cone, Johnson, Noel, Terrell, Grant, and Douglas.

is revealed to all of us who sin as the apocalyptic end of all our ways—as homocide, deicide and suicide. Jesus confronts us with this truth. He also confronts us with his, and God's, mercy. He will not cast us off, despite the sins we have perpetrated. By inviting us to join the sphere of the Spirit's power in which justice, mercy and the knowledge of God are integrated, Jesus reveals to us as sinners that there is no evil we might commit that is beyond the reach of God's forgiveness.[31]

For the victims, the resurrection also means the vindication of their rightful claims to life. The history of the new life, begun in Jesus's person and work, grows and cannot be squelched. The victims' experiences of apocalypse are shown to be penultimate. There is no evil we might endure that is beyond the reach of God's healing.[32]

THE HOLY SPIRIT'S ROLE IN SALVATION

Since the justice that Jesus the Just One establishes is not retributive but compensatory, reconciling and teleological, it cannot be concluded without our free participation in it. The Holy Spirit opens our eyes and moves us to accept the truth that we share in the trajectories of both human histories, which find their opposition and convergence in Jesus's life. For us as victims, the Spirit shows us a truth hidden and imponderable: the God who seemed to have abandoned us is, in fact, our companion. Jesus is beside us as victim of apocalyptic history, and thus we are no longer alone in it. The Spirit also shows that life, healing and justice are the final word, seen in the eschatological history begun in Jesus's birth and coming to fullness at the resurrection of Jesus from the dead.

For us as perpetrators, the Spirit shows us that despite our claims to right understandings of justice, of mercy, and of God, we in fact are frauds who do not do justice, love mercy, and walk humbly with our God. We kill God when we get the chance, and bend the cult, definitions of who is deserving of mercy, and the nature of justice to our own circumscribed collective or individual interests. The Spirit is not nice in showing us these things, but is loving and salvific. Further, when bringing us into the conversational space with the crucified and risen Jesus, the Spirit shows us that Jesus is not against us but for us. She reveals that,

31. See Williams, *Resurrection*, esp. chap. 1.

32. The resurrection as the basis for hope for victims of apocalypse is a common theme, shared again by theologians of the cross such as Moltmann and Hall, and African American and Womanist theologians like Cone, Grant, Johnson and Noel.

as with Paul, Jesus invites us to join the sphere of his power in which justice, routinized mercy, and an open and broad knowledge of God are interconnected.

OUR ROLE IN SALVATION

Our role in salvation is to allow ourselves to be confronted by Jesus, as well as by those we have harmed and those who have harmed us. This is extremely painful and threatening, but also the only route to liberation and the restoration of patterns of moral order within covenants. Our role is to accept baptism, to recognize in ourselves the old human history of violence which will lead to doom for all. It is also to recognize in Christ ourselves again, our identity in its ultimate form. He has established justice, the justice always tied to mercy and awaiting God's presence and guidance. We are to recognize the one we initially despised as being of no account as the one who alone is righteous, a human being of God.

Baptism initiates our presence in the sphere of power by which the divine Spirit spreads the new community based upon justice, the law of mercy, and knowledge of God. On the basis of the forgiveness of sins and the establishment of God's reign of righteousness, we live out of this new type of community in which everyone shares an identity rooted in Jesus, the rejected but just one. We cease to use forms of judgment rooted in our attempts to stabilize ourselves or our group by casting out others. Instead, we realize we all share two common histories: the one in which we all participate in self-destructive acts of violence, bringing us to the abyss; and the one in which the Spirit of new life fills all things.

10

Jesus, the Power of Reorienting Grace

Reorientation

All the natural *movements of the soul are controlled
by laws analogous to those of physical gravity.
Grace is the only exception.*[1]

MRS. TURPIN

RUBY TURPIN, THE PROTAGONIST in Flannery O'Connor's "Revelation," has the habit of summarily judging and classifying people based on how they look, how they talk, and the color of their skin. In the opening scene, Mrs. Turpin is sitting in a doctor's waiting room, considering the other people waiting with her. She primarily and succinctly classifies them by the shoes they wear. Across from her sits an overweight teenage girl, wearing Girl Scout shoes and reading the book *Human Development*. There is a mother in bedroom slippers, fitting Ruby's preconceived expectations of someone she considers "white trash." A well-dressed woman waits with suede shoes that match her outfit. She is a "lady" Mrs. Turpin considers her peer.

Placing people in their allotted social class in relationship to herself is an activity that often occupies Mrs. Turpin's imagination. The story's narrator explains:

> Sometimes at night when she couldn't go to sleep, Mrs. Turpin would occupy herself with the question of who she would have chosen to be if she couldn't have been herself. If Jesus had said to her before he made her, "There's only two places available for you. You can either be a nigger or white-trash," what would she

1. Weil, *Gravity and Grace*, 1.

have said? "Please, Jesus, please," she would have said, "just let me wait until there's another place available," and he would have said, "No, you have to go right now and I have only those two places so make up your mind." She would have wiggled and squirmed and begged and pleaded but it would have been no use and finally she would have said, "All right, make me a nigger then—but that don't mean a trashy one." And he would have made her a neat clean respectable Negro woman, herself but black.[2]

In fact, Ruby Turpin had developed an entire imaginary ladder of worth, with herself and her husband stationed comfortably near the top. The narrator continues:

> Sometimes Mrs. Turpin occupied herself at night naming the classes of people. On the bottom of the heap were most colored people, not the kind she would have been if she had been one, but most of them; then next to them—not above, just away from—were the white-trash; then above them were the home-owners, and above them the home-and-land owners, to which she and her husband Claud belonged. Above she and Claud were people with a lot of money and much bigger houses and much more land. But here the complexity of it would begin to bear in on her, for some of the people with a lot of money were common and ought to be below she and Claud and some of the people who had good blood had lost their money and had to rent and then there were colored people who owned their homes and land as well.[3]

RAY CHARLES

Once again, he learned that when people said they wanted to "help him," it meant they wanted to stiff him.[4] It was 1949, Ray Charles was nineteen, and he had revived the prospects of the *Rocking Chair* jazz club in Seattle. When Jack Lauderdale from Swing Time Records approached him about making a record, his manager Marlene and band partner Gossie excluded him from the negotiations. That's when the suspicious Ray was tipped off that Marlene and Gossie were taking 35% of the profits off the top, and Gossie was getting paid twice what Ray was making.

---

2. O'Connor, "Revelation," in *Everything That Rises Must Converge*, 195–96.

3. Ibid., 195–96.

4. The following is from the movie *Ray*.

"You need watching out for," Gossie had pleaded, but Ray repeated his mother's motto—"Scratch a liar, catch a thief"—and walked out.

Ray had two recurring daydreams. In one, he was a boy of seven, just turning blind. He saw his mother Aretha looking at him: "Always remember your promise to me. Never let nobody or nothing turn you into no cripple." While he had been trusting as a child, he slowly learned to trust no one. Not after his father had never shown up. Not after his former band manager on salary day had counted out fives but handed him dollar bills. As his mother had said, "Ain't nothing free in this world 'cept Jesus." He would trust no one. And he would take care of himself, stand on his own two feet. He learned to depend upon his ears, on his musical abilities, on his wits.

And from 1950 to 1965, on his drugs. He was always left alone by his band members after the show. They didn't want to "babysit a cripple." Fathead and another band member were doing heroin, and finally Ray wanted that high, too. "Come on, Fathead. I want in." You don't want this, Ray, Fathead responded. "This ain't weed, Ray. It's the null and void." "Null and void, just like my life," Ray responded. "I'll be right at home." And so he began using heroin while on the road, and eventually on the few occasions he was at home as well.

He had another recurring dream that came both during the day and in his sleep. Ray was five or six, his younger brother George maybe four. Aretha was doing the wash, and the boys were running through the hanging sheets, playing tag. "I don't want to play no more," George said, and moved off in another direction. He climbed the table where his mother's large wash tub sat full of water. Playing, he tripped, fell backwards, and landed in the water. Ray first thought George was fooling around, then stared, frozen, when George thrashed, then lay silent. Seeing George's feet quiet in the tub, Aretha runs out, tries to revive him, then holds him tight. She looks at Ray: "Why didn't you do something? Why didn't you call me?" At the funeral, Ray watched his mom throw herself on the casket, beside herself with grief.

He was on the road constantly. He had affairs with his lead singers, first Mary Anne, then Margie. Person after person warned him to get off the heroin, but he refused each time. In 1965, he was arrested for possession. Out on bail and at home, he felt a craving just as he was getting in a fight with Della Bea, his wife of eleven years. As he moved toward the bathroom, she confronted him.

"No, Ray, no! A needle ain't gonna solve this!"

"Get out of the way! Move!"

"Only thing that can help you is God, Ray."

"Don't you talk about God! Do you have any idea how it feels to go blind and still be afraid of the dark? And every day, you sit there and pray for just a little light, and you get nothing, 'cause God don't listen to people like me."

"Stop talking like that."

"As far as I'm concerned, me and God is even and I do what I please. And Goddamn it, if I want to shoot up, I shoot up."

Della Bea threatens to take the boys and leave.

"You know I love you and those boys more than anything."

"No, that is a damn lie, and you know it!" She mentions the little league banquet Ray missed, though their son won most valuable player. He was too loaded. "No, there is something you love more than me and them boys, more than all the women you ever slept with on the road, more than all the dope you ever took. Your music. And if you don't stop using that needle, they're gonna take away your music and put you in jail. Is that poison worth losing everything?"

THE REORIENTING POWER OF GRACE

In each story above, persons or communities live in a world without grace. They do not treat each other graciously, hospitably. Further, perceiving the world through lenses lacking in grace, they see an ungracious world. They tell themselves stories—about who they are, about who other people are or should be, about the way the world works—that are devoid of generosity and hope.

If salvation is to come, it must accomplish two things. It must first actualize a world of grace. It must then give persons and communities new lenses by which to see both the world of ungrace in which they live, and God's inbreaking, alternate, and superior world of grace. Because of the power of grace to transform persons and communities, I term this *the reorientation model of salvation*.

This model shares the strengths of chapter 5's enlightenment model, while overcoming its weaknesses. Similarly, it takes the strengths of Peter Abelard's "act of love" model and recent Girardian theories of atonement, while leaving behind their fatal flaws which make them as dangerous as the penal substitutionary theory.

THE PROBLEM WITHIN THE HUMAN CONDITION

O momentary grace of mortal men,
Which we more hunt for than the grace of God.[5]

The enlightenment model of salvation says that humans live in a fantasy world that does not cohere with reality. Further, like Ray, we are blind to our own ignorance. The reorientation model identifies this same blindness in individuals and communities. Certainly Mrs. Turpin and her Southern white culture of the 1950s, and Ray Charles are living in mental worlds of their own making.

If the enlightenment and reorientation models agree on the problem, they disagree on the origin of the problem and on its solution. While admitting that we play a role in the creation of our own blindness, the enlightenment model places the weight of origin upon the things that happen to us: natural psychological development; our families of origin; corporate sin's influence upon us. Further, we are not dead in our blindness, needing to be resurrected by another; we are only sleeping. Jesus acts as light, as lamp to guide the way to the divine, as catalyst to arouse us. If we are shown what is real, we will embrace it because we long for it like we long for the home from which we are estranged. We are trying to find our way back, but have simply gotten lost.

Our lostness, however, is more complicated than that. We long for home, and we despise home. Like the prodigal son, we want it, and we are running away from it (see Luke 15).

That our blindness and violent behaviors cannot be attributed primarily to mistakes we make or outside forces such as economics is evidenced by the slaveholding practices of the Tupinamba in preconquest Brazil. Like many primitive slaveholding peoples, they had no economic need for slave labor. Food was abundant. Yet the males continuously warred on their neighbors, yielding large numbers of enslaved women, children, and men. The foreign slaves were constantly required to humble themselves and show respect to their conquerors. Finally, the

---

5. Shakespeare, *Richard III*, quoted in Yancey, *What's So Amazing about Grace?* 28.

slaves would be reviled, released only to be recaptured in a "hunt," killed, and eaten.

"This behavior dramatizes the point that, wholly apart from later economic functions, slaves from the very beginning were perceived as dehumanized humans—humans deprived of precisely those traits and faculties that are prerequisites for human dignity, respect, and honor. By a depraved but all too human logic, this freedom to degrade, dishonor, enslave, and even kill and eat gave the Tupinamba not only solidarity but a sense of superiority and transcendence—of rising above the constraints and material conditions of life."[6]

While acknowledging the roles of human development, family of origin, and corporate sin in shaping our blindness, the reorientation model shifts the weight of emphasis to our own role in the creation and maintenance of our delusions. Three main elements of the human condition create this more-negative portrayal of individual and social blindness.

First, the problem is not merely that we do not see the truth, *but that we also do not want to see the truth*, because we do not want to let go of our understandings of reality, any more than Mrs. Turpin wants to let go of her hierarchical arrangement of social classes, with herself near the top, or Ray Charles wants to let go of his mistaken notion that he is keeping his promise to his mother to stand on his own feet while he remains daily addicted to heroin. We do not want to see the truth because our desires toward it are divided. God is omnipresent, and God is gracious, as the enlightenment model argues. But as almost every biblical character and community reveals (as well as characters of most Western literature and autobiographies), the human will is divided in relation to such realities. We long for God . . . and we mistrust God as One whom we believe seeks to dominate or belittle us. We long for grace . . . and we either do not believe grace exists, or we mistrust it as well.[7]

Second, it is true that we are hard-hearted (Borg); captive to the 'three powers' of ego, possessions, and violence (Soelle); and often self-centered egotists incapable of love (Abelard). Yet a deeper and broader problem exists, of which hard-heartedness and self-centeredness and the will-to-power are but manifestations. Partly, we do not want to see the

6. Davis, *Inhuman Bondage*, 28–29.

7. For recent works on the divided will, see May, *Addiction and Grace*, esp. chaps. 3 and 5; and Farley, *Wounding and Healing of Desire*, esp. chaps. 3–5.

truth about reality—the world's or our own—because *we live in a world without grace.* This means both that the world is ungracious, and that we perceive the world as lacking grace.

We live from and toward others in a social flow of grace and gratitude. Yet we resist grace, for we look ahead and see 'an ungracious horizon.'[8] We see that our human love is limited. It is limited by time; people die. Or it is limited by separation or estrangement; people grow apart. The world of nature and oftentimes of society is indifferent to our love relationships, making us anxious. Ray and his brother George were just playing, and then in a moment's time George was dead. Seeing that our loves will be lost, we perceive a horizon of nothingness. "The null and void" reigns.

Or alternately, we perceive a horizon of guilt. Like Ray, who had constant affairs and used connections to drive his career, yet who cast off everyone who ever cared for him—his longtime manager and best friend Jeff; Mary Anne and then Margie, when she became pregnant with his child; his sons; his wife—we are guilty of betrayal, and it weighs on us. There is no escape. Our acts of betrayal come back at us like assaults from the dead, like Ray's flashbacks in which he falls into the bloody water flowing out of the wash tub, and remembers his mother's accusations: "Why didn't you do something?" Though we erect excuses as walls, we fear being found out and seen through—by other humans, or by God at the Last Judgment. The people we have sacrificed, forgotten, or used for our self-benefit will confront us face-to-face. We were not gracious to them, so why should we expect a gracious neighbor? Or a gracious God? Ray called out for a gracious God, but did not find one. "For all of us must appear before the judgment seat of Christ, so that each may receive recompense for what has been done in the body, whether good or evil," Paul writes (2 Cor 5:10). Despite the repressions and excuses, we know we are responsible for our hideous betrayals.

This perception of a horizon of guilt is illustrated by Josef in the movie *The Secret Life of Words.* Josef, forty-five, was burned attempting to save someone during a catastrophic fire on an oil rig off the coast of Ireland. Hanna comes to care for him for two weeks. Though burned and temporarily blinded, he flirts with Hanna. In their conversations, they both reveal something about their inner lives and pasts. One day Hanna

8. The term is Helmut Gollwitzer's; see Gollwitzer, *An Introduction to Protestant Theology,* 160.

asks Josef if he has read *Letters to a Portuguese Nun*. He responds that he gave it to someone once, a woman.

> "I know I shouldn't have, but I did."
>
> "Why?"
>
> "Because it was another man's wife. A man who loved her. And whom she loved. And who even I loved. There are certain things one should never do."
>
> "Like what?"
>
> "One should never fall in love with one's best friend's wife. And above all, one should never tell one's best friend."

Hanna tries to comfort him, but he turns his head away.

> "Hanna?"[9]
>
> "Yes?"
>
> " How does one live with what has happened? The consequences of it? How does one live with the dead?"
>
> "I don't know. You'll have to go on, I suppose. Everybody keeps on living for the future, somehow. Or not. There are those who don't make it through. A helicopter is coming to pick you up tomorrow or the day after."
>
> "Are you coming with me? Will you hold my hand? Help me look at myself again?"

A third element makes our relation to our blindness more dire: *we are outnumbered, and we have given up*. In place of our longings for a gracious neighbor and a gracious God, we have substituted longings fit for the world we perceive to be without grace. These reduced desires have become entangled with our mistrusting worldview, and the entanglement goes all the way to our core, either as individuals or as communities. One part of the will may want to leave the world without grace. But the other part of the will wants to stay, and that part joins the physiology and the mind and the spirit in resisting the attempt to leave. For example, the part of Ray Charles that wants to quit his drug addiction is always outnumbered by the parts of him that want to keep it intact. Further, the part of Ray's will that wants to leave only does so occasionally, episodically. But the parts of him that insist on keeping the

9. In the movie here, he calls her Cora, because she had initially told him this was her name.

object of addiction—his hormones and neurons; his consciousness and subconscious; his spirit—are at work all the time. This is further complicated because a person's sense of identity is connected to the object of addiction and the security that it provides. Ray is someone who can handle his addiction, he tells himself; yet simultaneously he needs it to get through the darkness in which he as been abandoned. The ungracious elements of our worlds—our own inner life and behaviors, the things that have happened to us or that people have done to us—are woven into the stories that we tell ourselves. Or the multiple stories. And societies tell such narratives about themselves as well.

The stories we corporately and individually tell ourselves include our perceptions of an ungracious horizon, and such stories frame our senses of ourselves and of the meaning of our lives and of the world. That is why, though a part of us still longs for grace, we resist attempts by others to take away the ungracious elements and perceptions in our lives. Like Ray telling his wife the house is "his house" and "he will shoot up if he wants to," we are willing to shun or even murder others rather than give up our stories, for the loss of our stories feels like the death of us.

A mere "enhancement" to our stories, the providing of additional information, will not do. For the stories we tell ourselves and the lives lived under the guidance of such self-narratives are distorted to our center, from which spring our imagination of the world, self-perception and agency. An enhancement of a thoroughly distorted story will bring no change.[10]

THE MEANING OF SALVATION

In the reorientation model as in the enlightenment model, salvation is *sobriety*, the human imagination's restoration to reality. It is the embrace of God's inbreaking reign of *shalom*, a world in which Mrs. Turpin's hierarchies based upon classism, racism and sexism are replaced by a form of communal unity rooted in equality, reciprocity and mutuality. It is a yielding to a world of grace in which the warring parts of the self find

---

10. See May's discussion of the role of self-representation systems in maintaining our attachments to our objects of addictions (May, *Addiction and Grace*, 98–101). Our self-representation systems are not only determined by our addiction; they become objects of attachment themselves.

their reconciliation and healing. Ray Charles gives up his heroin habit and is able to attend to others in trust and fidelity.

THE COMING OF SALVATION

A simultaneous revealing of the worlds of ungrace and of grace is seen in an encounter between Inspector Javert and Jean Valjean in the film version of *Les Miserables*. Police Inspector Javert is a law-and-order man. Along with charging prostitutes and rounding up French rebels, he has been hunting for Jean Valjean, a small-time criminal who years before had broken his probation and deserved to be sent back to the quarries. Valjean lived in a world shaped by thievery, betrayal, self-interest, and violence until he encountered grace in a priest who protected him from re-arrest and gave him a large sum of money to begin a new life.

Late in the story, the revolutionaries have caught Javert, and want to kill him. "We don't want his blood in here with ours." Jean Valjean, who happens to be present, offers to do it. Valjean takes Javert into the alley. When Valjean takes his knife out, Javert sees that act according to his lens, one in which there are those who follow the law, and those who do not and are thus less-than-human. "A knife. That's right. It suits you better," he says to Valjean. Valjean, however, turns Javert around and uses the knife to cut his hands free. "That way, through the gate. You'll be safe." Javert continues to interpret the act in light of his ungracious world. "You're planning to shoot me in the back."

"I'm letting you go, Javert. Go on."

"You should kill me. I won't stop. Understand? I won't let you go. You should end this. Kill me."

"You're dead, Javert," says Valjean as he shoots his pistol into the air. Then he walks away.

Experiencing Valjean's gracious act, Javert does not yet fully understand its meaning, or its implications for himself or his view of the world. But it does allow him to transcend himself and realize that his perspective on the world's meaning is specific to him, not universal. There is another view, and it is not simply a different view, but a counterforce to his own.

The enlightenment and reorientation models share the same broad understanding of how salvation comes to those communities and individuals caught in delusion. It comes from the telling, and hearing, of two truths. The first truth is that one is living in a world without grace, and if continued, it will end in nothing but destruction. Intimations of this truth are seen as Javert, confused by Valjean's act, continues to pursue him, to his own and Valjean's detriment.

The second truth is this: another world exists, the world of grace. It is superior to the world of ungrace. We were made by God for grace, and it fulfills us.

Invited to live within the alternate world of grace, salvation also entails our yielding to such an invitation, and the corresponding transformation of our lives. We live in the world of grace, with its ethics.

At this point, however, it is unclear whether Javert will accept the invitation.

GOD'S ROLE IN SALVATION

The imagination is continually at work filling up
all the fissures through which grace must pass.[11]

The transformation of the human person presents a problem for God. On the one hand, if the sinful distortion in us goes all the way to the root of our identity, perceptions of the world and agency, then redemption requires a radical change, an about-face. As we saw in chapters 6 and 7, our propensity toward evil is universal, yet this enslavement is not intrinsic to our nature as finite creatures created all-good by God. We are the agents of transgression. The fact that our sin is historically contingent—not of our essence—is hopeful. For if our free choice is involved in our descent into sin, then it may yet play a role in our redemption.

This ubiquitous, unnatural propensity toward evil, furthermore, is not a defect peripheral to our identity. Rather, as we have seen, it is determinative of our identity and woven into its fabric. Thus while a person's nature need not change, her or his identity must change radically: it must be brought to an end, and then re-created in righteousness.[12]

If the change is to be redemptive rather than annihilating, however, there must be continuity of personhood across the change. Sufficient self-identity must remain continuous, so that "I" am both the "old man"

11. Weil, *Gravity and Grace*, 16.

12. As Paul describes it, as well as Jesus to Nicodemus in John 3 and to the disciples throughout the gospels, the change involves "death" and "rebirth." We need a new identity.

and the "new man."[13] Redemption does not mean God wipes the slate clean and starts over again. Who we are as particular persons or com-munities—our choices, our feelings of pain or joy, our experiences, our biographies—is necessarily brought into our fulfilled identity as adopted children of God.[14] God does not save us by destroying us.

How does God maintain continuity of the sinner's personhood if salvation necessitates bringing the sinner's identity to an end and re-creating it? God performs two particular acts, and both involve the accomplishments of God the Mother/Father's "two hands," the Word and Spirit. First, God creates the "second Adam," a person who is righ-teous. Chapters 7 and 8 describe the creation of this "New Being" in Jesus of Nazareth by the power of the Spirit. Such an act by the triune God accomplishes God's will for humanity while preserving human-ity's free will.

Second, through the living, risen Jesus and the Holy Spirit, God engages the person or group at the level of the human imagination, which is the source of self-representation or group-representation sys-tems. The two divine persons convince the sinner, in light of the victory of grace over a world without grace, to let go of the old understanding of the self and of the world, and to embrace the new understanding actualized and revealed in Jesus Christ. As with Javert, our encounters with the Word and Spirit enable us to transcend ourselves and see our story in a new light.

JESUS'S ROLE IN SALVATION

Only a small crack . . . but cracks make caves collapse.[15]

In the alternative models of penal substitution's sharp critics, Jesus is neither the second person of the Trinity incarnate, nor the savior of the world. He is a human being who has achieved what it is possible for

---

13. Jacob becomes Israel, Simon becomes Peter, and Saul becomes Paul; yet each transition of identity involves one and the same person.

14. Otherwise, the call for personal change would be indistinguishable from self-destruction. Concerning sin's entailing the need for drastic change of identity, see Reno, *Redemptive Change*, 197–213. Concerning the requirement for personal continuity across change, see ibid., 221–39.

15. Alexander Solzhenitsyn, quoted in Yancey, *What's So Amazing about Grace?* 122.

anyone to accomplish. He is one who has become open to the flow of divine, life-giving power in and all around us, particularly in communities of equality, mutuality and reciprocity. He is a piece of creation that has become luminescent, and he acts as a catalyst that awakens us to the presence of the divine all around us. He does this as a Jewish mystic, a subversive sage, a social prophet, and a charismatic leader. He shows us of what we are capable, once we allow our dormant abilities to be awakened.

Such descriptions by the generative and enlightenment models are true, but they stop short of a full description of who Jesus is and what he accomplishes. He is the second person of the Trinity incarnate, and the savior, and as such both his person and his saving accomplishments are unique in history. This is why the New Testament authors universally regard Jesus as "Lord" in their earliest descriptions of him: in other words, as One worthy of the worship that previously went to Yahweh alone.[16]

For the person or group awakened from delusion, what is realized is not layers of reality—eternal realities buried beneath the surface, which we then bring to fruition through our enlightenment and wise action. What is perceived by the once-deluded, rather, is that something has changed about the fundamental nature of the world, and that these ontological changes are somehow brought about by Jesus of Nazareth. Instead of layers of eternal realities, the main metaphors involve transitions. They tell the story of a decisive victory over death-dealing forces (chapter 7), of a definitive reconciliation (chapter 8), and of God's justice finally being done on earth as it is in heaven (chapter 9). What is seen by suffering and guilty people, thus, are not eternal truths, but new facts.

The triune God who is other than the world breaks through to delusional human beings from a location within the creaturely sphere. The disclosure to humanity of the twofold truth—God's judgment upon the world as ungracious, and God's offer of an alternative way to live, rooted in the world of grace—comes primarily through the incarnation, life and ministry of Jesus. Jesus shocks us with the two-fold truth *by being a different kind of human being*. While we succumb to the temptations

---

16. During the first five centuries of Christian history, the doctrines of the divinity of Christ and of the Trinity developed amidst a plurality of Christian views about Jesus. Perspectives on Jesus were never univocal, and what eventually became orthodoxy was often the minority stance. On the complex development of the doctrines of Christology and the Trinity, see Moule, *Origin of Christology*; Hurtado, *How on Earth Did Jesus Become a God?*; and Hurtado, *Lord Jesus Christ*.

of the demonic, he resists them completely. Through his continuous trust in God the Mother/Father and his hospitality to the Spirit of Life, Jesus carries within himself—as a human being!—the powers of life over death-dealing forces. Like Ray Charles, our selves are split between the part we show the world and the one that wrestles with the nightmares of the dark. We lie, to others and ourselves. We evade the truth, even when told by those who love us. We swing between evasions and stratagems for survival, and evasions and stratagems to gain power over others and climb to the top of whatever social status we crave. Everyone is suspect, no one trustworthy, even God. We use power demonically, a corruption evidenced by those who take advantage of Ray, by Ray using his wits to then take advantage of others, and by Mrs. Turpin solidifying kyriarchal structures from which she benefits.

But in Jesus of Nazareth, we encounter a human being who refuses to use power demonically. He lives with integrity, without a split between true and false selves, without masks or evasions and stratagems for survival. His being and his doing are one. He treats all as fellow subjects, never objectifying them. He offers himself without preconditions, refusing to cut himself off from God, self, or neighbor. In his deep sorrow for human sin in all its complexity and gravity, and his movement toward a different form of life, he tells a different story about human existence. He looks at us, as he looked at Peter after Peter's three denials. Like Peter, when we catch his gaze, we perceive not only Jesus's fidelity, but also our faithlessness and betrayals, and our unwillingness to face them. We see that we are completely implicated in the mess we have made. Like Montgomery Brogan in *25th Hour*, we see our need for grace, for forgiveness, for a second chance. We recognize our need for a level of transformation of which we are incapable.

In Jesus of Nazareth, we find our future form of humanity coming to meet us, who exist in a form of humanity gone wrong. He is unexpected. But as the second person of the Trinity incarnate, Jesus is also our God who comes to meet us. Not only is he a form of human being we did not expect; *he is a God we did not expect.* Jesus is born in an animal stall, and resides in the sticks. Though we are complicit with the demonic, he goes beneath our sin to us as suffering creatures. He is for our freedom, not against it. He reestablishes our freedom not by controlling evil through coercive force, but by refusing to yield to its ways. Jesus shows God's face to us, one of mercy, non-ambivalence and nonviolence. Yet he also reveals the God who brings our delusional identities and their entanglements with the world of ungrace to an end, but in such a way that he retains continuity between who we were and who we are, and that involves our free participation.

As the Johannine author reveals, God is love, and the power which changes the world is love. But this love does not come from the triune God as generic or diffuse, as a sentiment or general principle. It comes in the form of a concrete historical person, Jesus of Nazareth, and the changes he effects transform the world.[17]

Jesus's torture and execution also reveal our ungrace, and God's grace, but not in the way frequently described. In the twelfth century, Peter Abelard imagined God effecting human transformation by an act of extravagant love which "enkindled" a corresponding love within the human heart.[18] While Jesus revealed God's love through his teaching, example, and forgiveness of sins, for Abelard the central act of love occurs on the cross. As has so often been the case in Church history, Abelard identifies love with the willingness to sacrifice the self for others. The passion alone convinces us of God's love for us: "his rejection, agony, and torture . . . these mark the worth of sinners before God."[19]

It is not Jesus's suffering and passive victimization that save, however, but his actions. While love is nonviolent and non-retaliatory, love is not identified with the bare refusal to participate in mimetic violence, for such an identification defines love as the abnegation of power. The object of love is not simply "the other"; rather, it is all life. Reflecting the God who creates and cherishes every creature, love strives to protect and nourish all life, including that of others and the self. As we saw in chapter

---

17. As Reno says, "Christianity teaches that Jesus is the power of new life. Little that Christians say or do makes much sense without this basic affirmation" (*Redemptive Change*, 194); and see ibid., 193–94.

18. See Abelard, excerpt from "Exposition of the Epistle to the Romans."

19. Weingart, *Logic of Divine Love*, 122. Abelard's identification of the submission to torture and death with a display of love for others, and of a love that saves precisely the perpetrators of the violence, however, is a destructive theory of atonement. Pain and love are thoroughly conjoined and confused in this model. Thinking of oneself is the opposite of love. In contrast, love acquires its virtue and its disclosive and redemptive powers by its absorbing of the violence of perpetrators in a fathomless yielding. The victim's abnegation of power to resist violation has saving effect. Many recent atonement theories that employ René Girard's anthropological theories of religious sacrifice display the same problem. For the problems with Abelard's and Girard's models, see Brock and Parker, *Saving Paradise*, chap. 11: "Dying for Love"; and my chapter, "In Search of a Non-Violent Atonement Theory: Are Abelard and Girard a Help, or a Problem?"

7, Jesus enacts his striking love of life by bringing wholeness through his physical healings and raising of the dead, his appreciation of beauty and his nonviolent challenge to kyriarchal structures—such as when he chases the money-changers from the temple. As the emancipator, Jesus counters coercive power not by simply refusing to use power, but by wielding a different form of power—the generative power unleashed in relations of equality and mutual giving and receiving—and creating communities rooted in such power.

The cross, then, is a less-clear demonstration of the divine love which saves nonviolently than is the miracle of the loaves and fishes. In that miracle, Jesus confronts empire not with an opposing coercion, nor with an abnegation of power. Jesus confronts a world of ungrace—the Roman structures of domination and submission—by increasing a community built upon a different source of power, that of the Spirit of Life, and a different ethic, one that is hospitable and gracious.

And yet Jesus's last hours of suffering and death are essential for comprehending his love which acts to passionately embrace life, to create communities in which all members share equally in the resources needed for life, and to nonviolently resist kyriarchal forces which oppose such communities. In a world built upon scapegoating, codes of retaliation against the 'other,' and structures of domination and subordination, those who act compassionately also risk their life. In such a context, Jesus improvised. When threatened, he protected himself when he could, such as when he "disappeared from the crowd" when locals wanted his head, or when he slipped beyond Herod's jurisdiction to Caesarea Philippi after Herod executed Jesus's cousin John. But sometimes the act of supporting another's life, or refusing to yield one's embrace of the new communal ethos of life, puts a person in the path of those who find such love subversive of the hierarchical power structures from which they benefit. To step aside when threatened is to abandon the neighbor to the onslaught of coercive forces, or to abandon one's integrity and the new community. To put it differently, sometimes there are no good choices in the fight to preserve life (as the struggles of Bonhoeffer, King, and Romero display). Sometimes a choice to protect one's life would come at the self-defeating cost of severing connections to one's integrity, one's neighbors, the new community of love, and the God who calls us toward each of these.

Thus, while his torture and death are not salvific, Jesus's refusal to abandon the weak to the forces of empire, or curse his torturers, is salvific. This refusal is a constituent part of his life-act of compassion. If Jesus had attempted to avoid the cross at all cost, within such a contentious clash of communities based upon different forms of power, then the character of his life would have been changed. His willingness to risk his life because of his love of others, his love of his own life's integrity, his love of the God of life and of the new community of hospitality, is essential to the nature of love, a love that is redemptive.

Further, as we saw in chapters 7–9, the cross is a constituent part of God's new act in Jesus by which God effects ontological changes in the human situation and the God-world relation—including the creation of "the seed of a new humanity" and the deeper binding of God's own future to our own. Jesus's entire life-act has disclosive power, and the cross has no disclosive character whatsoever apart from his life of passionate acts of love. But as all four gospel authors perceived, the climax of his life-act's disclosive power occurs at Golgotha.

As is true in the emancipation, hospitality, and justice models, so with the reorientation model Jesus's power to save is undone without the resurrection. The first truth revealed is that we humans live in a world without grace, and it will destroy us. With its murder of the innocent, principle of mimetic violence, and deicide, the cross confirms this truth. But alone, it negates the second truth: That an alternate world of grace exists, that it fulfills us, and that it is ultimate. The fact that the forces of ungrace have done their worst, yet Jesus lives, confirms this second truth. This is why, despite the centrality of the cross in the gospel narratives, it is the resurrection which is the world-transformative and mind-altering fact. Jesus and his sacrificial love would not have been remembered if he had not been raised.

Further, he was not raised for private purposes. Jesus's ascension to "the right hand of God" the Mother/Father is also a part of the saving power of his life-act. As the living, risen Jesus, he is also the cosmic Christ who works broadly in different historical periods and contexts to bring about individual and communal reorientation. He continues to witness to himself, to give his love, a love which includes the particular goal of leading persons and communities to a transformative encounter with himself, and union with him through faith. He also seeks to reveal the two truths—that we live in a world without grace, and that an alternative life in grace exists—broadly, in all cultures, time periods and contexts.

THE HOLY SPIRIT'S ROLE, AND OUR OWN

Man is born broken. He lives by mending.
The grace of God is glue.[20]

MRS. TURPIN

"If it's one thing I am," Mrs. Turpin exclaims to the well-dressed woman while in the clinic's waiting room,

> "it's grateful. When I think who all I could have been besides myself and what all I got, a little of everything, and a good disposition besides, I just feel like shouting, 'Thank you, Jesus, for making everything the way it is!'"[21]

Before she knows it, the book hits her above her left eye. It comes from the girl reading *Human Development*, she sends it flying across the room. And then the girl attacks Mrs. Turpin, circling her neck in a death grip. After the doctor separates them, the girl stares directly at Ruby and whispers, "Go back to hell where you came from, you old wart hog."[22]

Later at home, Ruby can't let it go. She lies on the bed in the afternoon and cries. The image of an immense razor-back hog runs through her imagination. She says tearfully, "I am not a wart hog. From hell."[23] But she has her doubts.

Finally, Mrs. Turpin decides to go out and hose down the pigs. The sun is behind the wood, and no one else is around. As Ruby aggressively squirts the hogs, she speaks aloud:

> "What do you send me a message like that for?" she said in a low fierce voice, barely above a whisper but with the force of a shout in its concentrated fury. "How am I a hog and me both? How am I saved and from hell too?"[24]

Ruby blasts the old sow with water, and asks, "Why me?"[25]

---

20. Eugene O'Neill, quoted in Yancey, *Grace*, 270.

21. O'Connor, "Revelation," 205–6.

22. Ibid., 207.

23. Ibid., 210.

24. Ibid., 215.

25. Ibid.

"There was plenty of trash there. It didn't have to be me. If you like trash better, go get yourself some trash then," she railed. "You could have made me trash. Or a nigger."[26]

Ruby shakes her fist, sending the water flying. "I could quit working and take it easy and be filthy."[27] Finally, she gazes way across the pasture:

"Go on," she yelled, "call me a hog! Call me a hog again. From hell. Call me a wart hog from hell. Put that bottom rail on top. There'll still be a top and bottom!"[28]

And, a final, furious query to the spot beyond the horizon: "Who do you think you are?"[29]

The last question simply returns to her like an echo from beyond the pasture and highway and wood. She stares at the hogs for a long time. Finally, she lifts her head to look down the highway, and sees a purple streak cutting through the field, as if it were an extension of the road.

A visionary light settled in her eyes. She saw the streak as a vast swinging bridge extending upward from the earth through a field of living fire. Upon it a vast horde of souls were rumbling toward heaven. There were whole companies of white-trash, clean for the first time in their lives, and bands of black niggers in white robes, and battalions of freaks and lunatics shouting and clapping and leaping like frogs. And bringing up the end of the precession was a tribe of people whom she recognized at once as those who, like herself and Claud, had always had a little of everything and the God-given wit to use it right. She leaned forward to observe them closer. They were marching behind the others with great dignity, accountable as they had always been for good order and common sense and respectable behavior. They alone were on key. Yet she could see by their shocked and altered faces that even their virtues were being burned away.[30]

The vision quickly fades. Mrs. Turpin remains for a long time, then goes slowly back to the house.

---

26. Ibid., 216.
27. Ibid.
28. Ibid.
29. Ibid.
30. Ibid., 217–18.

RAY CHARLES

"No, No. Oh, George, I miss you. I miss you, George. I miss you." In his delirious flashback, he saw George fall back into a bucket of blood.

He had been at St. Francis Rehabilitation Clinic for weeks, insisting he go through withdrawals "on his own," without help from palliative medicines.

Finally off heroin, Ray is playing chess one day with his psychiatrist, who praises him for his progress. "I'm done with this dope and I'm finished."

"Who's George?" the psychiatrist asked, looking in his eyes.

Ray pauses, doesn't answer. "Forget the head shrinking, Doc. I can handle this." The doctor tells him he is far from whole, that he can't help him if he is unwilling to talk, then walks out of the room. Ray stands, gets angry, goes after him, trips on a chair.

As he falls, he has another daydream. He falls into the wash bucket. He digs madly in it for George.

"He ain't there."

Ray turns, sees the colored bottles hanging on the tree outside his boyhood home.

"Talk to me, son."

"Mama, I kept my promise."

"You got strong all right. Went places I never dreamed of. But you still became a cripple." Ray wept. "Come here, baby. Come here."

As Ray weeps, he hears a voice. "Ray?" He turns and sees George. "It wasn't your fault." They hug.

"Now promise us, you never let nobody or nothing turn you into no cripple ever again. That you'll always stand on your own two feet."

"I promise."

From that day, he never touched heroin again.

∼

Salvation comes to us when we perceive truths that make our life lucid. Yet the truths we encounter are not general. They are particular truths embodied in a particular person, the living, risen Jesus who is the one we humans crucified. From this encounter, the self is "shattered," reoriented, like Ruby Turpin's as she sees the procession going up to heaven, herself last. In the encounter with this lucid truth, we come to a dead stop and face a fork in the road, a choice about our existence. Like Mrs. Turpin, we have no capacities for this encounter, and can make no preparations for it.

When Jesus comes to meet us, we do not perceive him as an extension of ourselves or of our way of living. He does not appear as the destination of a route we ourselves are earnestly travelling. He does not seem to be our "elder brother." Rather, he comes to us as a countermove, a human being over against us and the world. It is not his ideals that confront our way of living and our self-definitions; it is his existence. He is not like us. He is someone else, a different form of human being. He does not fit our worldview (which is sinful and deluded). His narrative confronts our self-narrative and our social narratives. He comes with "the Day of the Lord."[31] In all this, we perceive him as threatening, for in Christ we recognize the end of the self, the end of our personal and social narratives in their present form. Like Paul's experience of Jesus on the road to Damascus, our end may be brought by catastrophe. With those words from Jesus—"Saul, Saul, why do you persecute me?"[32]—Saul realized that he had the meaning of his life and the world all wrong, that he had been filled with presumption and hubris. Or like the Samaritan woman at the well from whom Jesus asks for a drink of water, our end may be brought by what Tolkien called "eucatastrophe." Jesus's treatment of her with love and respect, his knowledge of her yet acceptance of her, his offer of living water helped her unbury her true self and live out of that self.[33] Good news shatters the self as fully as does catastrophe, as anyone who has ever been adopted or fallen in love can attest, particularly if the only news one has ever had is bad news.[34] "Come to me, all

---

31. See chapters 7, 9 above.

32. Acts 9:4. As was common with many ethnic groups in the Roman Empire, including diaspora Jews, Paul had two names. *Saul* was his Jewish name, *Paul* his Roman name; cf. Acts 13:9.

33. John 4.

34. As Serene Jones has indicated, talk of God's "shattering the self" may be appropriate in relation to the sins of those in power who are prideful and self-centered, and who wield dominating power. John Newton, for example, needed to have his self "shattered." But as we saw in chapter 2, such talk is highly problematic for victims of

you that are weary and are carrying heavy burdens," Jesus says, and this of course we expect. Living in a world without grace, with self-narratives devoid of grace, we all carry "heavy burdens." "And I will give you rest." That is the unexpected part, and the comic shock comes from both the gospel word he speaks and that it is he who speaks it.[35]

An analogous experience occurs when, in our worlds without grace, we encounter grace. The grace we encounter is also the work of the living, risen Jesus, this time as the Word at work broadly in various periods and cultures, causing a clash between worlds. Presenting the two truths, the Cosmic Christ shows us both the world of ungrace in which we live and which will destroy us, and the alternate world of grace which brings life to all. In his final daydream, Ray Charles hears the word which judges him from his mother. He didn't keep his promise. He became a cripple, through his failure to trust others who were faithful and generous, and his misplaced trust in his own dominating power and the power of his object of addiction to save him. But he also hears the words of grace, from his mother who loves him regardless of his abilities, and from George who insists it was not Ray's fault that he slipped and died in the wash tub. From both his mother and his brother, he encountered what he did not expect—a horizon of grace.

The living, risen Jesus also acts to challenge and reorient social narratives. For example, almost every civilization in human history, at least since 2000 BC, has kept slaves. And while there were some cultures that felt it was unnatural or due to the fall, many felt like Aristotle that certain groups of humans could be treated like beasts, since they were 'natural slaves.' "It is clear that there are certain people who are free and certain who are slaves by nature, and it is both to their advantage, and just, for them to be slaves," Aristotle argued.[36] Using arguments from ancient

---

abuse, who have already had their selves "shattered" by trauma, who are lacking a self because it is buried or split. They need to have their self unburied, lifted up, mirrored to them and restored, not shattered. (See Jones, *Feminist Theory and Christian Theology*, 61ff.; and Smith, *Risking the Terror*, 22.) We shall see that continuity of self is essential to whatever transformation Jesus effects in us. Yet in all cases, whether one's problem is that of having "too much self" or "not enough self," the encounter with Jesus and with grace brings an end to the narrative we tell ourselves. We are not who we thought we were, and the world does not work as we thought it did.

35. See Buechner, *Telling The Truth*, 58–59, and Matt 11:28. For examples of the shattering effect of good news, see chap. 3: "The Gospel as Comedy."

36. Quoted in Davis, *Inhuman Bondage*, 34. The only recorded all-out attack on slavery in antiquity came from Gregory of Nyssa in the late 300s CE. He argued that all

Greece and Rome as well as from the Bible, British and American apologists for slavery made similar arguments. Yet remarkably, within a generation during the mid-1800s in America, the act of enslavement that had once seemed natural or at least the will of God for a fallen world came to be seen by a majority as sinful and against the will of God. And through acts of Parliament, the British ended their participation in the slave trade (1807) and then abolished slavery in the empire (1833), though it cost them bitterly in economic terms. As was true with John Quincy Adams's argument before the Supreme Court concerning the *Amistad* case, part of what moved Americans was the principle of natural rights endowed by God. A gracious world in which God intended all human beings to live in freedom thus clashed with an ungracious world in which certain humans could be categorized and treated as sub-human, and the clash created a fork in the road, forcing a choice.

The one who brings the catastrophe and the one who brings the eucatastrophe are the same person, Jesus of Nazareth. Similarly, the revelation that we are living in a world of ungrace comes with the revealing of the alternative world of grace, for the presence of grace reveals both truths. This simultaneity is seen in Mrs. Turpin's final vision, which reflects the new community based on equality, mutuality and reciprocity. As she gazes upon it, she knows that her hierarchical order based upon domination and subjection will not last, that it is judged by God as "for nothing."[37]

Surprisingly, like Javert and Mrs. Turpin, what we find so threatening is the offer of a gift of life in a world of death. "I came that they may have life, and have it abundantly," Jesus said. But certainly the leaders and beneficiaries of the kyriarchal systems did not perceive it this way.[38] Our role in salvation is simply to accept the gift being offered. Yet we resist it, and there is a logic to our resistance. Accepting the gift of grace feels like a "death," because it means giving-up one's image of oneself and one's understanding of how the world works. The change required of the

humans had been made in the image of God, and so no human could enslave another (ibid.).

37. Alongside "Revelation," O'Connor's short story "The Artificial Nigger" equally illustrates the simultaneity of revelations. The presence of grace reveals one's own lack of grace.

38. John 10:10. "What has come into being in him was life, and the life was the light of all people.... He came to what was his own, and his own people did not accept him" (John 1:4, 11).

individual or social imagination is all-encompassing, for it reaches down to our self-representation systems and communal narratives which integrate all the other systems of a person's self or a group's unified daily life. Such self-representation systems exist at the level of our "basic acts," the wellspring not only of our identity but of our emotions, desires, free deliberations and choices. To give them up feels like the end of the self— at least, the only self one has ever known.

We may also resist the gift of grace because doing so may alienate us from those still living in the world of ungrace. "Do not think I have come to bring peace to the earth; I have not come to bring peace, but a sword," Jesus told his disciples bluntly. "For I have come to set a man against his father, and a daughter against her mother, and a daughter-in-law against her mother-in-law; and one's foes will be members of one's own household."[39]

Most of all, the presence of a world of grace threatens us with the sting of shame: we must admit to God, to others, and above all to ourselves that we were wrong. Not just wrong about bits of our self-representation, or portions of our worldview, but—being wrong about the most basic truth, the ultimacy of grace—wrong about everything. Like Ray Charles in his confrontational conversations with his wife Della Bea and his psychiatrist, we have to admit that we are not just deluded, but self-deluded. We have conned ourselves. Like Mrs. Turpin, we have to admit that part of us despises the world of grace. We have to admit that whatever part of us seeks freedom from the gloom of an ungracious world and its horizons of nonbeing and guilt, that part of us is outnumbered by the rest of our being that wants to remain.

It is at these moments of pause, of no-movement, that the element of divine risk and human freedom becomes clear. Mrs. Turpin, sitting for a long while after the vision of the swinging bridge has ceased. Javert, his hands released, staring at Valjean. No one, not even God, can force a person to change her or his imagination, the way she or he interprets who she or he is and what the world means. As Abelard and Dostoyevsky rightly perceived, love and grace do not coerce people to accept them.

The role of the Holy Spirit in salvation is to convince us to accept a life in the world of grace. When Christ approaches us, or Christ hidden in acts of grace, the Teacher Spirit converses with us about the meaning of the word of grace. Like the three ghosts speaking with Ebenezer

39. Matt 10:34–36.

Scrooge about scenes of gravity and grace from his past, present and future, the Holy Spirit shows us our life in ungrace and its inevitable fall into the void, the alternate basis for identity and life in a world of grace, then encourages us to take the latter.

Our role in salvation is clearly essential, revealed in the fact that our acceptance cannot be vouchsafed. Paul, the Samaritan woman, and Ray Charles accepted the new self-definition and the offer of grace. But certainly many in Britain and America did not accept the "natural law" or Christian arguments for the equality of all peoples and the divine judgment upon slavery. And after the American civil war, Cuba and Brazil actually became more invested in their slave systems. Lacking competition from the English and Americans, the economic value of slavery lurched upward. Planters were confident in the 1860s and 1870s that slavery would last for many more decades. Further, they hardly saw emancipation movements as embodying the hand of God. Stories are often left open-ended to highlight this role of the recipient of grace. We do not know what Mrs. Turpin decided as she walked home from her vision. We do not know what the disciples in Mark decided after they encountered a young man in a white robe who told them Jesus was not in the tomb, but had been raised and would meet them in Galilee (see Mark 16:8). In *The Brothers Karamazov*, when the cardinal finishes ranting at Jesus for loading the burden of freedom on humanity, Jesus simply kisses him. We are not sure how his encounter with grace affected him. "The old man shuddered. His lips moved," and he told Jesus to leave, releasing him. Then Dostoyevsky's last line: "The kiss glows in his heart, but the old man adheres to his idea."[40]

As all those who accept a life rooted in grace discover, there is continuity of self-identity across the chasm of death that occurs to one's self-identity and worldview. Our self-deception may be "shattered," but not we ourselves. While our ungracious self-narratives and social narratives are thrown down by grace, our narratives themselves are protected and lifted up. Though we "die" with the letting go of our most basic self-representation and social representation systems, our life "is hid with Christ in God," with all of its particularities (Col 3:3). Our life-story is placed within Jesus's life-story; our narrative of ungrace is set within the larger, more ultimate narrative of grace. Placed within such a context, the events and choices, joys and sorrow of our life do not disappear, but they

---

40. Dostoyevsky, *Brothers Karamazov*, 241.

take on a radically different context, like tragic elements placed within a drama which ends as a comedy. They are taken up and used. Israel knows he is Jacob, too. Peter knows he is Simon. But Jacob and Simon are penultimate; it is Israel and Peter that last into the new age . . . indeed, are the new age even here in the old.[41]

As Abelard perceived, love is not a mere sentiment. It is a form of power which can transform broken hearts. Previously we mistrusted God as one who sought to dominate the self, or to belittle it. But in the face of Christ, we encounter grace and realize that God seeks to dominate or belittle no one. God wants our freedom, as the Grand Inquisitor exclaimed, the kiss still burning on his lips. The door is opened by which we may then move from mistrusting God to trusting God, if we are willing to allow the sting of letting go our false conceptions. If we are willing to let everything go, to descend below the water, and be raised to a new name.

This willingness to let grace be done to us, to be baptized, is our first act in our salvation, and the most difficult. As Kierkegaard said, "our greatest achievement is to let God help us."[42] Our second role is to allow Christ and the Holy Spirit, who both indwell us, to teach us how to live in the new world of grace, to resist the forces of ungrace and instead reshape the world according to grace. This does not necessarily mean we throw out our present systems wholesale and try, in utopic fashion, to build structures which perfectly reflect God's reign of grace. For example, it may mean that we place an economic system based fundamentally in patterns of exchange—capitalism—into conversation with alternative economic ideas gained from what Kathryn Tanner calls God's "economy of grace." That economy includes principles of economic interdependence and noncompetitiveness, as well as practices of welfare and unconditional giving, stewardship of nonmarketable goods and noncompetitive possession and use of goods instead of a sole focus upon private goods.[43]

Jean Valjean attempts to live in that world of grace, being generous toward others as well as himself. Ray Charles learns to live, day by day,

41. Before Jesus gave him the new name of "Peter" upon calling him to be a disciple, his name was "Simon." See John 1:42, and Matt 16:13–23.

42. The phrase comes from Kierkegaard, *Søren Kierkegaard's Journals and Papers*, vol. 1, entry 54, VB198.

43. Tanner, *Economy of Grace*.

without heroin and open to his wife, his sons, his coworkers. Abolitionists not only change social narratives, but also laws and economic and political structures. In this new way of living with a new identity, we are confident because we matter: we are consequential, as our encounters with the crucified and risen Christ, with grace, make clear. It is true that our new identities are tied to Christ's identity. Jesus lives first and primarily, and we live in him and he in us. All this is by the power of the Holy Spirit who connects us to Christ and makes all things new.

And yet, we say with Paul, "I live."[44]

44. See Gal 2:19–20.

11

Jesus, the Securer of Meaning

Restoration

FRANK ARTRESS AND SUSAN GUSTAFSON

Frank Artress knew he was going to die. As a cardiac anesthesiologist, he knew the signs of high altitude pulmonary edema. It was the fifth of a six-day climb up Mt. Kilimanjaro. He had neglected to thaw his water that morning, and so did not tell his wife, Susan Gustafson, or any of the twenty-two African porters that he was thirsty. After hiking all day to Crater Camp at 18,500 feet, he finally told his wife that his lungs were slowly filling with fluid, as if someone were squeezing his throat. "We are in a really, really bad place." The only cure was to descend, but the route up was too rocky and dangerous to descend. Though it was dark, their only hope was to climb 840 feet more to the top and descend on the other side. It seemed undoable.

Frank and Susan were sitting together on a rock above the clouds when he realized something. He was not afraid to die; he was ashamed. He had lived only for himself—practicing medicine in a Modesto hospital, traveling with Susan, purchasing luxury vacation homes and collecting art. He felt as if he had nothing to show for his fifty years, as if his life had been a waste. They both realized they were living for the wrong reasons.

They held each other and wept.

FREDERICK, MARIE, AND ELIZABETH MASOUDI

At 6:30 a.m., Ruth Johnson-Reimann and her daughter Sarah were in the kitchen. Her son Christopher and daughter Julie were still asleep, as were

238

nephew Sam Masoudi and Grace Masoudi. This was to be the first day of a two week-long family vacation in a house they rented in Gearhart on the northern Oregon coast.[1]

And then the plane fell from the sky. The pilot and his passenger, both fathers of two children each, were well-respected in Gearhart. The Cessna 172 had just taken off from the municipal airport. But the engine died, its wing clipped a tree, and the plane hit the roof at 398 N. Marion Avenue.

There were twenty seconds before the house exploded into flames. Ruth, Sarah and Christopher escaped, but were burned severely. Within a minute and a half, the house was a torch, and Ruth's daughter Julie, two Masoudi children, and the pilot and passenger were dead.

Frederick and Marie Masoudi had awoken early, and went for a walk on the beach with their daughter Elizabeth. They returned to find their two other children dead.[2]

HANNA

In *The Secret Life of Words*, Hanna also has secrets. When she first arrives on the oil rig to care for Josef's burns, she lies about her name. She works in a factory, eats the same things daily for her meals—chicken, rice, apples. Finally, she tells him. She had once been so cheerful, before the Balkan wars. Unsure what to do when the war shut her college, she got in her car and drove toward her hometown. Two kilometers from home, soldiers from her own ethnic group stopped her and some other women and took them to a hotel, holding them prisoner for weeks and raping them. UN soldiers came through but did nothing to stop it. The Balkan soldiers made a woman kill her own daughter. One day, a soldier cut Hanna repeatedly with a knife. During the torture, she let the old person she was die, so that that original Hanna would no longer suffer.

A different person survived, but it wasn't the twenty-year-old, eager for life, who had once been a little girl who loved to laugh.

1. Ruth Johnson-Reimann is 47 years old; Sarah is 11; Christopher is 13; Julie was 10. Her nephew Hasem (Sam) Masoudi was 12; her niece Grace, 8.
2. Elizabeth is 14 years old. The accident occurred at 6:37 a.m. on August 4, 2008.

SOPHIE ZAWISTOWSKI

Sophie Zawistowski does not sleep anymore, not since the war.[3]

Her father had been a law professor in Cracow. She loved him dearly until she heard him give an anti-Semitic speech in which he encouraged the extermination of the Polish Jews as the 'solution' to their ethnic problem. Her father loved the Nazi's because they hated Jews as much as he did. Her husband was also anti-Semitic.

She had an affair with a member of the Polish resistance. Two weeks after the Gestapo caught him, they arrested her and put her and her two young children, Jan and Eva, in the cattle car to Auschwitz.

They arrived at night. She stood in line with the thousands of Jews with yellow stars, holding Eva with Jan clutching her leg. The camp doctor was walking along the line and noticed her fair complexion and golden hair.

"Are you also one of those filthy communists?"

"I am a Pole! I was born in Cracow. I am not a Jew! Neither are my children! They're *not* Jews. They are racially pure. I'm a Christian. I'm a devout Catholic."

"You are not a communist? You are a believer?"

"Yes, Sir. I believe in Christ."

"So you believe in Christ ... the Redeemer? Did he not say, 'Suffer the little children to come unto me?' You may keep one of your children."

"I beg your pardon?"

"You may keep one of your children. The other one must go [immediately to the crematorium]."

"You mean, I have to choose?"

"You're a Polock not a Yid. That gives you a privilege, a choice."

"I cannot choose ... I cannot choose."

"Choose! Or I'll send them both over there!"

"Don't make me choose! I can't!"

"Take *both* children away," the doctor tells the guards. "Move!"

---

3. This story is from the movie, *Sophie's Choice*, based on the book by William Styron.

As the guards come, Sophie screams, "Take my little girl! Take my baby! Take my little girl!"

Little Eva is screaming for her mother as the guard carries her away down the road.

The day after she tells this story for the first time, she commits suicide.

THE VOID OF MEANINGLESSNESS

Writing in 1943 at the height of the Second World War, the American Christian ethicist H. Richard Niebuhr did not think many people in Europe and America encountered the benevolence of God firsthand. Coming off the Depression, Stalin's starvation of twenty million Russians, the rise of fascism in Europe and Japan, and the persecution of the Jews, many experienced instead the failure of traditional structures and values to hold barbarism at bay. Many in that generation experienced "the twilight of the gods," the fact that none of our personal or communal centers of value on which people rely for meaning in their lives is able to supply meaning that lasts.

> The causes for which we live all die. The great social movements pass and are supplanted by others. The ideals we fashion are revealed by time to be relative. The empires and cities to which we are devoted all decay. At the end nothing is left to defend us against the void of meaninglessness. We try to evade this knowledge, but it is ever in the background of our minds . . . We know that "on us and all our race the slow, sure doom falls pitiless and dark." All our causes, all our ideas, all the beings on which we relied to save us from worthlessness are doomed to pass.[4]

In each of the stories above, the problem of the human condition is not guilt or alienation from God because of rebellion. It is not the problem of feeling unloved. The problem is the shattering of meaning, and doubts about whether life as a whole has any meaning at all. Salvation comes as the restoration of meaning, and its placement upon a foundation that will last. As such, I call this model *the restoration model of salvation.*

---

4. Niebuhr, "Faith in Gods and in God," 122.

THE PROBLEM WITHIN THE HUMAN CONDITION

Guilt and death are still strong elements in human experience. Yet in the modern, technologically 'developed' societies, achievements in standards of living and health care have postponed death.[5] As these societies also experience the loss of standards of normative behavior by which to judge actions, guilt becomes relativized and its sense diminished. In these societies, *despair* has become the predominant problem within the human condition. *Individuals and societies feel bereft of any credible system of meaning.*

In the developed societies of Europe and North America, for example, there is a social loss of purpose as people question the meaning of the entire Western exercise in progress and the pursuit of happiness. Some of this comes from the secular banishment of transcendence. Since Darwin's theory of natural selection, a transcendent Designer is no longer needed to explain the process of change. People experience the one-dimensional quality of a secular world devoid of transcendent realities. Religious pluralism suggests that whatever transcendent realities we have are personally or culturally chosen.[6] For those who long for God, there is an abiding sense of aloneness. Many are suspicious that there is no objective correlate to their devotion. Nor is there Someone or Something with a definite plan or purpose for creaturely, or our own personal, existence.

Societies in Europe and North America influenced by the European Enlightenment and the scientific and technological revolutions began to see history as containing within itself a *telos* and drive toward ever-higher levels of human achievement. A technocratic mind-set replaced one in which the world was enchanted with the presence of God and humans lived their lives before God. There seemed no limits to nature's bounty or human ingenuity. "Science is power," said Francis Bacon, for

5. By 2007, several countries reached life-expectancy rates at birth above eighty years old. For example: Canada, 80.34; France, 80.59; Australia, 80.62; Sweden, 80.63; Singapore, 81.8; Japan, 82.02. The United States was at 78.06. See Central Intelligence Agency, *CIA World Factbook 2007*.

6. Peter Berger argues that in the premodern world, a person or community was orthodox simply by existing in the dominant community. Heretics were those who chose to embrace religious beliefs outside the community's traditional framework of belief. Cultural and religious pluralism in the modern world, however, forces everyone to *choose* the object of their religious devotion—an act previously committed only by heretics. See Berger, *Heretical Imperative*.

it allowed humans to understand the cause-and-effect processes of nature's inner-workings, and thus gain a mastery over them. Power was interpreted as invulnerability, the growing human ability to affect nature and other persons without being affected by them.

But in the history of the West since the Enlightenment, the deification of the power principle has gone hand-in-hand with the suspicion of transience. The twentieth century brought the collapse of the Enlightenment worldview and revealed its bankruptcy. Instead of optimism, progress, and human mastery, the century revealed human life as absurd, futile, tragic. A self-contradiction in Western societies' way of being displayed itself: In the very process of achieving mastery, we could destroy our natural and social environments, and thus ourselves. We have created the downward movement toward our own demise, for as communities we face disintegrating spirals of destruction in ecology and society of our own making, yet now seemingly beyond our ability to alter.[7] Our embrace of a triumphalist ideology seems to carry within itself a flirtation with Nothingness. Instead of a glorious ascent, we perceive an approaching tragic end, and we wonder if we are living in the "last era."[8]

The demise of Enlightenment optimism is furthered by the experience of those who achieve its goals, but find they do not satisfy. Though the standard of living has increased steadily and markedly since the 1950s, Americans report increasing levels of dissatisfaction. Their wealth has not made them happy.[9] Unlimited self-expansion paradoxically leads to self-deflation, an internal sense of emptiness and a perception of one's life as shallow.

The loss of transcendence, the seeming drive to corporate suicide, and the felt emptiness of even those who achieve society's goals lead Westerners to question whether the human enterprise has any purpose. To the question, "To what end?" we are suspicious that the answer is, "There is none."

7. As Jared Diamond documents, modern Western societies are not alone in exhibiting such self-destructive values and life patterns. Examples of such societies can be found across time and culture. See Diamond, *Collapse*. What is new is Western societies' capacity to destroy, not just its way of life, but life on earth.

8. The phrase is Moltmann's; see *Way of Jesus Christ*, 159, 191, 194.

9. See Easterbrook, *Progress Paradox*.

Frank Artress and Susan Gustafson on top of Kilimanjaro suspect that life is vain beyond the goals we arbitrarily impose upon it.

Random and catastrophic events contravene one's agency, bringing on the threat of meaninglessness. Frederick and Marie Masoudi come home from an early-morning walk to find that a plane fell out of the sky, hit their vacation home and killed two of their children. All of their hard work to shape lives and participate in the meaningful rhythms of family life disappear in the space of two minutes.

Random events of human evil steal the sense of life's rationality. After her trauma, Hanna was never the same. Existing only by spare routines, she had found a "way to go on," but not a way to live.

The meaningfulness of existence is assaulted as well by tragic events in which a combination of sinful choices and chance occurrences lead to a devastation of one's life. Sophie Zawistowski displayed both virtue and opportunism. When the Nazi doctor came by, she disassociated herself from the thousands of Jews around her, using Nazi ideology to her benefit. Then the doctor gave her a "privilege" not given to Jews: She may choose one child to live. Her sense of the meaningfulness of being a faithful mother was destroyed in a moment's time.

All of these people—Frank Artress and Susan Gustafson; Frederick and Marie Masoudi; Hanna; Sophie—may begin to ask whether life is simply absurd.

THE MEANING OF SALVATION

As Frank and Susan lay shivering under blankets that night, he thought of "how stupid it would be to die without ever giving anything back to society." He also knew he would be dead by morning if he did not act.

Gustafson awakened the camp, and they set off in the darkness for the summit. It took eight hours to climb 840 feet. Their guide Kitaba and the porters wrapped arms around Frank and sang Swahili songs to encourage him. At some point on the way down the other side of Kilimanjaro, Frank passed out. He awakened to find four porters holding the corners of a military cot upon which he was strapped. A wheel was beneath it, and they were running down the mountain, still singing Swahili prayer songs. Climbing in the darkness, these men had risked their lives for his. Artress was overwhelmed with gratitude.

The next day, a doctor said, "You know, Dr. Frank, we need doctors here in Africa way more than they need them in California."

Frank and Susan stayed up all night talking about how to live a life of purpose. What better way to thank the people who had saved Frank's life than by returning to their medically deprived village so he could save theirs? "We're in," they told the doctor the following morning.

When they returned to Modesto, they quit their jobs, and then sold everything—the Montana ranch, the condos in Colorado and Palm Springs, the $40,000 garden sculptures. The material possessions they normally missed no longer appealed to them. It looked like "junk," they said.

Their new African home was a tiny apartment on one of the noisiest streets in Arusha. Their electricity was intermittent, their tap water brown. They took cold showers.

And they were at peace.

After two years at the clinic, they bought a 20-foot bus with running water, oxygen, and solar electricity, and began a mobile practice in the villages around Mt. Kilimanjaro.

One day Frank came to the village of his former guide Kitaba. "For a *mzungu*—a white person—to come here and care so much is a really amazing thing," Kitaba said. "When he comes, people ask me how much it will cost them and they can't believe it when I tell them it's free." Frank's arrival was greeted with a feast of chicken, rice, and cooked bananas.

Before dinner, Frank saw the first patient, Abraham, a thirtyish man who looked 50. He had an ulcer. As he was touching Abraham, Kitaba ran and got a camera. "He thinks you are an angel who came with medicine," Kitaba explained. "He wants a picture to prove it was true, because nobody will believe it. He will put it on his wall and remember you forever."

Frank hugged Abraham, overcome by the compliment. This is what doctoring is supposed to feel like. This is the moment he will think about when he is at death's door.[10]

∿

Salvation is hope, the hope of a meaningful life gained by the restoration of a purposeful framework in which to live, both personally and socially. God restores personal and social meaning by placing them within the larger framework of God's purposes for human life: the human participation in the free movement of grace and gratitude that flows between

10 See FAME online: www.fameafrica.org, and the linked news stories.

God and humanity, humans with one another, and human beings with other creatures.

That Frank is saved from a vain life is revealed by two comments he makes. The first is when he says he is overcome with gratitude for Kitabi and the twenty porters who lifted him up, sang him songs, and bore him at their own risk down the mountain. He is overcome by their graciousness. The second is when he says he is overcome by the compliment given to him by Abraham wanting to take his picture and keep it, for he is to Abraham "an angel who came with medicine." To accept grace, and to give grace; to accept the thanks of others, and to be thankful: For this we were created.

We are *homo sapiens* and *homo faber*, as Frank shows with his use of intelligence and creativity to bring medicine to those lacking it through his bus. But primarily we are *homo adorans*. We receive the world from God in joy, then give it back again in generosity and gratitude.[11]

THE COMING OF SALVATION

While Hanna stayed with Josef as he rode the helicopter from the oilrig to the mainland, she left afterward despite his cries for her to stay. She returned to her factory job, though now she brought spinach soufflé to work.

During his recuperation and then back home, Josef thought frequently of Hanna, and decided he wanted to spend the rest of his life with her. Finally tracking her down, he met her outside her factory.

"I thought you and I would go away together . . . Today . . . Come with me, Hanna."

"No, I don't think that is going to be possible. Because I'm afraid one day I may begin to cry, and the tears will fill the room, and we'll both drown."

"Then I'll learn how to swim."[12]

---

11. This understanding of the purpose of human life is presented by Eastern Orthodox Church theologian Alexander Schmemann in *For the Life of the World*. See for example 15, 118–21.

12. One of the early secrets Josef told Hanna is that though he works on an oilrig, he doesn't know how to swim.

In the final scene, Hanna is in a farmhouse kitchen. She and Josef have been married for several years. She watches as their two sons laugh and run in the grass outside.

When alone, Hanna at times still thinks about the past. But what saves Hanna is hope, hope that the end of her story could be changed by the introduction of something new and life-giving and meaningful. That newness was human fidelity, embodied in the actions and promises of Josef. She was afraid no one had the grace to endure beside her a descent into the hellacious flashbacks from the past. He convinced her that at the least, he wanted such grace.

Sheer power is almost useless in helping someone overcome despair, as Josef discovered, because one cannot force another who is despairing to have hope. Instead of coercion, Josef meets her with nothing but himself and an honest statement of his desires. He has already walked part way with her in her descent into hell, listening to her story while on the oil rig. Both then and when he met her outside her factory, he offered her solidarity and the promise of fidelity in relation to the future. Through this approach, he respects her free will, while giving her hope.

This is how God also overcomes our personal and social despair.

GOD'S ROLE IN SALVATION

Frank, Susan, and Hanna are able to move from despair over the meaninglessness of their lives to a sense of the purposefulness of life. How is God able to help someone make this transition? How is God able to respect the free will of the despairing person while also giving her or him a reason to live again?

The way that God secures the meaning of our personal and corporate lives is through two moves. First, God determines the end of the human story. One way or another, despite our choices, we will find the fulfillment of our life's meaning. While a possibility, this truth does not necessitate a belief in universal salvation. It is possible to miss the purpose of our life, if we continuously refuse God's end for our life as participation in the movement of grace and gratitude. But for those who do not steadfastly refuse, fulfillment is guaranteed. We get back even that which we rejected—the form of life which satisfies us because it fulfills God's intent for our lives.

God's second move, however, is this. Though the end is determined, the route to the end is indeterminate. We determine the route to the end through our choices, and our choices have consequences. Losses are real, as Frank and Susan discovered on the mountain, looking back at fifty years of a life wasted. The route to our and the world's fulfillment can be hard, or relatively easy, depending on choices we make. This openness of the route makes our life choices meaningful.

Yet the choices we make, with real consequences, are made within the context of a divine promise and guarantee: We will not be dropped by God.

JESUS'S ROLE IN SALVATION

God the Mother/Father sends the Son to secure the meaning of creaturely existence. Jesus's role is teleological. That he secures the meaning of existence has a positive import: There is a purpose to life, and the triune God gives us access to this meaning. This provides those in despair the very thing they are missing: a reason to hope.

That Jesus secures the meaning of existence can also be perceived as a threat. The meaning made real and lasting by Jesus may not be the meaning a person or society has chosen for themselves. For Satan, for the demons Jesus encounters in the gospels, for those who benefit from kyriarchal forces, like Caesar and Hitler, Jesus's teleological actions are rightly seen as a counterforce to their life efforts. The same would be true of someone like Nietzsche, of cynics or nihilists who find their identity in their cold-eyed realism: "There is no meaning to life."

Jesus acts in three ways to secure the meaning of human existence. First, by becoming a human being like us, God the Son joins us in our experiences, including those of meaninglessness. God binds God's history to our own history, the meaning of God's existence to the meaning of the world's existence: This is the significance of the incarnation and the cross. In Christ, God is Emmanuel, God-with-us.

This presence of God with and beside us in our desperate moments helps to overcome the loneliness we feel in our suffering. We find a companion in our suffering. God is with Sam and Grace Masoudi and Julie Johnson-Reimann when the flames engulf the house. God is with Ruth, Sarah, and Christopher John-Reimann in the burn unit. God is with Frederick, Marie, and Elizabeth Masoudi when they return from their walk to find two children and siblings gone. When the randomness and searing catastrophes appear to make our lives cheap, we find Someone beside us who affirms that we are of infinite worth.

When Nicholas Wolterstorff lost his son Eric to a climbing accident, he eventually realized that God was present with Eric when he fell, and sat beside Nicholas on the mourning bench. It was a great comfort, he wrote, but it did not answer all questions. It did not explain why God allowed the catastrophes in the first place. Envisioning God falling down the mountain with Eric, God "scraped and torn," Wolterstorff asked God, "Why do you permit yourself to suffer, O God? If the death of the devout costs you dear (Ps. 116:15), why do you permit it? Why do you not grasp joy?"[13] He did not find an answer to that question.

But if Nicholas did not find an answer, he found an Answerer, a God who answers not with theodicy theorems but with God's own covenantal presence.[14] For those in Western societies in which they question whether there is a correlative object to their longings for the divine, the presence of God overcomes that loss. Further, the One who is with them in experiences of meaninglessness has experienced the suffering of meaninglessness as well, in his moments of doubt and struggle in Gethsemane, and through his cry of dereliction from the cross. Jesus knows what it is like to be disappointed, including being disappointed in God.[15] Further, the One who knows our sufferings and who suffers alongside us is also the One through whom all things were made. "He himself is before all things, and in him all things hold together" (Col 1:17; see vv. 15–20). The One who sits beside us and refuses to ever leave us is the Maker of all things, including the meaning of all things. Again, this does not answer why the horrific things happen, or exactly how all things will be "brought together in him" and made whole. But we have the assurance that God has not cast us aside as those beyond hope of a meaningful existence, that God's determination to see God's own purposes fulfilled entails with it God's covenanted determination to see our lives brought to their full meaning. As Wolterstorff wrote of the incarnate God whose thirty-three years on earth ended on a cross:

> We're in it together, God and we, together in the history of our world. The history of our world is the history of our suffering together. Every act of evil extracts a tear from God, every plunge

13. Wolterstorff, *Lament for a Son*, 80.

14. See Hall, *God and Human Suffering*, 94.

15. On God as a suffering God, see Hall, *Professing the Faith*, chapter 3; on God's solidarity with us through incarnation and cross, see ibid., chapter 9; on Jesus's experiencing meaninglessness in Gethsemane and at Golgotha, see ibid., 535–37, 544–48.

into anguish extracts a sob from God. But also the history of
our world is the history of our deliverance together. God's work
to release himself [sic] from his suffering is his work to deliver
the world from its agony; our struggle for joy and justice is our
struggle to relieve God's sorrow.[16]

Second, in Jesus Christ, the end of creaturely existence is determined.
"Today this scripture has been fulfilled in your hearing," he told those in
Nazareth as he began his public ministry (Luke 4:21). In his person and
his public ministry, he brings to earth "the Day of the Lord," the time
when God reigns directly upon earth and God's purposes are fulfilled.
History has meaning, and as we saw in the emancipation, hospitality, and
justice models of chapters 7, 8, and 9, Jesus is that meaning come to fruition, its "first fruits," the new human being. Following his murder, Jesus's
resurrection from the dead is God's seal of promise and guarantee that
God's purposes for creation will be fulfilled. Along with the incarnation
and cross embodying God's solidarity with us in our meaninglessness,
the resurrection is another basis for hope. As Wolterstorff concluded,
the general resurrection of the dead, of the bodies of the dead, is God's
assurance that the final word will not be the meaningless ripping of relationships of love, but meaning. "The poor will be raised from the dust;
the sorrowing, lifted up from their ashes."[17]

That the meaning of the world's existence, and of our own, is secured
can be a great relief. We no longer have to keep justifying ourselves, proving that we have made our lives meaningful. Securing our life's meaning
is no longer our job. In an interview about her autobiography *Audition*,
Barbara Walters said that even late in her career, colleagues would ask
her, "When are you going to stop auditioning?" Despite her phenomenal
success as a journalist, each step in her career and indeed in her life she
felt like she was on stage, proving she was good enough.[18]

But since Jesus secures life's meaning, we can let go of our desperate and futile attempts to do it on our own.[19] In Jesus, God is with us.
In Jesus, the movement of God to human beings in love, and the free

16. Wolterstorff, *Lament for a Son*, 91; see also ibid., 108.

17. From the Song of Hannah, quoted in Wolterstorff, *Lament for a Son*, 111. On the
crucial role of the resurrection of the body in securing meaning, see ibid., 101–2, 111.

18. Walters, *Audition*, 4.

19. On this positive element of Jesus bringing in "the Day of the Lord," see Barth,
Church Dogmatics, IV/1, 233–35.

response of love from humans back to God, is actualized. As *homo ador-ans*, the meaning of our existence is to participate in that flow of grace and gratitude, to accept our identity as a gift: We are the ones whom God loves. That end of all things for us is determined. "Who will separate us from the love of Christ? Will hardship, or distress, or persecution, or famine, or nakedness, or peril, or sword?" As one who had the meaning of his existence shattered in a conversation with Jesus, and who certainly endured frustrations to his missionary vocation, Paul nevertheless knew the purpose of his life was secured. "No," he wrote. "In all these things we are more than conquerors through him who loved us" (Rom 8:35, 37).

While Jesus secures the end, his third action is to leave the route to that end indeterminate. As we have seen, the prophesied "Day of the Lord" was split into two "days." The God who Comes to us comes first in Jesus of Nazareth. But God will come again, as will Jesus, at the end of history. This two-day configuration of God's fulfillment of all things opens up space for a human role in determining the precise shape that guaranteed fulfillment will take. Our choices matter, not in whether God will succeed in fulfilling the world's purpose, but in the exact way it gets fulfilled. We are given the role of stewards of God's creation, and co-partners in effecting the particular shape of the fulfilled new creation.

It matters whether Frank Artress and Susan Gustafson come down from the mountain and choose to move to Africa and drive their bus to villages that have never had medical care. It matters whether Hanna takes the risk to join Josef in a life together, or shrinks back into her old patterns of hopelessness.

THE HOLY SPIRIT'S ROLE IN SALVATION

The Holy Spirit is the divine improviser. The Spirit of the resurrection, of the new future and thus of hope, tries to get us to perceive God's pres-ence with us in our sufferings, and God's guarantee that in Jesus our life's meaning is and will be fulfilled.

The Holy Spirit also interacts with us to encourage us to take the quickest and easiest way to our and the world's fulfillment. Since we can quench or resist the Spirit's guidance, as Frank and Susan did initially in choosing the pursuit of prestige over love, the Spirit then finds another way to lead us to our fulfillment. The Spirit finds other ways to use our gifts for the building of God's kingdom. These other ways may involve more pain and struggle for us, and for God, than the original option the

Spirit intended for us. It may have been easier, for example, if Frank and Susan had decided at age 30 to devote their medical skills to those lacking it, rather than to an American hospital with twenty anesthesiologists.

OUR ROLE IN SALVATION

In the movie *Romero*, Salvadoran archbishop Oscar Romero comes to a moment of defeat. His friend and compatriot Father Grande has been murdered. Other members of his parish who have fought for the human rights of the poor have been abducted in the middle of the night, tortured, and left for dead on side streets. The military has threatened his life. Visiting the sight where Father Grande was killed, Romero walks into a field and falls to his knees. "I can't," he says to God. "You must." He has given up, it seems. If anyone is to make any meaningful sense of the disorder of a society ruled by death squads and oppression, God must do it. But then Romero says, "Show me the way." Despite the long odds of change, he is still willing to be used by God to bring in God's reign of justice and peace.

Romero went on to rise up again and challenge the ruling oligarchy. Though the death threats increased, he responded, "If they kill me, my blood will arise in the Salvadoran people."[20] He did not know how God would fulfill God's promise of a just world, but he knew that the end was guaranteed. This fact gave him the hope and courage needed to offer himself to causes that were risky, uncertain, and indeed, seemingly hopeless.

Frank Artress has a similar perspective on the meaning of his work. For three months, Amber Croft, a Kaiser pediatric nurse, joined Artress for checkups on six hundred Tanzanian school children. She had been looking for more meaning in her ten-year nursing career. Just a few days into it, she did not know how she could continue on without feeling overwhelmed. How, she asked Frank, can you pass out medicines and antibiotics and multivitamins when the kids are most likely going to be just as sick again in a month? He told her that every little bit helps. Even the littlest bits are better than no bits at all in a starving country. The life expectancy in Tanzania is 43, but maybe their medicine could help them reach 45, or even 50. It was a start, not a stopping point.

---

20. Romero in a telephone interview with a Mexican newspaper two weeks before his death; quoted in Woodward, *Making Sense*, 46.

"For to me, to live is Christ, and to die is gain," Paul wrote while in prison awaiting trial (Phil 1:21). And in Romans, he wrote: "We do not live to ourselves, and we do not die to ourselves. If we live, we live to the Lord, and if we die, we die to the Lord; so then, whether we live or whether we die, we are the Lord's. For to this end Christ died and lived again, so that he might be Lord of both the dead and the living" (Rom 14:7–9).

That the meaning of his existence and of all things is guaranteed by Christ's work does not make Paul passive or apathetic, stealing the meaning of his life's decisions and efforts. Rather, it frees him up to do "fruitful labor" by enabling him to let go of the results of that labor (Phil 1:22). The world's purposes are fulfilled by God, and if the specific texture and route of fulfillment is not done through him in one way, then it will be done through some other way. Like Paul and Romero, so also Bonhoeffer and Martin Luther King Jr. found the freedom for action, for a meaningful vocation as God's creature, empowered by the hope secured in the incarnation, public ministry, cross and resurrection of Jesus.

We are freed to strive for a life in which, attentive to God's grace, we may be overwhelmed with joy and gratitude; and serving God with our lives, we may also be overwhelmed by the compliments of others, their expressions of gratitude for our grace. As Frank Artress discovered, in both experiences, we shall find the meaning of our existence fulfilled, and peace.

Postlude: The Center Holds

THE GOAL OF THIS book has been to sever the connection between the decisive salvific change in the human situation brought about in Christ from the myth of redemptive violence. It has sought to combine the strengths of the penal substitutionary theory of atonement and the generative and enlightenment theories of salvation, while leaving behind their fatal flaws. It has sought a nonambivalent, nonviolent God-image allied with the New Testament's herald that something *new*—a definitive resolution to the problems of human sin and the world's kyriarchal resistance to the life-giving purposes of God—has occurred in Jesus Christ.[1]

Womanist theologian Delores Williams says, "There is nothing of God in the blood of the cross,"[2] and from the perspective of God's ultimate and intentional wills, she speaks truth. God the Mother/Father sent the Son to inaugurate "the Day of the Lord," and with it, the new reign of God's justice and *shalom*. God's *intentional will* was for Jesus to recreate life. The five constructive models in Part Three affirm that there is no intrinsic saving significance to the torture Christ endured. They deny the myth that good comes out of torture, thereby preventing the cross from symbolically supporting the sacrificial mentality which funds scapegoating and mimetic violence. God and the gospel stand for life, and call followers to the twin virtues of obedience to God and revolt against the forces of death.

And yet, while violence does not save, given the circumstances of fallen humans resisting Christ's world-upending, life-restoring acts, the cross is a locus of God's saving act. In sending the Son to become incarnate, the three persons of the Trinity knew his murder—while not necessary—was likely, if not inevitable. The three were prepared

---

1. The former is the strength of the generative and enlightenment models; the latter is the strength of the penal substitutionary theory.

2. Williams, "Black Women's Surrogacy," 32.

to enact the salvation of the world through that brutal murder of the beloved Son.

From different angles, the *emancipation, hospitality, divine justice, reorientation,* and *restoration* models describe how the nonviolent God saves us through the cross of Christ. Like the generative and enlightenment models, they affirm God's unconditional love and nonviolent intentions toward humanity. Yet while the generative and enlightenment models are not untrue in their descriptions of Jesus, they simply do not go far enough in describing his saving work. Jesus does not merely point to redemptive possibilities within us that we may or may not actualize; he effects salvation in his own person and work.

Like the penal substitutionary theory, these five models affirm redemption, but one with a different shape. Instead of using the lenses of retributive justice and mimetic violence for reconciling divine justice and mercy, the five models see redemption as God's "making good" God's promise to humanity to secure human life, and as humanity's "making good" (through Jesus) of their covenant commitments to God and to their fellow creatures. Redemption entails restorative justice more than retributive; it thus functions to support the former as the basis for criminal systems and international relations, rather than the latter.

The five models' combination of salvific actualism and divine nonviolence empowers mission and evangelism. It allows the Church to return to its core message, the good news about the saving power of Christ, which it tells in narrative and demonstrative forms through worship and resistance to the kyriarchal forces of death. The good news of the saving act in Christ by a nonviolent God allows the Church in its witness to avoid mystagoguery—the implicit or explicit claim by the Church that we do not know how God saves us in the cross, but our worship centers around it anyway. It likewise allows the Church to stop avoiding discussions of atonement and the cross for a preferred shift in focus to supposed ideals taught by Jesus—ideals that can be garnered elsewhere anyway, thus undercutting the necessity of Christian witness. In concrete ways, the *emancipation, hospitality, divine justice, reorientation,* and *restoration* models enable the Church to speak about atonement and the cross, and to relate them to particular situations of human distress. With confidence, we know the redemption God has accomplished in Christ, and give thanks for it. Further, with the five models' reassertion of the saving role of the Holy Spirit into the doctrine of atonement, we can also know our role in God's salvation, and do it.

By reimagining the relation of divine love, violence, and the cross, the five models present a viable center for our faith, a center that can hold.

Glossary of Terms

act of love theory of atonement   For Peter Abelard (a twelfth-century contemporary of Anselm), love is a form of power which can transform broken hearts. Developed by Abelard and reconfigured by nineteenth- and twentieth century liberal Protestants, the "act of love" theory (also called the *moral influence* or *exemplarist* theory) believes the change that needs to happen is not in God's attitude toward humanity—God is always loving toward the ones whom God has made—nor in the power of the Devil, but rather in distorted human hearts. Humans mistrust God, thinking God seeks to dominate the self, or to belittle it. God overcomes this mistrust through an act of extravagant love which enkindles a corresponding love in the humans who witness it. While Jesus's teachings and moral depth exhibit God's love, his willingness to sacrifice his life for others clarifies that he, and God, seek to empower rather than belittle humans. This passionate act opens the door for a human renewal of trust in God, and a desire to follow God's way of self-giving love.

ambivalent God-image   An image of God as both loving and death-dealing, attitudes and actions rooted in an internal conflict within God concerning God's valuation of the created "other"—humans and nature. This divine posture induces confusion, fear, mistrust, and the sacrificial mentality into human beings.

apocalypse, apocalyptic   An apocalypse is a disclosing of things hidden, particularly related to God's will for the future. Jewish and Christian apocalyptic literature emerged during periods of great persecution from the second century BCE to the second century CE. The genre describes the (often imminent) return of God to Israel to destroy the ruling forces of evil and free the righteous from their dominion. This event overturns a history of the domination of corrupt powers and empires to establish God's reign on earth. Jewish apocalyptic literature describes the coming of a messiah who will bring the corrupt era to an end and deliver the righteous into the new freedom of God's reign. Many New Testament scholars hold that John the Baptist and Jesus were apocalypticists who preached that the corrupt aeon's end would happen within their lifetimes.

apocalyptic history Jürgen Moltmann argues that two conflicting histories—apocalyptic and eschatological—meet in the incarnation, life, death, and resurrection of Jesus. Apocalyptic history describes the downward spiral toward corporate self-annihilation brought on by human histories of betrayal and violence, and God's definitive act through the Messianic One with integrity to reveal these histories' nihilistic end. This action represents divine judgment, God's "No," against that self-destruction—truly bringing it to an end. [See *day of the Lord's wrath*.]

atonement In the context of relational concord broken by betrayal and violation, atonement has two meanings. It means the opposite state: being "at onement" in the Middle English, "in harmony" or "concord." It also can mean the act by which the perpetrator brings about that new state of reconciliation. Often the word refers to an act of repentance and reparations. In Christian theology, atonement refers to God's act to restore harmonious relations with humans, and that reconciling act finds its centerpiece in the incarnation, life, death, and resurrection of Jesus. A multitude of images of atonement is found in the Bible, and no single formal doctrine of atonement has been put forth by the Church (as has been put forth for the incarnation and the Trinity). Significant theories of atonement in the Church's history include the sacrifice metaphors prevalent in the New Testament texts; the "Christ the Victor" theory prominent in the early church and still the dominant view of the Eastern Orthodox churches; the satisfaction theory created by Anselm; the penal substitutionary theory favored by the Reformers and many Protestants since; and the "moral influence" or "act of love" theory advocated by Abelard and by many nineteenth and twentieth century Protestants.

biophilic A view of redemption in which life flows out of life, rather than from suffering and death (*necrophilic*). This view imagines a living and life-giving entity (a gardener, a mother) birthing and nurturing life in the other, simply because it is good that it exists. The giving of life is the central activity of God, not the bringing of death. Jesus' power of life gives life to others (the hemorrhaging woman, Jairus's daughter), not his last days of suffering and state execution.

Christ the Victor theory of atonement Perhaps the earliest theory of atonement—prominent in the writings of the early Greek Fathers including Irenaeus, Origen, Athanasius and Gregory of Nyssa—it perceives humans as captive to the malevolent forces of the demonic, and the degenerating power of death. Christ battles and defeats both the Devil and death itself, particularly through the incarnation, his death and subsequent resurrection. In this model, God the Mother/Father and Christ remain mostly nonviolent, focused solely on liberating captive humans. The Devil needs the death of Jesus, not God or Jesus himself, and the Devil is the agent behind the death.

day of the Lord's wrath Also called "the day of the Lord," "the day of wrath," "the day of vengeance of our God," and "the day of judgment," this phrase in the Hebrew Scriptures refers broadly to the prophets' warnings of divine judgment of the continuously sinning Israel (before the Assyrian conquest and then Babylonian Exile; see for example Amos 5:18–20; 8–11; Jer 5–6; Zeph 1:14–18) and the nations (after the Exile, when it became more a day of rescue and hope for scattered Israel; see for example Isa 13–23; 61:2). In later apocalyptic literature, the phrase refers to the anticipated day of judgment when God will return to punish and destroy the forces of evil and reestablish God's rule of righteousness over Israel and the nations. Humans would suffer the penalties for their hubristic violence—their just recompense—and God's law would be upheld.

demonic, the (the "third factor") Alongside humans and God in strained covenantal relations, there exists a "third factor" which the New Testament calls "the demonic." It seeks to destroy all life and threatens God's creatures. Whether conceived in personified terms (a personal Devil and demons) or not, it goes beyond mere human motive and agency. This destructive force is suffused within social structures and even nature, but is also present deep within the human springs of mind and will. While its origin is mysterious, it appears whenever anxiety leads individuals or groups to treat any part of the good creation as if it were a god, one able to convey ultimate power and meaning. The finite force, now corrupted, eventually doubles back upon the worshippers with destructive power and an enslaving hold. While Paul identified five such demonic tyrants (sin, the Law, the principalities and powers, distorted regularities in the natural world, and death), the religious mystical traditions find the demonic lodged in attitudes and social structures based upon ego, possessions, and violence.

divine justice model of atonement   Through acts of escalating violence fueled by envy, avarice, and hatred of the "other," humans unleash a collapse of civil society and ecological sustenance which they are then powerless to reverse. Salvation entails a rescue operation in a fallen, self-annihilating planet through a restoration of God's just, fecund order of creation. God effects this restoration through a divine judgment which is simultaneously a divine "No" to human disorder and a lifting-up of human life into its true order. In the history of Jesus, the violent, self-annihilating trajectory of the perpetrators (the *apocalyptic history*) is carried to its inevitable and just end of collapse. Yet in that same history of Jesus and his disciples, simultaneously a new form of human being and community, filled with the Spirit of life and "the breath of the resurrection," is constituted and commences its unimpeachable growth (the *eschatological history*). God judges the world by making it right.

double agency   In contrast to synergistic models which imagine God and creatures as existing on the same level of agency—and thus either competing or contractually cooperating with one another—the double agency model conceives of God and creatures as existing on qualitatively different levels of being and agency. God is thus able to act in and through the free acts of the creature to bring about a single effect, without threatening their freedom. God's agency creates genuine creaturely agents.

emancipation model of atonement   In a tragic context in which humans have allowed themselves to become enslaved to the "third factor"—demonic forces within and without—God saves by sending the Son to defeat the demonic and free us. The Son, who wields the power of life over death, gains victory by non-violently pushing back evil; by resisting temptation, thereby disentangling the demonic from the good creation in his own humanity; and by constituting a form of community not based upon domination and subjugation.

enlightenment model of atonement In a context of blindness and delusion about reality—particularly about the nature of power—God saves through illumination and the invitation to switch from participating in false forms of power to true power. True power gives life within communities of equality, mutuality, and generosity.

eschatological history Jürgen Moltmann argues that two conflicting histories—apocalyptic and eschatological—meet in the incarnation, life, death, and resurrection of Jesus. Eschatological history is God's salvific countermovement to the apocalyptic history of human sin and self-destruction. Through the "standing up" of the Messianic One who has integrity and the Spirit of the resurrection and life, the "new creation" breaks into this world. Like yeast in dough, it begins to move the world toward its true end of a communal unity not based on domination and subjugation. [See *eucatastrophe*.]

eschatology, eschatological The doctrine of "the final things." In the three Western religions, eschatology refers to the "last aeon," the period when God defeats evil and brings the created order to its fulfillment in the "new heaven and new earth." In the Christian version, God consummates God's purposes for creation through the return of Jesus the Messiah (the "second coming of Christ"); the general resurrection of all the dead; the final judgment by God of all human beings, the dead and the living; and the establishment of God's dwelling within a healed creation on earth, in which there is no more suffering or death. The doctrine also discusses the possibility of an eternal hell. Jesus's preaching of "the coming reign of God" reflects a central eschatological theme in the New Testament.

eucatastrophe A term coined by J. R. R. Tolkien to describe not an ending of the tragic thrust of a narrative, but a sudden, joyous turning of events. The protagonists (and readers) glimpse a reality of goodness and wholeness beyond that tragic history; this goodness is more ultimate and will finally win the day.[1] Bertrand Russell named tragedy "the proudest, the most triumphant" of all the arts, for he saw the human condition as one of staunch defiance against "the trampling march of unconscious power." He wrote that "we see, surrounding the narrow raft illuminated by the flickering light of human comradeship, the dark ocean on whose

---

1. See Tolkien, "On Fairy Stories."

rolling waves we toss for a brief hour."[2] From one angle, Tolkien was even more pessimistic, for those who live through real tragedies experience only being smashed by those uncaring forces; they experience only the absurdity of life. Tolkien declared history a "long defeat": "man, [sic] each man and all men, and all their works shall die. A theme no Christian need despise."[3] Yet for Tolkien, human life is not utterly meaningless, for it is connected to another world, one of divinely-created human fulfillment and purpose. When this divine purpose from time to time enters into history, reversing the "long defeat," letting a gleam of final victory shine, bringing for the protagonists hope—"a catch of the breath, a beat and lifting of the heart"[4]—the shattering moment is eucatastrophic. For Tolkien, the incarnation is the eucatastrophe of "the long defeat" of history, the resurrection that of the gospel story begun at the incarnation.[5] The eucatastrophic moment does not halt history's downward spiral, nor deny that catastrophes occur, but it denies universal final defeat. It shows that the end is goodness, not absurdity, and though we die, our deaths will not be in vain.

generative model of atonement   Kyriarchal forces dissipate energies for living by blocking the flow of life giving, mutual power between persons, communities, and God. Salvation occurs when God overturns kyriarchal structures and opens the flow of power, generating new capacities for flourishing. This model imagines God's power as *biophilic*, with new life flowing out of life.

hospitality   To live hospitably is to trust both self and others, for one sees God as nonambivalent toward humanity, and one's neighbor as a fellow beloved creature of God. Instead of cutting oneself off, one lives open to God, neighbors, and God's inbreaking reign of *shalom*. The kinship of this hospitable community is found in mutual regard, forgiveness of faults, and the glad receiving and giving of aid.

---

2. Quotes from Russell, "A Free Man's Worship," 112, 116, and 113 respectively.

3. On history as a "long defeat," see Tolkien's letter dated December 15, 1956, in *The Letters of J. R. R. Tolkien*, 255. For the latter quote, see Tolkien, "*Beowulf*: The Monsters and the Critics," 119.

4. Tolkien, "On Fairy Stories," 86.

5. Ibid., 88. See Mary Magdalene's cry, "Rabbouni!" upon seeing Jesus outside the tomb on Easter morn, John 20:16.

hospitality model of atonement   When creation has been made a wasteland, defiled by multiple betrayals of promises, escalating cycles of violence, and a cynical hopelessness, salvation is levity: the opening up within history of a future different than the past, one hopeful and life-giving. This new future brings a restored life for victims of violence, cleansing for perpetrators, and the reconciliation of perpetrators, victims, and God within a renewed community of trust. On behalf of humanity, God the Son effects this reconciliation through an act of hospitality. Instead of closing himself off from any parties, he remains open, offering a "two-fold sacrifice" on behalf of perpetrators toward God: he tells the truth about what humans have done, and he commits to a different kind of relationship with God and neighbors in the future. God accepts this representative response, and forgives and reconciles with humanity.

justice, restorative   A theory of justice that seeks to heal victims' wounds, restore offenders to law-abiding practices within the community, and repair broken webs of trust. It sees crimes as primarily against individuals or the community rather than the state or abstract laws. Victims are given an active role in the dispute, and offenders are urged to take responsibility for their crimes, attempt to repair the damage, and become reintegrated into communal life.

justice, retributive   A theory of justice that rewards good deeds and inflicts punishment on offenders. It sees crimes as primarily against the state and its laws. The theory argues that the offender through her or his behavior has gained unfair advantages in securing a community's limited resources, and that punishment will set this imbalance straight. The severity of penalty must be proportionate to the severity of the crime (a principle argued, for example, in the Code of Hammurabi and the Law of Moses [Deut 19:16–21; Exod 21:23–27, the *lex talionis*]).

kyriarchy   Kyriarchy refers to a community in which relations of super- and subordination are deemed natural, preferable, and/or divinely ordained. In her book *But She Said*, feminist New Testament scholar Elisabeth Schüssler Fiorenza introduced this neologism to broaden the social analysis of oppression beyond "patriarchy's" merely gendered perspective. Like patriarchy, kyriarchy describes a society structured by a pyramid of relations of domination and subordination. These structures are justified with socially-constructed notions of superior and inferior persons. Power is understood as domination of "the other." However, while patriarchy recognizes the father as the head of the household, kyriarchy broadens the definition to include "the rule of the emperor/master/lord/father/husband over all his subordinates." Schüssler Fiorenza notes that such fathers also function as lords and masters over multiple other persons. Most patriarchal cultures entail complex webs of super- and subordinate relations involving not just gender, but also property, education, race, ethnicity, sexual orientation, and geography. Further, persons who are victims can be at the same time masters over others, and collaborators in maintaining the system of graduated dominations and subordinations. For example, the lady in a ruling class is "the other" of the lord, but she may collaborate in treating all other women as "inferior" by race, class, or ethnicity. Moreover, not all men dominate and exploit women in equal fashion. Underlying the multiple webs of oppressive relationships in a kyriarchy is the insistence that society needs a "servant class" (or race or people) to function—a class maintained by law, ideology, and brute violence.

logic (law, principle) of mercy, grace, forgiveness　The *logic of mercy* is rooted in two elements of the Hebrew Bible which become basic to later messianic hope, and of which the New Testament claims fulfillment in the experiences around Jesus and Pentecost. The first element is the interconnections between three forms of laws in the Exodus-covenant materials: the stipulations regulating justice, laws concerning mercy, and instructions for cultic life. The second element is the promises of the Spirit who would fulfill a universal realization of justice, mercy, and knowledge of God, each trait strengthening the other. While the justice laws uphold equity of treatment, the companion mercy laws—found in all bodies of law in the Hebrew Bible—cultivate a society expectation that stands as a counterforce to and deep qualification of the meaning of the principle that "people should get what they deserve." The logic of mercy carries with it the expectation that the privileged will withdraw their own claims—perhaps even forgoing their legal rights—to benefit those who are weak. These mercy laws move logically toward the dismantling of systematic structures of oppression.[6] Justice provides stability by equitably resolving disputes, while mercy insures sensitivity that weaker persons are not systematically overlooked in regard

6. See Welker, *God the Spirit*, 18–20.

to communal resources. Those using the logic of mimetic exchange believe that people should only get what they deserve, and presume to know the meanings of the terms "justice," "mercy," and "God." In contrast, those using the law of mercy believe they must look to God to reveal the meanings of those terms, and that the inclusion and uplifting of the weaker members may entail one forfeiting one's rights. In the New Testament, the law of mercy insures that none can be cast out, for all share the same identity, rooted in Jesus, of healed victims and forgiven sinners. God, who establishes the universal reign of righteousness (which brings the communal coalescing of justice, mercy, and the knowledge of God), resembles the prodigal father of the lost son.

logic (law, principle) of mimetic exchange, mimetic violence In interpersonal or intercommunal relations, actions should be repaid in kind. Beneficial action earns merit which deserves to be repaid by the other. If a person harms another, he must compensate the other for damages. While this principle of Roman law can fund *restorative justice*, the transactional logic of mimetic exchange more frequently feeds *retributive justice*: offenders must endure retributory sufferings commensurable with the evils they have inflicted if the balance of justice—a "fair exchange"—is to be restored. Violence is responded to with equal violence. God becomes the exacting and punitive judge who upholds the cosmic order of "an eye for an eye," a king who uses violence to solve violence, and a father whose forgiveness of sinful children is contingent upon the penalty of suffering unleashed upon someone. This God oversees a world in which nothing is free.

love Throughout the tradition, Christian love has commonly been identified with the willingness to sacrifice the self—even to the point of death—for the wellbeing of a beloved. But to love as Christ loved is *to love life*, a definition which includes loving the life of the self as well as that of others (whether a beloved or an enemy). What is "sacrificed" in such loving is not the self, but the ego's desire for dominance over others. Love entails pure attending—to self or the other—as well as doing things without calculation of *quid pro quo*. Such love brings a form of unity with the 'other' that is not based upon dominance.

myth of redemptive violence The erroneous belief that salvation comes through violence. The violent perpetrator may be saved by the innocent victim's endurance of pain, just like violent humans are saved by the blood of Jesus. The victim is also redeemed through adopting the holy trait of selflessness, a trait exemplified by Jesus who freely chose to die "for others." They myth may suggest to perpetrators that violence against other groups is salvific in some mysterious fashion.

panentheism   Literally "all things in God," pan-en-theism believes that God is greater than all things, yet all things exist within God or are part of God. In some forms, God is not the creator, but is the eternal force of life generating and interpenetrating the universe. In other forms, all things are eternally part of God's being, though God transcends the material world (as a personality/mind transcends a body, even as it is inextricably connected to it). Also in most forms, as the universe which is in God evolves, God also changes, becoming "more than" God was before. This view of the God-world relation is ancient, being held by many North and South American native peoples, several schools of Hinduism, and mystical schools of Greek philosophy (Neoplatonism), Islam (Sufism) and Judaism (Kabbalah) in the Middle East and Europe. In contemporary Christian theology, it is frequently also the philosophical foundation in process, feminist, and eco-spiritual theologies.

pantheism   The physical universe is equivalent to God. One form sees God as immanent within the world; another form believes God is the only reality, the physical universe merely appearing to be real.

patriarchy   Literally "rule by the father," patriarchy refers to a social system, historically derived from Greek and Roman law, in which the father (or eldest male) is head of the household, men have authority over women and children, and descent is traced through the male line. Based on this familial unit, patriarchy also refers more broadly to a larger system of government by males, and the dominance of men over women in wealth, status, and public power.

penal substitutionary model of atonement   Humans are sinners who willfully and egregiously break God's laws, and thus deserve the punishment for their sins—death. God satisfies the claims of divine justice in a way other than killing all the humans, by mercifully transferring the obligation to a vicarious substitute—strikingly, God's own person, incarnate and dying on the cross. Thus God makes forgiveness and divine-human reconciliation possible.

polytheism The belief that multiple gods exist. In some schools of Hinduism, certain indigenous religions of the world, as well as ancient Egyptian, Greek, and Roman religions, such gods were separated; in other forms of Hinduism, distinct gods were seen as subsumed within a greater divine whole.

power used demonically In the demonic exercise of power, individuals or groups objectify fellow subjects, using them as means for their own purposes, or as expendable to an imagined future. The imagined end may not in itself be evil. Nevertheless, by gaining mastery over others' freedom, those who use power demonically seek a communal unity that solidifies relations of domination and submission.

power, erotic This view conceives of power as grounded neither in dominance and willful assertion, nor in its seeming opposite, *agapic* love. Instead, true power is rooted in *eros*. A person with *eros* has a posture of wise, compassionate openness to the self, to all other beings, and to the interconnecting web of relationships that links all things. Erotic power, moving through such open channels, either increases or diminishes simultaneously for all creatures. Through the reciprocal giving and receiving of life, power, and love, all things flourish. Erotic power as the force for life—identified with the divine Spirit—is located deep within each being and also in the web of connections (immanence), yet cannot be controlled or possessed by any individual (transcendence). With such an understanding of power, self-possession and the capacity to engage with and give to the world are directly linked.

process theology Influenced by the process philosophy of Alfred North Whitehead and Charles Hartshorne, this twentieth-century and contemporary theology in Britain and North America conceives the fundamental nature of reality as *becoming* rather than *being*. Reality is not constituted by unchanging "substances" but by events in time, all of which are necessarily related. Each event is rooted in past events which form its environment, perceives a range of possible moves for the next moment, and acts with relative freedom to creatively choose from that range what it will next become. God, who is also constituted by events in time, both takes in every moment of the universe's experience (God's "consequent," or receptive, nature), holding them for the next moment, and lures each entity toward the best from amongst its range of next possible moves (God's "primordial" nature). God is in time rather than above it, is the most-influential (without having all the power), feels the sufferings and joys of each creature, and demonstrates the patient power of love rather than coercion.

ransom theory of atonement   A subset of the *Christ the Victor* theory, this image popular in patristic writings describes how it is that God defeats the most intelligent of the fallen angels. God does not directly challenge the Devil's right to dominion over sinners. Instead, God sends the Son to take on lowly human form. The Devil does not perceive the deity hidden in Jesus of Nazareth and, like a fish that swallows the bait on a hook, grabs hold of him and condemns him to death. However, the Devil has no right to the sinless Jesus. Through his act, the Devil forfeits his control of sinners to Christ, who restores them to their original glory as human beings created in God's image.

reorientation model of atonement   We live in a world without grace. Looking ahead, we see only the ungracious horizons of judgment upon our just guilt, or the annihilation of death. In our delusion, we cling to the ungracious world, believing it can save us, or that there is nothing else. Salvation is sobriety, which is effected through God's telling of two truths to us: We are living in a world without grace, and if continued, it will end in our destruction. At the same time, another world exists, the world of grace. It is superior to the ungracious world, and it fulfills us. In the Son, God both creates a human life filled with grace, and engages lost humans at the level of the imagination. Jesus' way of grace simultaneously reveals both truths, and invites us to form a new basis of the self in the gracious world.

restoration model of atonement   In contexts of hopelessness, in which meaning is shattered by random events of suffering or tragic events (which combine sin and chance), God saves by restoring a purposeful framework in which to live, both personally and socially. Through two moves, God respects the free will of the despairing person while also giving her a reason to live again: in Jesus, *God determines the end* of the human story, God's fulfillment of *shalom*; yet though the end is determined, *the route to the end is indeterminate*. We determine the route, and thus our choices matter.

sacrificial mentality   When relations of love or justice become distorted by patterns of domination and submission rather than reciprocity and equality, this psychological attitude rooted in fear and contempt may appear. The dominated individual or group takes it on when the character and motives of the other seem ambivalent and heteronomous. In the face of a moral watchdog unwilling to accept imperfections, the dominated one feels a lack of such perfected worth, and a corresponding fear of punishment or abandonment. The individual or group comes to believe that sacrificing something or someone may resolve the tension. Through *asceticism*, the dominated one "freely gives up" a part of the self to preserve the needed relationship—either the part that is deemed imperfect or, paradoxically, the parts that are lofty. Such internal violence can also be turned outward, toward others perceived as competitors for the blessings of the exacting, dominating party (as occurred, for example, between Cain and Abel). The sacrificial mentality simultaneously manifests itself in *moralism*. The ascetic willingness to "give up" parts of the self to gain approval leads to a willingness to liquidate individualistic and human qualities—kindness, humanity, an inner sense of self, freedom of conscience—for the sake of group acceptance. One attempts to become "perfect" by agreeing with external norms.

salvation   God bringing the world to its intended wholeness, a liberating and fulfilling act of which *atonement* is a part. The doctrine presumes a negative anthropology and cosmology, for it assumes that the human and creaturely situation is hopeless without aid from outside the human and creaturely sphere. The problem within the human situation is multivalent, and thus the saving act of the triune God must overcome all the elements of the problem simultaneously. Each of the theories about salvation attempts to convey a portion of the problem and of the mysterious, comprehensively saving act, which is why multiple models are needed to portray it fully. Two tensive relations are seen in the New Testament's and church history's descriptions of salvation. First, from one angle, God saves humanity and creation *by rescuing them from forces which threaten their very existence*, forces which include: individual and corporate guilt and the resulting divine-human and intra-human estrangement and violence; suffering and the dissipation of life, brought on by random or tragic events or diseases; the tragic twining of good and evil in human hearts and societies, threatening to bring both to collapse; the "third factor" of demonic forces; and death itself. From another angle, God saves humanity and creation *by bringing them to their divinely-purposed end*, the end of the new community which fulfills their hearts' longings. Salvation here means healing brokenness, wiping away tears, creating a form of life which is indestructible, establishing a community based on equality, forgiving faults, sharing resources, and loving hospitably. The Synoptic Gospels' identification of salvation with entry into the kingdom of God (see for example Mark 10:23–26) reflects this first tension, for God comes to both break the reign of tyrants, freeing captives, and to establish God's true way of *shalom*. Reflecting the second tension in the New Testament, the descriptions portray *salvation as already actualized in Jesus's life and work* (we "have been saved" [Eph 2:1–10; see also Luke 10:9]); yet also *longed for as a comprehensive event of the future* (we "shall be saved" [Rom 5:9–10; see also 1 Thess 5:8]). The Christian splitting of the messianic *day of the Lord* into two "days"—the first occurring in Jesus' life, death, and resurrection, the second when he returns again at the Last Judgment to comprehensively end evil—embodies this second tension. Finally, while the tradition rightly focuses upon the saving work of Jesus, a Trinitarian view of the divine action (which incorporates the roles of the Holy Spirit and humans who respond to Jesus and the Spirit), and the doctrine of eschatology are also essential to a full description.

satisfaction theory of atonement   Developed by Anselm in the 1090s, this theory perceived the human problem as the transgression of boundaries of civility, threatening the order and beauty of God's beloved creation. Justice requires the satisfaction of God's demands that the world order be set right, either by punishing the sinners, or through satisfaction from some other source. God chooses the later route, and acting as the Just One in the Son, through a life of perfect obedience even unto death, God restores the right relations which heal social communities and the divine-human covenant.

sin, corporate sin, and original sin   Broadly, sin is anything that goes against God's life-giving purposes for the human creation: It is "what was not meant to be." To some extent, God's good purposes may be discerned in one's conscience, through reason, or by observing the general order of creation. Explicitly, God's purposes are revealed in the "book end"

Biblical texts of creation and eschatology; in God's dealings with Israel; in the Ten Commandments and prophetic texts; and paradigmatically for Christians in the life, ministry, death and resurrection of Jesus. More specifically, sin is vandalism of God's good creation, and a distrustful and hubristic or despairing rejection of the community formed with God and others by the hospitable giving and receiving of grace. Such acts incur guilt in relation to God and concrete persons, and bring estrangement from these others and from the true nature of the self. Both individuals and communities sin in multiple ways. Values (love of ego, wealth, and violence, for example), presuppositions (power as domination), and behavior patterns of the "way without grace" all work to infect a community's ethos and its societal structures (*corporate sin*; as seen for example in patriarchy, kyriarchy, racism, militarism). The concept of *original sin* points to the paradoxical experience that sin is universal, yet freely chosen. The universal distortion of social systems and human attitudes affects all persons, so that no one has access to the original purity of the created order; we affect each other in disastrous ways. And yet the sinning we all do is self-chosen and is not inevitable.

sophia Sophia, God's "Wisdom" (*hokmah* in Hebrew, *sophia* in Greek) is used to personify God's presence and activity in the world (as God's "Spirit" or God's "Word" are similarly used). The term is grammatically feminine, and consistently depicted in female roles. Divine Wisdom is not only seen as a sister, a mother, a beloved, but also as a preacher of God's truth, a judge, a liberator, and an establisher of justice. Both in natural and human communities, Wisdom is the transcendent power of God in their midst, delighting in them and luring all things toward justice and life. Some feminist New Testament scholars argue that the gospels more consistently portray Jesus as the incarnation of Wisdom than as that of the Word (*logos*).

soteriology The technical term for the doctrine of salvation.

synergy, synergism Literally "working together," synergy occurs when two or more forces or agents work together to produce an effect greater than the sum of their individual effects. In Christian theology, synergism refers to the belief that salvation is achieved by the partial and joint efforts of divine and human agency.

theism   Broadly, theism is belief that a God or gods exist. Specifically, in the monotheistic context of the West, theism is the belief in one personal God who transcends the universe, created all things out of nothing, and sustains and governs all things towards God's purposes.

theodicy   A theodicy is a reasoned attempt to justify God's trustworthiness in the face of experiences of horrendous moral and natural evils which seem to thwart God's purposes. The problem is brought on by the three affirmations held by the three major Western religions: God is all-powerful; God is all-good; evil is real. It is difficult to see how all three affirmations can be true, for if God is able to prevent evil and gross suffering on the innocent but will not, then God is not good; if God wants to prevent evil and suffering, but cannot, then God is not omnipotent. With either case—an indifferent or sadistic God, or a weak one—it becomes difficult to trust God.

theological norm   While Christians draw from four sources to develop their views of God and humanity—Scripture, tradition, reason, and experience (including the sciences)—they also have a theological norm by which they judge the strength of a theological statement. Almost anything can serve as a norm, from autobiographical experiences to doctrinal or ethical principles (such as "salvation by grace through faith alone," or "all religions provide equal access to the Divine"); from elements of a narrative ("Jesus Christ, and him crucified") to other fields of inquiry ("the statement must fit with what science knows about reality").

tragedy   Against the notion that the suffering of the innocent is redemptive and is supported by God, tragedy points to forms of suffering that are radically destructive, utterly meaningless, and against the will of God. Further, we act in self-destructive ways, unleashing forces of evil that escape our control and that bring sufferings far beyond any culpability of our original act. We freely sin, yet exist as slaves to our own sinning. In our hearts and motives, good and evil entwine; we sin inspired by lofty intentions and executed with glorious skill. Despite all our powers, we cannot separate the evil without destroying the good. And as German Catholic theologian Eugen Drewermann points out, beneath the genuine moral culpability of the fall lies a true tragedy: though God walks in the Garden as ever, now the humans see God only in ambivalence, as One perhaps protecting, but perhaps annihilating.

Vicarious substitute, punishment, death   Someone who takes upon her- or himself the punishment due another, though not the guilt associated with the crime.

violence   To violate is to take an inalienable subject and treat it as an object. This act can be done to the self or others, to nature, and even to God. Such acts to harm can include killing, physical injury to bodily integrity, damage to a person's dignity and self-esteem, and the dehumanizing practices found in the systemic violence of kyriarchal structures. Perpetrators often commit violence to solidify relations of dominance and submission.

Yahweh   The sacred name of Israel's deity, as transliterated from the Hebrew consonants YHWH. It is represented nearly 7,000 times in the Old Testament.

Yahwist   The name scholars give the oldest of four major sources of the Pentateuch (the first five books of the Hebrew Bible), as postulated by the Documentary Hypothesis. The writings of this anonymous author or compiler, produced around 950 BCE, include half of Genesis, the first half of Exodus, and pieces of Numbers.

Bibliography

Abelard, Peter. "Exposition of the Epistle to the Romans (Excerpt from the Second Book)." Translated by Gerald E. Moffatt. In *A Scholastic Miscellany: Anselm to Ockham*, edited and translated by Eugene Fairweather, 276–87. The Library of Christian Classics 10. Philadelphia: Westminster, 1956.

Abraham, Arthur. *The Amistad Revolt: An Historical Legacy of Sierra Leone and The United States*. Washington, DC: U.S. Department of State, International Information Programs, 1998.

Anselm. *St. Anselm, Cur Deus Homo*. Translated by Sidney Norton Deane. Chicago: Open Court, 1903.

Apted, Michael, director. *Amazing Grace*. DVD. Presented by Bristol Bay Productions in association with Ingenious Film Partners, a Sunflower production. Produced by Edward Pressman et al. Written by Steven Knight. Beverly Hills, CA: Twentieth Century Fox Home Entertainment, 2007.

Arendt, Hannah. *Eichmann in Jerusalem: A Report on the Banality of Evil*. 1963. Reprint, Penguin Classics. New York: Penguin, 2006.

August, Bille, director. *Les Miserables*. DVD. Written by Rafael Yglesias, based on the book by Victor Hugo. Produced by Caroline Hewitt et al. Presented by Mandalay Entertainment. Culver City, CA: Sony Pictures, 1998.

Balakian, Peter. *The Burning Tigris: The Armenian Genocide and America's Response*. New York: HarperCollins, 2003.

Barth, Karl. *Church Dogmatics* III/2. Edinburgh: T. & T. Clark, 1960.

———. *Church Dogmatics* IV/1. Edinburgh: T. & T. Clark, 1956.

———. *Church Dogmatics* IV/2. Edinburgh: T. & T. Clark, 1958.

———. *Church Dogmatics* IV/3.1. Edinburgh: T. & T. Clark, 1961.

Bartlett, Anthony. *Cross Purposes: The Violent Grammar of the Christian Atonement*. Harrisburg, PA: Trinity, 2001.

Beier, Matthias. *A Violent God-Image: An Introduction to the Work of Eugen Drewermann*. New York: Continuum, 2004.

Beilby, James, and Paul Eddy, editors. *The Nature of the Atonement: Four Views*. Downers Grove, IL: InterVarsity, 2006.

Belt, Don. "Struggle for the Soul of Pakistan." *National Geographic Magazine* 212 (September 2007) 32–59.

Berger, Peter. *The Heretical Imperative: Contemporary Possibilities of Religious Affirmation*. New York: Anchor, 1979.

Boesak, Allan Aubrey. *Farewell to Innocence: A Socio-Ethico Study on Black Theology and Black Power*. Maryknoll, NY: Orbis, 1976.

Bond, L. Susan. *Trouble With Jesus: Women, Christology, and Preaching*. St. Louis: Chalice, 1999.

Bondi, Roberta C. *Memories of God: Theological Reflections of a Life.* Nashville: Abingdon, 1995.

Borg, Marcus. *The God We Never Knew: Beyond Dogmatic Religion to a More Authentic Contemporary Faith.* San Francisco: HarperSanFrancisco, 1997.

―――. *The Heart of Christianity: Rediscovering a Life of Faith.* San Francisco: HarperSanFrancisco, 2003.

―――. *Meeting Jesus Again for the First Time: The Historical Jesus and the Heart of Contemporary Faith.* San Francisco: HarperSanFrancisco, 1994.

Borg, Marcus J., and N. T. Wright. *The Meaning of Jesus: Two Visions.* San Francisco: HarperSanFrancisco, 1999.

Brock, Rita Nakashima. "And a Little Child Will Lead Us: Christology and Child Abuse." In *Christianity, Patriarchy, and Abuse: A Feminist Critique,* edited by Joanne Carlson Brown and Carole Bohn, 42–61. New York: Pilgrim, 1989.

―――. *Journeys By Heart: A Christology of Erotic Power.* New York: Crossroad, 1988.

Brock, Rita Nakashima, and Rebecca Ann Parker. *Proverbs of Ashes: Violence, Redemptive Suffering, and the Search for What Saves Us.* Boston: Beacon, 2001.

―――. *Saving Paradise: How Christianity Traded Love of This World for Crucifixion and Empire.* Boston: Beacon, 2008.

Brown, Joanne Carlson. "Divine Child Abuse?" *Daughters of Sarah* 18.3 (1992) 24–28.

Brown, Joanne Carlson, and Carole Bohn, editors. *Christianity, Patriarchy, and Abuse: A Feminist Critique.* New York: Pilgrim, 1989.

Brown, Joanne Carlson, and Rebecca Parker. "For God So Loved the World?" In *Christianity, Patriarchy, and Abuse: A Feminist Critique,* edited by Joanne Carlson Brown and Carole Bohn, 1–30. New York: Pilgrim, 1989.

Brueggemann, Walter. "David and His Theologian." *Catholic Biblical Quarterly* 30 (1968) 156–81.

Buechner, Frederick. *The Son of Laughter.* San Francisco: HarperSanFrancisco, 1993.

―――. *Telling The Truth: The Gospel as Tragedy, Comedy, and Fairy Tale.* New York: Harper & Row, 1977.

Burton, David. *Buddhism, Knowledge and Liberation: A Philosophical Analysis of Suffering.* Ashgate World Philosophies Series. Aldershot, UK: Ashgate, 2004.

Bynum, Caroline Walker. *Jesus as Mother: Studies in the Spirituality of the High Middle Ages.* Publications of the Center for Medieval and Renaissance Studies 16. Berkeley: University of California Press, 1982.

Cahill, Thomas. *Desire of the Everlasting Hills: The World Before and After Jesus.* Hinges of History 3. New York: Anchor, 1999.

Calvin, John. *Institutes of the Christian Religion.* 1536 Edition. Translated and annotated by Ford Lewis Battles. Bibliotheca Calviniana. Grand Rapids: Eerdmans, 1986.

Carbine, Rosemary P. "Contextualizing the Cross for the Sake of Subjectivity." In *Cross Examinations: Readings on the Meaning of the Cross Today,* edited by Marit Trelstad, 91–107. Minneapolis: Fortress, 2006.

Case-Winters, Anna. *God's Power: Traditional Understandings and Contemporary Challenges.* Louisville: Westminster John Knox, 1990.

Central Intelligence Agency. *The 2007 CIA World Factbook.* Dulles, VA: Potomac, 2007.

Chalke, Steve, and Alan Mann. *The Lost Message of Jesus.* Grand Rapids: Zondervan, 2004.

Chang, Iris. *The Rape of Nanking: The Forgotten Holocaust of World War II.* New York: Penguin, 1997.

Coixet, Isabel, writer and director. *The Secret Life of Words*. DVD. Produced by Augustín Almodóvar et al. Presented by El Deseo SA. Universal City, CA: Universal Studios, 2007.

Collins, Billy. "On Turning Ten." In *The Art of Drowning*, 48–49. Pitt Poetry Series. Pittsburgh: University of Pittsburgh Press, 1995.

Collins, Sheila D. *A Different Heaven and Earth?* Valley Forge, PA: Judson, 1974.

Cone, James H. *God of the Oppressed*. New York: Seabury, 1975.

Crysdale, Cynthia S. W. *Embracing Travail: Retrieving the Cross Today*. New York: Continuum, 2001.

Darabant, Frank, director and screenwriter. *The Shawshank Redemption*. DVD. Produced by Nicki Marvin. Castle Rock Entertainment. Burbank, CA: Warner Home Video, 1999.

Davaney, Sheila Greeve. *Divine Power: A Study of Karl Barth and Charles Hartshorne*. Harvard Dissertations in Religion 19. Philadelphia: Fortress, 1986.

Davis, David Brion. *Inhuman Bondage: The Rise and Fall of Slavery in the New World*. Oxford: Oxford University Press, 2006.

de Gruchy, John W. *Reconciliation*. Minneapolis: Fortress, 2002.

Demarest, Bruce. *The Cross and Salvation: The Doctrine of Salvation*. Foundations of Evangelical Theology 1. Wheaton, IL: Crossway, 1997.

Deyle, Steven. "Origins of the Domestic Slave Trade." *Journal of the Early Republic* 12 (Spring 1992) 37–62.

Diamond, Jared. *Collapse: How Societies Choose to Fail or Succeed*. New York: Viking, 2005.

Dickens, Charles. *A Christmas Carol*. Salzburg, Austria: Neugebauer, 1988.

Dinesen, Isak. *Anecdotes of Destiny and Ehrengard*. New York: Vintage, 1993.

Dostoyevsky, Fyodor. *The Brothers Karamazov: A Novel in Four Parts and an Epilogue*. Translated with an introduction and notes by David McDuff. Penguin Classics. New York: Penguin, 1993.

Douglas, Kelly Brown. *What's Faith Got To Do With It? Black Bodies/Christian Souls*. Maryknoll, NY: Orbis, 2005.

Duigan, John, director. *Romero*. DVD. Written and produced by John Sacret Young. Also produced by Ellwood Kieser et al. Presented by Paulist Pictures. Santa Monica, CA: Lions Gate, 2000.

Dupuis, Jacques. *Toward a Christian Theology of Religious Pluralism*. Maryknoll, NY: Orbis, 1997.

Easterbrook, Gregg. *The Progress Paradox: How Life Gets Better While People Feel Worse*. New York: Random, 2003.

Eastwood, Clint, director and producer. *Unforgiven*. DVD. Written by David Webb Peoples. Presented by Warner Bros. Pictures. A Malpraso Production. Burbank, CA: Warner Home Video, 2000.

Farley, Wendy. *Tragic Vision and Divine Compassion: A Contemporary Theodicy*. Louisville: Knox, 1990.

———. *The Wounding and Healing of Desire: Weaving Heaven and Earth*. Louisville: John Knox, 2005.

Fiddes, Paul. *Past Event and Present Salvation: The Christian Idea of Atonement*. Louisville: John Knox, 1989.

Finlan, Stephen. *Problems With Atonement: The Origin of, and Controversy about, the Atonement Doctrine*. Collegeville, MN: Liturgical, 2005.

Forbes, Robert P. "Slavery and the Meaning of America." PhD diss., Yale University, 1994.

Fortune, Marie M. *Sexual Violence: The Unmentionable Sin*. New York: Pilgrim, 1983.

———. "The Transformation of Suffering: A Biblical and Theological Perspective." In *Christianity, Patriarchy, and Abuse: A Feminist Critique*, edited by Joanne Carlson Brown and Carole Bohn, 139–47. New York: Pilgrim, 1989.

Gebara, Ivone. *Out of the Depths: Women's Experience of Evil and Salvation*. Translated by Ann Patrick Ware. Minneapolis: Fortress, 2002.

Girard, René. *Violence and the Sacred*. Translated by Patrick Gregory. Baltimore: Johns Hopkins University Press, 1977.

Gollwitzer, Helmut. *An Introduction to Protestant Theology*. Translated by David Cairns. Philadelphia: Westminster, 1982.

Grant, Jacquelyn. *White Women's Christ and Black Women's Jesus: Feminist Christology and Womanist Response*. American Academy of Religion Academy Series 64. Atlanta: Scholars, 1989.

Grey, Mary. *Feminism, Redemption, and the Christian Tradition*. Mystic, CT: Twenty-Third, 1990.

Gunton, Colin E. *The Actuality of Atonement: A Study of Metaphor, Rationality, and the Christian Tradition*. Edinburgh: T. & T. Clark, 1989.

Gutiérrez, Gustavo. *The God of Life*. Translated by Matthew J. O'Connell. Maryknoll, NY: Orbis, 1991.

———. *A Theology of Liberation: History, Politics, and Salvation*. Translated and edited by Sister Caridad Inda and John Eagleson. 15th anniversary ed. Maryknoll, NY: Orbis, 1988.

Hackford, Taylor, writer and director. *Ray*. DVD. Also written by James White. Produced by Alise Benjamin et al. Presented by Anvil Films. Universal City, CA: Universal Studios, 2005.

Hall, Douglas John. *God and Human Suffering: An Exercise in the Theology of the Cross*. Minneapolis: Augsburg, 1986.

———. *Professing the Faith: Christian Theology in a North American Context*. Minneapolis: Fortress, 1993.

Hart, David Bentley. *The Beauty of the Infinite: The Aesthetics of Christian Faith*. Grand Rapids: Eerdmans, 2003.

Heim, S. Mark. *The Depth of the Riches: A Trinitarian Theology of Religious Ends*. Sacra Doctrina. Grand Rapids: Eerdmans, 2001.

———. *Salvations: Truth and Difference in Religion*. Faith Meets Faith. Maryknoll, NY: Orbis, 1995.

———. "Saved by What Shouldn't Happen: The Anti-Sacrificial Meaning of the Cross." In *Cross Examinations: Readings on the Meaning of the Cross*, edited by Marit Trelstad, 211–24. Minneapolis: Fortress, 2006.

———. *Saved from Sacrifice: A Theology of the Cross*. Grand Rapids: Eerdmans, 2006.

Herman, Judith Lewis. *Trauma and Recovery*. New York: Basic Books, 1992.

Heyward, Carter. *The Redemption of God: A Theology of Mutual Relation*. Lanham, MD: University Press of America, 1982.

———. *Our Passion for Justice: Images of Power, Sexuality, and Liberation*. New York: Pilgrim, 1984.

Hodge, Charles. *Systematic Theology*, Vol. 2. 1871–1872. Reprint, Peabody, MA: Hendrickson, 2001.

Howe, Daniel Walker. *What Hath God Wrought: The Transformation of America, 1815–1848*. Oxford History of the United States. New York: Oxford University Press, 2007.

Hurtado, Larry W. *How on Earth Did Jesus Become God? Historical Questions about Earliest Devotion to Jesus*. Grand Rapids: Eerdmans, 2005.

———. *Lord Jesus Christ: Devotion to Jesus in Earliest Christianity*. Grand Rapids: Eerdmans, 2003.

Jackson, Peter, director and producer. *The Lord of the Rings—The Two Towers*. New Line Cinema presents a Wingnut Films production. Los Angeles: New Line Home Entertainment, 2004.

Japinga, Lynn. *Feminism and Christianity: An Essential Guide*. Abingdon Essential Guides. Nashville: Abingdon, 1999.

Johnson, Elizabeth A. *Consider Jesus: Waves of Renewal in Christology*. New York: Crossroad, 1995.

———. "Redeeming the Name of Christ." In *Freeing Theology: The Essentials of Theology in Feminist Perspective*, edited by Catherine Mowry LaCugna, 115–37. San Francisco: HarperSanFrancisco, 1993.

———. *She Who Is: The Mystery of God in Feminist Theological Discourse*. New York: Crossroad, 1992.

Johnson, Matthew. "Lord of the Crucified." In *The Passion of the Lord: African American Reflections*, edited by James A. Noel and Matthew V. Johnson, 1–32. Facets. Minneapolis: Fortress, 2005.

Jones, Serene. *Feminist Theory and Christian Theology: Cartographies of Grace*. Guides to Theological Inquiry. Minneapolis: Fortress, 2000.

Julian of Norwich. *Showings*. Translated by Edmund Colledge, and James Walsh. The Classics of Western Spirituality. New York: Paulist, 1978.

Kelsey, David H. *Imagining Redemption*. Louisville: Westminster John Knox, 2005.

Kierkegaard, Søren. *Søren Kierkegaard's Journals and Papers*. Vol. 1. Translated and edited by Howard V. Hong and Edna H. Hong. Bloomington: Indiana University Press, 1967.

Kim, Bok-dong. Testimony No. 6. The Korean Council for Women Cyber *Memorial: Remember the Past; Testimonies*. Online: http://www.womenandwar.net/bbs_eng/index.php?tbl=M04028&cat=&mode=V&id=6&SN=0&SK=&SW=/.

Kwok, Pui-lan. "God Weeps with Our Pain." In *New Eyes for Reading: Biblical and Theological Reflections by Women from the Third World*, edited by John S. Pobee and Bärbel von Wartenberg-Potter, 90–95. Geneva: World Council of Churches, 1986.

LaGravenese, Richard, director and screenwriter. *Freedom Writers*. DVD. Hollywood: Paramount Home Entertainment, 2007.

Lee, Spike, director. *25th Hour*. Touchstone Pictures presents a 40 Acres and a Mule Filmworks Production. An Industry Entertainment, Gamut Films production. Hostage Productions, 2002.

Lindbeck, George. *The Nature of Doctrine: Religion and Theology in a Postliberal Age*. Philadelphia: Westminster, 1984.

Linklater, Richard, director. *Before Sunrise*. DVD. Written by Richard Linklater and Kim Krizan. Presented by Castle Rock Entertainment. Atlanta, GA: Turner Home Entertainment, 1999.

Love, Gregory Anderson. "In Search of a Non-Violent Atonement Theory: Are Abelard and Girard a Help, or a Problem?" In *Theology as Conversation: The Significance of*

Dialogue in Historical and Contemporary Theology, edited by Bruce McCormack and Kimlyn Bender, 194–214. Grand Rapids: Eerdmans, 2009.

MacDonald, George. *Life Essential: The Hope of the Gospel*. Edited by Rolland Hein. The Wheaton Literary Series. Wheaton, IL: Shaw, 1978.

Malick, Terrence, director and screenwriter. *The New World*. Produced by Sarah Green. Burbank, CA: New Line Home Entertainment, 2006.

Masuzawa, Tomoko. *The Invention of World Religions, Or, How European Universalism Was Preserved in the Language of Pluralism*. Chicago: University of Chicago Press, 2005.

May, Gerald G. *Addiction and Grace: Love and Spirituality in the Healing of Addictions*. San Francisco: Harper & Row, 1988.

McEwan, Ian. *Atonement: A Novel*. New York: Doubleday, 2001.

Metzger, Bruce M., and Roland E. Murphy, editors. *The New Oxford Annotated Bible: The New Revised Standard Version*. New York: Oxford University Press, 1994.

Migliore, Daniel L. *Faith Seeking Understanding*, 2nd ed. Grand Rapids: Eerdmans, 2004.

Moltmann, Jürgen. *The Spirit of Life: A Universal Affirmation*. Translated by Margaret Kohl. Minneapolis: Fortress, 1992.

———. *The Way of Jesus Christ: Christology in Messianic Dimensions*. Translated by Margaret Kohl. 1990. Reprint, Minneapolis: Fortress, 1995.

Moltmann, Jürgen, and Elisabeth Moltmann-Wendel. *Passion for God: Theology in Two Voices*. Louisville: Westminster John Knox, 2003.

Morrow, Lance. "I Spoke . . . as a Brother." *Time* (Jan 9, 1984) 27–33.

Moule, C. F. D. *The Origin of Christology*. Cambridge: Cambridge University Press,

Niebuhr, H. Richard. "Faith in Gods and in God." In *Radical Monotheism and Western Culture*, 114–26. New York: Harper & Row, 1943.

Nolan, Christopher, director and producer. *The Dark Knight*. 2 DVDs. Presented by Warner Bros. Pictures, Legendary Pictures, DC Comics, and Syncopy. Burbank, CA: Warner Home Video, 2008.

North, Douglass Cecil. *The Economic Growth of the United States, 1790–1860*. Englewood Cliffs, NJ: Prentice-Hall, 1961.

O'Connor, Flannery. "The Artificial Nigger." In *The Complete Stories*, 249–70. New York: Farrar, Straus & Giroux, 1971.

———. "Revelation." In *Everything That Rises Must Converge*, 191–218. New York: Farrar, Straus & Giroux, 1993.

Packer, J. I. *Concise Theology: A Guide to Historic Christian Beliefs*. Carol Stream, IL: Tyndale, 1993.

Pakula, Alan J., writer, producer, director. *Sophie's Choice*. Santa Monica, CA: Live Entertainment, Artisan Home Entertainment, 1999.

Parfit, Derek. *Reasons and Persons*. Oxford: Oxford University Press, 1984.

Pasewark, Kyle A. *A Theology of Power: Being beyond Domination*. Minneapolis: Fortress, 1993.

Patterson, Orlando. *Rituals of Blood: Consequences of Slavery in Two American Centuries*. Washington, DC: Civitas/CounterPoint, 1998.

Piper, John. *Fifty Reasons Why Jesus Came to Die*. Wheaton, IL: Crossway, 2006.

———. *Seeing and Savoring Jesus Christ*. Wheaton, IL: Crossway, 2004.

Placher, William C. "The Cross of Jesus Christ as Solidarity, Reconciliation, and Redemption." In *Many Voices, One God: Being Faithful in a Pluralistic World*, edited by Walter Brueggemann and George W. Stroup, 155–66. Louisville: Westminster John Knox, 1998.

———. *Narratives of a Vulnerable God: Christ, Theology, and Scripture*. Louisville: Westminster John Knox, 1994.

———. "The Vulnerable God." In *Narratives of a Vulnerable God: Christ, Theology, and Scripture*, 3–26. Louisville: Westminster John Knox, 1994.

Poling, James N. *The Abuse of Power: A Theological Problem*. Nashville: Abingdon, 1991.

———. "The Cross and Male Violence." In *Cross Examinations: Readings on the Meaning of the Cross Today*, edited by Marit Trelstad, 50–62. Minneapolis: Fortress, 2006.

Purvis, Sally B. *The Power of the Cross: Foundations for a Christian Feminist Ethic of Community*. Nashville: Abingdon, 1993.

Rae, Murray. "A Remnant People: The Ecclesia as Sign of Reconciliation." In *The Theology of Reconciliation*, edited by Colin Gunton, 93–108. London: T. & T. Clark, 2003.

Reno, R. R. *Redemptive Change: Atonement and the Christian Cure of the Soul*. Theology for the Twenty-first Century. Harrisburg, PA: Trinity, 2002.

Ricoeur, Paul. *The Symbolism of Evil*. Translated by Emerson Buchanan. Religious Perspectives 17. New York: Harper & Row, 1967.

Rizzuto, Ana-Maria. *The Birth of the Living God: A Psychoanalytic Study*. Chicago: University of Chicago Press, 1979.

Rogerson, John W. "Sacrifice in the Old Testament: Problems of Method and Approach." In *Sacrifice*, edited by M. F. C. Bourdillon and M. Fortes, 45–59. London: Academic, 1980.

Russell, Bertrand, "A Free Man's Worship." In *Why I Am Not a Christian: And Other Essays on Religion and Related Subjects*, 104–16. New York: Touchstone, 1957.

Saussy, Carroll. *God Images and Self-Esteem: Empowering Women in a Patriarchal Society*. Louisville: Westminster John Knox, 1991.

Schama, Simon. *Rough Crossings: Britain, the Slaves and the American Revolution*. New York: HarperCollins, 2006.

Schmemann, Alexander. *For the Life of the World: Sacraments and Orthodoxy*. Crestwood, NY: St. Vladimir's Seminary Press, 1973.

Schüssler Fiorenza, Elisabeth. *In Memory of Her: A Feminist Theological Reconstruction of Christian Origins*. New York: Crossroad, 1983.

———. *Jesus and the Politics of Interpretation*. New York: Continuum, 2000.

———. *Jesus: Miriam's Child, Sophia's Prophet; Critical Issues in Feminist Christology*. New York: Continuum, 1994.

Smith, Christine M. *Risking the Terror: Resurrection in This Life*. Cleveland: Pilgrim, 2001.

Soelle, Dorothee. *Beyond Mere Obedience*. Translated by Lawrence W. Denef. New York: Pilgrim, 1982.

———. *The Silent Cry: Mysticism and Resistance*. Translated by Barbara and Martin Rumscheidt. Minneapolis: Fortress, 2001.

Spielberg, Steven, director. *Amistad*. DVD. Produced by Steven Spielberg, et al. Written by David Franzoni. Presented by DreamWorks Pictures in association with HBO Pictures. Universal City, CA: DreamWorks, 1999.

Stanton, Andrew, director. *WALL-E*. DVD. Pixar Animation Studios. Presented by Walt Disney Pictures. Produced by Jim Morris. Burbank, CA: Walt Disney Home Entertainment, 2008.

Stott, John R. W. *The Cross of Christ*. Downers Grove, IL: InterVarsity, 1986.

Streufert, Mary J. "Maternal Sacrifice as a Hermeneutics of the Cross." In *Cross Examinations: Readings on the Meaning of the Cross Today*, edited by Marit Trelstad, 63–75. Minneapolis: Fortress, 2006.

Styron, William. *Sophie's Choice*. New York: Random House, 1979.

Tanner, Kathryn. *Economy of Grace*. Minneapolis: Fortress, 2005.

Taylor, Jill Bolte. *My Stroke of Insight: A Brian Scientist's Personal Journey*. New York: Viking, 2006.

Taylor, Mark Lewis. "American Torture and the Body of Christ: Making and Remaking Worlds." In *Cross Examinations: Readings on the Meaning of the Cross Today*, edited by Marit Trelstad, 264–77. Minneapolis: Fortress, 2006.

———. *The Executed God: The Way of the Cross in Lockdown America*. Minneapolis: Fortress, 2001.

———. *Remembering Esperanza: A Cultural-Political Theology of North American Praxis*. 1990. Reprint, Minneapolis: Fortress, 2004.

Terrell, JoAnne Marie. "Our Mothers' Gardens." In *Cross Examinations: Readings on the Meaning of the Cross Today*, edited by Marit Trelstad, 33–49. Minneapolis: Fortress, 2006.

Thompson, Deanna A. "Becoming a Feminist Theologian of the Cross." In *Cross Examinations: Readings on the Meaning of the Cross Today*, edited by Marit Trelstad, 76–90. Minneapolis: Fortress, 2006.

Tillich, Paul. *Systematic Theology*. Vol. 2, *Existence and the Christ*. Chicago: University of Chicago Press, 1957.

Tolkien, J. R. R. "*Beowulf*: The Monsters and the Critics." In *Beowulf: A Verse Translation*, translated by Seamus Heaney. New York: Norton, 2002.

———. *The Letters of J. R. R. Tolkien*. London: George Allen & Unwin, 1981.

———. *The Lord of the Rings: Return of the King*. New York: Ballantine, 1976.

———. "On Fairy Stories." In *The Tolkien Reader*. New York: Ballantine, 1966.

Trammel, Madison. "Cross Purposes." *Christianity Today* (July 2, 2007) 16–17. Online: http://www.christianitytoday.com/ct/2007/july/7.15.html/.

Trelstad, Marit, editor. *Cross Examinations: Readings on the Meaning of the Cross Today*. Minneapolis: Fortress, 2006.

———. "Lavish Love: A Covenantal Ontology." In *Cross Examinations: Readings on the Meaning of the Cross Today*, edited by Marit Trelstad, 109–24. Minneapolis: Fortress, 2006.

Ulanov, Ann, and Barry Ulanov. *Cinderella and Her Sisters: The Envied and the Envying*. Philadelphia: Westminster, 1983.

Volf, Miroslav. "Love Your Heavenly Enemy." *Christianity Today* (October 23, 2000) 94–97.

Walters, Barbara. *Audition: A Memoir*. New York: Knopf, 2008.

Weaver, J. Denny. *The Nonviolent Atonement*. Grand Rapids: Eerdmans, 2001.

———. "Violence in Christian Theology." In *Cross Examinations: Readings on the Meaning of the Cross Today*, edited by Marit Trelstad, 225–39. Minneapolis: Fortress, 2006.

Webster, John. "The Ethics of Reconciliation." In *The Theology of Reconciliation*, edited by Colin Gunton, 109–24. London: T. & T. Clark, 2003.

Weil, Simone. *Gravity and Grace*. Translated by Emma Craufurd. London: Routledge, 1987.

Weingart, Richard. *The Logic of Divine Love: A Critical Analysis of the Soteriology of Peter Abailard*. Oxford: Clarendon, 1970.

Welker, Michael. *God the Spirit*. Trasnalted by John F. Hoffmeyer. Minneapolis: Fortress, 1994.

White, Vernon. *Atonement and Incarnation: An Essay in Universalism and Particularity*. Cambridge: Cambridge University Press, 1991.

Williams, Delores S. "Black Women's Surrogacy Experience and the Christian Notion of Redemption." In *Cross Examinations: Readings on the Meaning of the Cross Today*, edited by Marit Trelstad, 19–32. Minneapolis: Fortress, 2006.

Williams, Rowan. *Resurrection*. Cleveland: Pilgrim, 2002.

Wolterstorff, Nicholas. *Lament for a Son*. Grand Rapids: Eerdmans, 1987.

———. *Until Justice and Peace Embrace: The Kuyper Lectures for 1981 Delivered at the Free University of Amsterdam*. Grand Rapids: Eerdmans, 1983.

Woodward, Kenneth L. *Making Saints: How the Catholic Church Determines Who Becomes a Saint, Who Doesn't, and Why*. New York: Touchstone, 1990.

Yancey, Philip. *Soul Survivor: How My Faith Survived the Church*. New York: Doubleday, 2001.

———. *What's So Amazing about Grace?* Grand Rapids: Zondervan, 1997.

Young, Iris Marion. *Justice and the Politics of Difference*. Princeton: Princeton University Press, 1990.

Author and Name Index

Subject Index

Scripture Index

~

~

EARLY CHRISTIAN WRITINGS